NEW
PROFITS
FROM THE
MONETARY
CRISIS

Also by Harry Browne

———————

COMPLETE GUIDE TO SWISS BANKS
YOU CAN PROFIT FROM A MONETARY CRISIS
HOW I FOUND FREEDOM IN AN UNFREE WORLD
HOW YOU CAN PROFIT FROM THE COMING DEVALUATION

NEW
PROFITS
FROM THE
MONETARY
CRISIS

Harry
Browne

WILLIAM MORROW AND COMPANY, INC.

NEW YORK   1978

Library of Congress Cataloging in Publication Data

Browne, Harry (date)
    New profits from the monetary crisis.

    Includes index.
    1. Investments. 2. Currency question. I. Title.
HG4521.B698   332.6'78   78-12778
ISBN 0-688-03373-3

BOOK DESIGN   CARL WEISS

Printed in the United States of America.

First Edition

1   2   3   4   5   6   7   8   9   10

To Ute

CONTENTS

Part III
Investment Survey

Part IV
Investment Strategy

Part V
Investment Tactics

Epilogue

Appendices

Index

PROLOGUE

1

THE THIRD
INVESTMENT ERA

Two periods since World War II have allowed an investor to relax his vigilance and still make money. Unfortunately, both of them are over.

The first era lasted twenty-three years—from 1942 to 1965. During that time, you could invest the bulk of your savings in blue-chip U.S. stocks, turn your attention to other things, and simply let the profits accumulate.

There were only two requirements for success: (1) choose well-known stocks that could be expected to move in step with the overall market, and (2) diversify. You needed no sense of *timing*. If you happened to buy when stock prices were temporarily high, the price decline that followed was soon reversed.

The great U.S. super-bull market ended on February 9, 1966. But by then many investors had come to think of a rising stock market as part of the natural order of things. And so they held on too long, suffering terrible losses that some of them are still waiting to recover.

The second era lasted from 1970 to 1974. This was the era of "hard-money" investments—gold, silver, and strong foreign currencies. As with stocks in the earlier era, an investor who saw what was coming could place his bets, ignore timing considerations, and go on about his business.

The rewards were handsome. Many investors doubled or

tripled their money. Not all of them bought at the bottom, of course, and there were reversals along the way that had to be waited out. But for those who understood what made the hard-money bull market inevitable, the waiting was rather painless.

The various hard-money investments peaked at different times, but, in general, we can say that the era ended at the close of 1974. These investments haven't been idle, however; the currencies have reached new highs, and gold and silver were in the middle of new rallies when I wrote these words. But the reasons for, and the patterns of, the present price movements are different from those that investors saw during 1970 to 1974. And the differences create the need for more precise timing.

Precious metals and strong currencies will continue to trend upward, with new price peaks being reached. But the trend won't be as intense as during the golden era of 1970–1974. We will need to know when to step onto the hard-money bandwagon—and when to step off.

And stocks will continue to trend downward. Mirroring gold, the trend will be neither steep nor steady. Amid the general decline, mini-bull markets will appear and offer opportunities to investors who recognize the transient nature of these false recoveries.

SUPER-BEAR MARKET

Despite its ups and downs, the U.S. stock market has been in a long-term downward trend since 1966. Three times the market has approached the 1966 high (the 1,000 area of the Dow Jones Industrial Average), and three times it has retreated into a new bear market. It might appear that the stock market has been going nowhere, but that isn't the case.

During a time of price inflation, the dollar prices of investments can be misleading. Only by translating investment prices into terms of purchasing power can you see whether you've gained or lost.

The stock market has actually been declining in value since 1966—because of price inflation. If you're lucky, the stock you bought in 1966 for $30 might also sell today for $30; but the $30 you receive today will purchase only 49% of the products and services that $30 could purchase in 1966. Thus, a share of stock that still sells at its 1966 price has lost half its purchasing power.

The graph on page 16 shows the Dow Jones Industrial Average from January 1941 to May 1978. The chart was constructed by adjusting each month's Dow Jones closing figure for that month's change in the consumer price index. With this adjustment, you can see the gain or loss in the purchasing power value of the Dow stocks from one date to another.

As the graph shows, the period from 1942 to 1965 was a super-bull market. There were bull markets and bear markets along the way, but the long-term trend was upward—a conservative investor's paradise.

Since early 1966, however, stock values have been declining. Again, there have been bull markets and bear markets, but each bull market has topped out at a progressively lower level. And each bear market has fallen lower than its predecessor. Thus, we now have the opposite of the super-bull market of 1942–1965.

Such long-term bear markets discredit the conventional buy-and-hold wisdom that invites you to ignore market cycles. From 1942 to 1965, you didn't have to worry; you would come out ahead eventually. Now that trend has been reversed; in the long run, you come out behind.

Of course, this super-bear trend will end someday. In the *very* long term, stocks that you buy today may justify themselves. But I'm not sure that any of us is prepared to wait for the very long term.

The average stock purchased in 1929 didn't return to a nominal break-even point until 1952. In terms of purchasing power, the break-even point didn't come until 1955. That's twenty-six years—a very long time to postpone your child's dental work, the purchase of a new home, or your own retirement.

RATIO SCALE

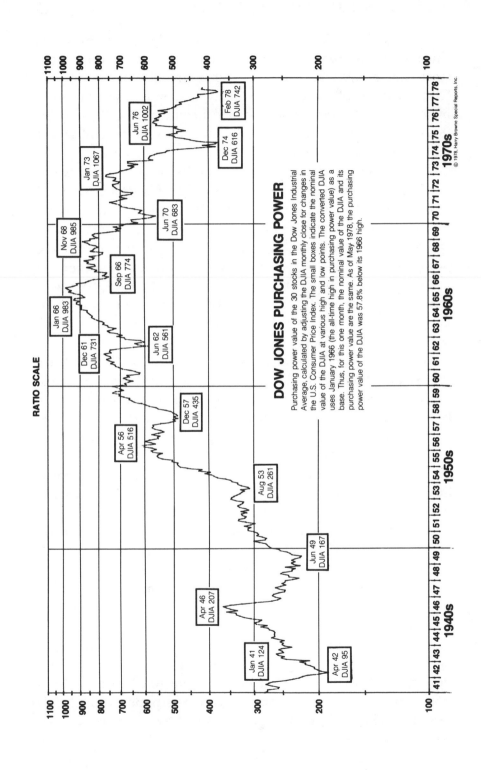

DOW JONES PURCHASING POWER

Purchasing power value of the 30 stocks in the Dow Jones Industrial Average, calculated by adjusting the DJIA monthly close for changes in the U.S. Consumer Price Index. The small boxes indicate the nominal value of the DJIA at various high and low points. The converted DJIA uses January 1966 (the all-time high in purchasing power value) as a base. Thus, for this one month, the nominal value of the DJIA and its purchasing power value are the same. As of May 1978, the purchasing power value of the DJIA was 57.8% below its 1966 high.

Jan 41
DJIA 124

Apr 46
DJIA 207

Apr 42
DJIA 95

Jun 49
DJIA 167

Aug 53
DJIA 261

Apr 56
DJIA 516

Dec 57
DJIA 435

Dec 61
DJIA 731

Jun 62
DJIA 561

Jan 66
DJIA 983

Sep 66
DJIA 774

Nov 68
DJIA 985

Jun 70
DJIA 683

Jan 73
DJIA 1067

Jun 76
DJIA 1002

Dec 74
DJIA 616

Feb 78
DJIA 742

1100 1000 900 800 700 600 500 400 300 200 100

41 | 42 | 43 | 44 | 45 | 46 | 47 | 48 | 49 | 50 | 51 | 52 | 53 | 54 | 55 | 56 | 57 | 58 | 59 | 60 | 61 | 62 | 63 | 64 | 65 | 66 | 67 | 68 | 69 | 70 | 71 | 72 | 73 | 74 | 75 | 76 | 77 | 78

1940s   **1950s**   **1960s**   **1970s**

Many stock market studies have indicated that stocks, in the long term, show an appreciation of around 9% per year, including dividends, if held for long periods. These studies encourage the attitude that you'll come out quite well in the long run if you simply buy high-grade stocks and resist the temptation to trade in and out of the market.

But a closer look at the studies shows that it was far more profitable to start your buy-and-hold program in the 1930s than in the 1920s. And it will be far more profitable to start the next long-term buy-and-hold program after this super-bear market has bottomed—not now.

The first great investment era of the postwar period, the bull market in stocks, ended in 1965. And, from all indications, it won't be repeated for many years.

From 1966 to 1970, no investment was a simple, sure bet. These years were difficult ones for investors. But an alert investor, using a proper strategy, could make money even then. And the period was laying the groundwork for the *second* great investment era.

THE GOLDEN ERA OF GOLD

The prices of gold, silver, and strong foreign currencies didn't begin moving dramatically until 1972 and 1973. But anyone who bought as early as 1970 was well ahead by the end of 1973. And by 1975, he could average his gain back to show a spectacular yearly return since 1970. Gold had increased in price by over 400%, silver by 150%, and the Swiss franc by 70%.

Of course, investment strategies are always more obvious in retrospect. Who could have known that these investments would do so well?

Many people knew. And they weren't "insiders" or fortune-tellers. They were people who paid attention to what had been going on in America for many years. They knew that dramatic changes would have to follow. They may not have known *when* those changes would come, but they knew that it was a matter of months or years, not decades.

Many such people intuitively saw gold, silver, and foreign currencies as hedges against uncertainty, chaos, or inflation. But the price increases enjoyed by hard-money investments were caused by more than just the disorders of the early 1970s. And some investors may not understand that those additional causes no longer exist. If so, they may be expecting more from gold, silver, and foreign currencies than the investments have left to give.

I believe higher prices are still to come for these investments. But there will be some wide price swings along the way. And the intermediate price declines may last long enough to try the patience of the most faithful gold bug.

It's helpful to understand why these investments appreciated so dramatically from 1970 to 1974.[1] It's important, too, to understand what can be expected from them in the next ten years or so.

But it's most important to understand that the second great investment era, the hard-money era, is over—and that a different strategy is called for now.

CHAOS

Another era made its debut around 1970—and it will probably be with us for a long time. It is the era of economic and monetary chaos, both national and international.

The seeds planted by so many years of misguided government policies finally began to produce their bitter fruits in 1970. Brief periods of disorder had appeared before, but not since World War II had there been such intense, prolonged chaos.

Since 1970, we've had high unemployment rates, chronic price inflation, volatile currency prices, banking scandals, failures of "first-class" corporations, and a multitude of other trials—trials that, as recently as 1970, those without foresight swore could never happen.

[1] My explanation is given in Chapter 5.

The crises have been blamed on everything from greedy Arabs to bad weather to sunspots. But sooner or later, most people will recognize that the crises aren't haphazard, unlucky, isolated events. They aren't the result of bad luck; they're the result of bad government.

Those who understood the nature of the New Deal, the Fair Deal, the New Frontier, The Great Society, "enlightened" social legislation, Keynesian economics, the welfare state, the "Whip Inflation Now" campaign, and the "barbarous relic" view of gold—those people could see the crises coming and were prepared for them.

You don't have to be a fortune-teller to realize that if you take money from one person and give it to another, neither person has much incentive to earn more. And you don't have to be an economic scholar to know that issuing more paper money doesn't add to the real wealth of the nation; it only debases the money already in existence, distorts the structure of prices, and encourages investments that have no real economic purpose.

Unfortunately, the belief that the crises stem from too much government is still a minority opinion. The prevailing viewpoints are that (1) the crises were just bad breaks and will go away soon enough, or (2) the crises are symptoms of the anarchy of free markets and will end only when the government tightens its control.

So we can have little hope that the crises will disappear in the near future. On the contrary, the crises often are excuses for new government programs—creating new problems that grow into new crises.

This means you'll be hindered even more in the next few years in your efforts to make a living, to invest profitably, and to live your life as you want. Who knows what the government will dream up tomorrow to solve the problems created by its previous dreams? Will we see a tax on savings accounts? Work permits in order to get jobs? A surtax on investment profits?

Do these possibilities sound like science fiction? Think back to July 1971—and remember how alien then, how un-

American, was the concept of wage and price controls. And yet the following month we had them. Did you believe in 1970 that the U. S. dollar, the reserve currency of the world, could ever be devalued?

A few years' ago you might have thought that only a police state would require that you give your Social Security (identification) number in order to open a bank account. Or that the government would demand that all checks be microfilmed for future inspection.

Before, you may have believed those things could never happen. But now that they have happened, you may not find them so remarkable. A human being assimilates the past so quickly that, in a short while, he stops thinking of last year's revolution as revolutionary. The changes of the past appear, in retrospect, to have evolved quite naturally. And, of course, they did. But they didn't seem natural *before* they happened.

Although he has accepted and assimilated past changes, the average person somehow expects the present to be frozen into the future. He takes each upheaval to be final; he can't accept the possibility that more revolutionary changes may be on the way. He can't imagine "his" government denying him the basic freedoms he takes for granted—even though that same government has already taken away a great deal of the freedom he once had.

And so he continues to plan his future with the rules of the present in mind—heedless of the possibility that the future will have rules of its own.

Of course, change is inherent in civilization. The difference today is that changes are more abrupt, more violent, and more destructive. Change has become so traumatic because now its dominant source is an ever-busier government. Normal change results from new knowledge, improved technology, and evolving tastes. Anyone can ignore new knowledge or new tastes, if he chooses; normal change touches only those who welcome it. But no one can ignore a new government policy that's backed up by the power to tax, to spend, and to punish.

THE FUTURE

The changes of today are imposed upon the economy by political leaders who know nothing of economics, but who want to be seen as "doing something."

For example, Jimmy Carter stated (on October 13, 1977) that higher oil and gas prices were inevitable. But, he added, "The question is who will profit from these prices and to what degree." He questioned whether these "billions and billions of dollars should be given partially to the American people in a *fair* way, or whether it should all be *grabbed* by the oil companies at the expense of the American consumer." (Emphasis added.) [2]

Think about that for a moment. America has an "oil shortage." Why? Possibly it's because price controls and restrictions have been placed upon American oil producers. Who wants to risk his savings in a venture that can't appreciate in value, when there are other ventures available that *can* appreciate?

Whatever the reason for the oil shortage, there seems to be general agreement that the situation is serious. If so, we should be thankful for *any* oil available to us—not complain that the producers aren't giving it away. But the politicians expect to grab the oil and then pay for it according to some contrived standard of "fairness."

Our concern here isn't with what really is "fair." In making investment plans, we should look only at the consequences of an act, fair or unfair.

One logical consequence is that the Carter rule might be applied directly to you. If an oil company's profits can be confiscated under the cloak of "fairness," should you believe that *you* will be allowed to keep the profits from *your* investments? After all, if you invest in something that appreciates in price, won't your profits be made "at the expense of the American consumer"?

[2] *International Herald Tribune,* October 14, 1977.

Of course, I realize that politicians say many things—and that they must eventually compromise with reality. But they only *compromise* with reality; they never accept it. They continually peck away at the laws of supply and demand; they persistently hope to take from producers without discouraging production; they repeatedly put obstacles in our way and then are surprised that we go around the obstacles instead of lying down in front of them.

The crises we see are nothing more than the conflict between politics and reality. The crises occur because governments assume that people won't act in their own self-interest, while people respond by continuing to act in their own self-interest.

Reality always triumphs over politics. But because we've been taught to believe otherwise, the triumph of reality appears to us as a crisis.

The fall of the dollar is the realistic consequence of years of dollar debasement; no one will hold a currency that doesn't keep its value. High interest rates are the realistic consequence of years of funny money; no one will lend money at a rate that won't compensate him for the money's declining value.

And chronic unemployment is the realistic consequence of years of political tinkering with the investment and labor markets. When a politician says that no one may be employed at a wage of less than $2.50 per hour, he expects everyone to be paid at least $2.50 per hour. And anyone who is worth $2.50 per hour *will* be. But anyone whose work isn't worth $2.50 per hour will find that he's been legislated out of a job. When reality triumphs, we have unemployment —a crisis.

The examples are endless, of course. But I'm not trying to build up a catalog of problems. The point is that the trend hasn't been reversed. While Rome burns, the politicians discuss free medical care, job quotas, new restrictions on business, wage and price controls, "incomes policies," and fictitious tax cuts.

It would be unrealistic to foresee an early end to the crises.

INVESTMENT STRATEGY

I'm not trying to discourage you. But it's necessary to know where we stand before we attempt to plan our strategy. As I see them, here are the major considerations:

1. The economic and monetary crises that burst upon the scene in the early 1970s will be with us for many years to come.

2. The government will react to these crises by creating new programs that will lead to even worse crises.

3. Each new program will make it more difficult to find profitable investments, and each new program will erase profits that many investors believe they've already earned.

4. You can no longer rely upon *any* long-term, buy-and-hold investment strategy to take care of you. The swings between bull and bear markets in any investment will be too extreme to tolerate.[3]

To cope with these problems in the third investment era, we need a strategy that will satisfy several standards:

1. The strategy must enable you to take advantage of bull markets, as they occur, in several different investments—since you won't enjoy sitting through the swings in any single investment.

2. The strategy must minimize your exposure to the government's future surprise packages. You won't be able to anticipate everything, so you must insure that no single surprise can cause an intolerable loss.

3. The strategy must provide a way to make timing decisions—without an unrealistic expectation that you become a full-time investor or a ticker-tape watcher.

---

[3] Although my words are directed toward U.S. investors, the situation is little different in any country of the world. And the word *government* can be assumed to apply to any government in the world today.

The timing consideration is important. Not too long ago, you could have been a year too early or too late in making an investment in gold or the Swiss franc. But I don't think you have that luxury any longer.

So I'm going to suggest that you move in and out of gold, silver, and foreign currencies as the circumstances dictate. And what will you do with your funds when they're not invested in these assets? I'm going to suggest several possibilities—including apparently discredited investments such as U.S. stocks and U.S. Treasury bills. However, the strategy will include methods for minimizing the risks—the risk of bad timing and the risk of government interference.

In my previous books, I suggested that you stay away from these investments. The potential for additional profit didn't justify the additional effort and risk. Now, however, I believe the strategy must be broadened. But it must be broadened in a way that keeps the risks at a tolerable level.

The new strategy will require that you watch your investments more closely than before. But I don't expect you to go beyond your interest or capability. For most people, a program of checking investment prices at least weekly, and being prepared to make changes once or twice a year, if necessary, will be sufficient.

The strategy will allow you to choose your own degree of involvement. I offer no single program that must be followed slavishly by everyone. Instead, I hope you'll find that you can choose a plan that fits your own objectives. There's even a plan for those who are determined not to make any changes over the next few years.

CONTENTS

My investment suggestions will be meaningless if we ignore the principles upon which they're based. So you must decide first whether you agree with my appraisal of economic conditions and with the philosophy that I bring to investment planning. Only then can my suggestions be helpful.

And if your view of the world isn't similar to mine, there's little chance that you'll find my investment suggestions useful. But if we agree somewhat on basics, my suggestions will provide important alternatives from which you can choose.

Part I of the book will deal with the economic background. I won't attempt to provide the more thorough background presented in two previous investment books.[4] Telling the same story again would take space away from the more detailed new investment strategy that's the purpose of this book.

Part II will present my view of the way investments behave. These ideas may help to keep you from falling prey to some common investment errors. And, because these investment errors are so widespread and popular, an understanding of them can help you to decipher investment price trends.

Part III will survey the investment alternatives available to us. In it, I'll state my views concerning the outlook for each of these investments for the next few years.

Part IV will discuss the investment strategy that I believe will be the most useful for investors. The strategy is built on the foundation laid in the first three parts of the book, and the discussion will include ways in which you can adapt the strategy to fit your own situation.

Finally, Part V will suggest tactics and guidelines that can be used to carry out the strategy. Again, because each investor is different, you can choose the tactics that match your capabilities and the amount of attention you want to give to your investments.

LET US BEGIN

Most investors tend to lose money—despite the economy's underlying tendency toward growth. It isn't that they lack information or advice. What they lack is a well-founded investment philosophy that would equip them to evaluate the information and advice they receive.

---

[4] *How You Can Profit from the Coming Devaluation* and *You Can Profit from a Monetary Crisis.*

The investor who understands where our economy is today
—and who understands the process of investing—needs much
less information. He knows what information is important,
and he can ignore the endless irrelevancies that other investors try to assimilate.

And this man needs no advice at all. He appreciates new
ideas and suggestions that reveal new alternatives, but he
wouldn't trust his decisions to anyone but himself.

The suggestions I'll make in the latter part of the book
are based on the economic ideas explained in the earlier
parts of the book. The suggestions will make sense only if
the economics make sense.

And so I ask you to examine the foundation first. I've done
my best to make the explanation interesting and understandable, because I know that you won't profit from it if you can't
follow it.

I hope I've succeeded.[5]

---

[5] If you come across a word that's unfamiliar, or if you're not sure what *I* mean
by a word, there's a good chance that the word is defined in the Glossary beginning
on page 433.

PART I

INVESTMENT
CRISES

2

WHY THERE
ARE CRISES

IN THE POLITICAL WORLD, MUCH IS SAID ABOUT "SUMMONING the national will" to cope with inflation, the energy crisis, or whatever problems the politicians currently believe are pressing. It is hoped that a team spirit will develop, inspiring everyone to do what is right (as the politicians see it) to help the nation overcome the problems.

In the real world, each individual is preoccupied with his own problems. He may want to see inflation go away, he may worry about the energy crisis, he may wish that unemployment would decline. In fact, he may admire all the national goals the politicians claim to pursue. But he won't forsake his own goals.

Those who are truly willing to give their own lives for their country, or even to make voluntary personal sacrifices, are so few and far between that they affect the whole picture very little.[1]

The concept of national goals is simply incompatible with the realities of human action. Programs to pursue national goals never succeed because they require individuals to forsake their own goals. If a national program were compatible

---

[1] Of course, the "sophisticated" intellectual who boycotts grapes, refuses to cross a picket line, or takes part in study groups and "action" committees is just having a good time.

with individual goals, it would be unnecessary; the goals would be achieved without it as each individual went about his own business. If the national program isn't compatible, it will fail; and the failure will be called a crisis.

Today much of the study of economics is the study of government policies—because governments dominate national economies. To anticipate the general shape of the economic future, one needs to recognize the probable consequences of major government programs, past and present.

This book's main purpose is to discuss investment strategy, so I'll resist the temptation to restate the detailed explanation of markets and governments presented in my earlier books. However, as a foundation for the suggestions to follow, I think it's necessary to go a little deeper into the subject than I did in the first chapter.

THE FORGOTTEN MAN

William Graham Sumner spoke of the "forgotten man." He said that when A takes from B to give to C, the world is well aware of the benevolence of A and of the plight of C; but B is the forgotten man.

The relevant point for us is not that B is being treated unfairly; the point is that B isn't going to stand still for this. He'll look for ways to prevent A from stealing from him. He may begin avoiding or evading taxes; he may earn less so that less will be taken from him; he may move out of A's jurisdiction; or he may start pretending to be C.

The end result is a society in which everyone wants to be C (or A), and no one wants to be B. But B was the person who originally financed A's generosity; and without him, there will be little to redistribute. In addition, if C doesn't have to pay for his own needs, it's inevitable that his needs will grow larger.

And so a society develops that has boundless needs and no one to pay for them. We can see how this happens if we look at one sample of the A-B-C process.

Many politicians believe, for example, that people have a "right" to free medical care. Since no "rights" can be asserted against nature, the politicians must not be thinking of a right to live without disease. They are, in fact, thinking that no citizen should have to pay for medical treatment—that it should be free.

Since nature doesn't provide medical care, it must come from other human beings. So one person's right to medical care is nothing more than a claim upon some other person's time, energy, money, or knowledge. The man on whom this claim will be made is B, the forgotten man. The politician offers free medical care, but he never says, "You will have free medical care because we are going to force B to pay for it."

The plan is unrealistic from the start—in that it assumes that B will submissively pay the bill without looking for loopholes. It's unrealistic, also, to believe that the costs of the program won't change when the economics of it change.

The politician sees that people presently spend $100 billion per year on medical care. So he plans to collect $100 billion in new taxes (or medical insurance "contributions"), and use the money to pay for doctors, nurses, medicine, X rays, etc. He believes that this will make medical care free.

But once the program is underway, the economics change drastically. The $100 billion was what people had spent yearly when the money came from their own pockets. Now that medical care is free, their medical needs suddenly increase. Why forgo that operation, checkup, or treatment that might have some value?

Or if you're lonely, why not go talk to the doctor? Or if you need a place to stay, check into the hospital; they'll find *something* wrong with you. Many people will see that this is wasteful—for the nation. But for each individual, the consideration is always that it costs zero dollars to obtain something that *might* prove to be valuable. So free medical care turns out to cost far more than $100 billion per year.

And after a while B decides that he's tired of paying for these loafers—and he checks into the hospital, too.

Or at least he stops working so hard. His income is taxed to pay for free medical care and for all the other government programs. And so leisure (unpaid and therefore untaxed) seems more attractive to him. He earns less; and he saves less, too, because he'd just have to pay tax on the interest his savings earn. And because he and all the other Bs are earning less taxable income, the politicians have to raise tax rates even higher than they planned—to collect the money they need for free medical care.

Because even the government's resources are limited (it can't tax what doesn't exist), it is forced eventually to do something to limit the costs of the program. Naturally it won't *end* the program; it will declare that a crisis exists and impose rationing.

So when the cost of free medical care has reached double or triple or quadruple the original estimate of $100 billion, the government announces that *it* will decide who gets to see the doctor first. You will have to go without—unless you have the right disease or fill out the right form or know the right people.

And most people will have no choice but to wait in line for free medical care. The billions spent on the program will have bid up the price of medical services; only the very wealthy (of whom there are fewer) will be able to afford to hire a doctor on their own.

Just as the politicians promised, medical care is free; it just isn't available.

We can already see the first symptoms of such a medical program. The government already subsidizes medical schools and hospitals, regulates medical insurance companies, prohibits the practice of medicine without a government license, and subsidizes the medical care of a large portion of the population. As a result, we already have crowded doctors' offices and waiting lines at hospitals.

But this isn't a warning to a politician. It's an excuse to enlarge the government's program.

If good medical care were his real purpose, the politician would be sobered by the medical situation in most European countries. Government medical and "Social Security" programs are far advanced there, compared to the U.S. The shortage of medical care is chronic because doctors emigrate to the U.S. and other countries where there are greater opportunities to earn money. Waiting lists sometimes are years long. Mr. B. has long since disappeared.

I've used the medical-care issue as one example of the way crises develop. The crisis is always a conflict between the government's goals and the actions of individuals. Many individuals will sympathize with the government's position, but none will sacrifice his personal interest.

It isn't a matter of selfishness vs. unselfishness. *Every* individual acts in his own self-interest; that's a principle of human action. The conflict is between the individual who selfishly pursues what he believes is best for himself and the politician who selfishly wants the individual to act under his direction.

INTERNATIONAL CRISES

The fall of the dollar overseas provides another example of how the government creates a crisis. The dollar's fall means that other currencies become more expensive for someone to purchase with dollars. And the price of a dollar, when measured in any other currency, goes down.

The government fights to stop the fall—supposedly fighting against greedy "speculators" who are trying to bring the dollar down. But who are these speculators? Well, let's see.

The dollar is falling because many foreigners can no longer afford to pay the high prices of American products—high prices caused by the U.S. government's inflationary policies. There are better bargains elsewhere. And because foreigners buy less from the U.S., they need to acquire fewer dollars for purchases. The demand for dollars in the currency markets is reduced.

At the same time many Americans find it advantageous to buy foreign products—as a lower inflation rate in a foreign country makes that country's products more competitive. Every American may like the idea of a strong dollar, but none will pay extra for U.S. products simply to help the dollar out. Even if every Toyota owner puts a "Buy American" sticker on his bumper, the pressure on the dollar will continue. Just as the demand for dollars by foreigners has been reduced, so has the supply of dollars being offered to foreigners been increased.

And if the dollar is heading downward, many people will transfer their savings from dollar assets into other currencies —in order to protect the value of the savings. This further increases the downward pressure on the dollar.

To fight all this the government uses a variety of weapons. It may sell foreign currencies or other assets from its reserves —buying dollars in the currency markets in order to create an artificial demand. Or it may borrow foreign currencies from other governments for this same purpose. Or it may impose restrictions upon its citizens—forbidding them to send money out of the country or imposing heavy taxes on foreign imports.

These weapons are powerful and may succeed in slowing the dollar's fall. But such success only delays the crisis. The overpriced dollar will continue to make U.S. products unattractive to foreigners, and foreign products will continue to be attractive to Americans.

The conditions that caused the imbalance will be perpetuated. And so the crises will continue to erupt.

If the government had stayed out of the currency market all along, there wouldn't have been a crisis. The dollar's price would have adjusted to changing conditions in a gradual, orderly fashion.

Instead the government tried to perpetuate an unrealistic price long after underlying conditions had changed. Once again, the government has challenged reality—and lost. And whenever that happens, it appears to us as a crisis.

Who, then, are the greedy speculators the government has been fighting? They are the foreigners who refuse to buy overpriced American merchandise. They are the Americans who refuse to pay high domestic prices when lower prices are available. They are the individuals who are afraid to see their savings erode. And they are currency traders who create the market through which international trade is possible.

I've used the dollar in this example, rather than another currency, so that the story would be easy to follow. But, of course, other national governments create currency crises. And, in practice, the dollar situation is complicated by the actions of other governments who may be buying or selling dollars in order to satisfy *their* objectives.

The net result is always the same, however. Governments spend great amounts of their citizens' resources in pursuit of the impossible.

THE JOB GETS HARDER

The crises recur because politicians, past and present, have created a multitude of laws and programs that make it harder for individuals to achieve their goals. And as the consequences of these programs pile up, the politician's job becomes harder; for the programs are, in many cases, contradictory—and the politician must try to reconcile irreconcilable goals.

For example, price inflation can be reduced only by first reducing the rate at which new paper money is created. But if the government reduces the supply of new paper money, banks will have to foreclose on shaky corporate loans. Even the corporations that are able to repay the loans will have to reduce their payrolls to stay in business.

But the corporations can't reduce their payrolls because the politicians have imposed minimum wage laws and given labor unions the power to prevent work-force reductions. A corporation might be able to survive if it could offer its products and services at prices consumers would be willing to pay in a noninflationary world. But it's prevented from doing so by minimum wage laws that forbid matching wages to the value (to consumers) of what is being produced. And labor-union laws prevent employers from hiring workers who are willing to accept such wages.

Every wage and every price must be free to rise or fall if the economy is to be efficient. Only in that way can businessmen be alerted to the products that consumers want most. And only through wage differences are workers attracted to the industries where they're most needed.

The government's floor under wages makes a special contribution to the current crises. Price inflation is *mandatory*; it is the method by which unrealistically high wage rates are made less expensive. If price inflation were to stop, workers with unrealistic wage rates would be priced out of their jobs.

So the politician can't reduce price inflation and fight unemployment at the same time; his own policies and those of his predecessors have boxed him in.

Even back in the good old days of the 1950s and 1960s, the government was an expensive drag on the economy. But the problems the politicians were creating rarely surfaced, because they were offset by an economy that was vigorous enough to circumvent political obstacles. Now the problems have accumulated, and the economy that is supposed to pay for the political programs is being suffocated. C has been encouraged to assert far more rights than B could possibly pay for. And A hasn't the faintest idea what to do about it.

As a result we now have constantly recurring crises.

THE FUTURE

There's no reason to hope that things will improve in the near future. Even if the politicians were determined to undo the real causes of the crises, there still would be terrible damage to repair. But unfortunately we haven't reached even that point yet, so the damage will grow worse.

Meanwhile the politicians tell us that the same government that brought us the Post Office can bring us medical care; that more oil can be available if we pay the oil producers less for their efforts; that *we* (outside the government) are responsible for stopping inflation.

Unhappily the problems will continue to get worse because the government is trying to solve them with the same old formulas. Alvin Lowi once said, "It won't help to move faster if you're on the wrong road."

And as long as the government is on the wrong road, the most we can hope for is that it will break a leg and be slowed down.

3

THE
MONETARY CRISES

THE AMERICAN ECONOMY HAS CHANGED CONSIDERABLY OVER the past fifty years. Not only does the government have a great deal more influence, but changes in communications, investment markets, and banking practices have altered the structure of the economy.

During the late 1960s and early 1970s, many observers were fond of saying that the government's greater involvement made a repetition of the 1930s depression impossible. The steady stream of government spending, stabilizing actions by the Federal Reserve, and the confidence created by government insurance of bank deposits would keep the economy on an even keel.

Now many of the optimists are not so sure. Too many impossible things have happened during the past eight years. But, through it all, they may have been right.

It's quite possible that we won't see a repetition of the 1930s depression. Nothing can overrule the economic laws of cause and effect, but changes in the country's economic structure can alter the way in which the laws of economics assert themselves.

Each depression in American history has been unique in

some way. And it would be a mistake to make all one's plans in anticipation of a rerun of the last depression.

There is a limitless variety of possibilities, but I believe it can be reduced to three basic scenarios:

1. We could have a deflationary panic and crash. Stock prices would tumble (the Dow Jones Industrial Average might drop to the 200s); the unemployment rate could reach 15% to 25%; many businesses and banks would fail.

2. We could have a runaway inflation. The present high inflation rates could escalate to a pace at which prices would be rising 1% to 5% *every day*. And this would be followed by a deflation even worse than that of number 1 above. The economy might even return to barter for a while.

3. Present conditions could continue for many years, slowly deteriorating but avoiding the extremes of the first two possibilities. Every so-called "recovery" from a recession would fail to fulfill its promise. Progressively higher rates of price inflation and unemployment would be considered to be "acceptable." In other words, a very long period of poor, but not outwardly catastrophic, economic conditions.

Of course, possibility number 3 is already with us. National *goals* for price inflation and unemployment rates are already considerably above rates that would have been labeled dangerous twenty years ago.

The three possibilities I've given are not mutually exclusive. We could see a combination of any two of them—or all three.

Of course, there will be periods when the economy will appear to be on the road back to prosperity (just as in 1972 and 1976). But the good economic news will be mostly projections for "next year"—not actual accomplishments. And each "recovery" should be superseded by a recession that's a little deeper than the previous one.

It's easy to predict the future. The hard part is being right. All we can be sure of is that the many years of monetary inflation and governmental interference will have painful consequences. But if we're prepared for all possibilities, we don't have to predict the future precisely.

INFLATIONARY EFFECTS

To understand how the various possibilities could arise, it's necessary to understand the nature of monetary inflation.

An increased money supply (monetary inflation) results in higher retail prices—which is the effect that most people notice. But price inflation is actually the least of the problems monetary inflation creates. More important, it sets in motion a chain of economic distortions.

The newly created money doesn't enter the economy evenly—as though everyone received a $20 bill in the mail. It enters the economy at a specific place, and encourages or subsidizes certain types of activity.

The Federal Reserve System's principal tool for expanding the money supply is its purchase of bonds in the open market. It pays for these bonds with newly created money, making the bond market the first beneficiary of the monetary inflation. Because the Fed's purchases are so large, they push bond prices upward, and that pushes interest rates downward.

The stock market is usually the next stop in the path of the new money. The investors who sold some of the bonds the Fed bought will look for a place to reinvest the proceeds. And the stock market is a liquid, ready market for that money. Consequently, the stock market reacts sensitively to changes in the money supply. Other investment markets follow soon after.

Most of the new money reaches commercial banks very quickly. Banks are usually among the largest sellers of the bonds the Fed purchases. And the money received by other sellers will wind up in someone's bank account somewhere. Thus, the banking system is the next beneficiary of the new money. This leaves the banks with more money available for loans to their customers, providing further downward pressure on interest rates.

As a result, corporate managers take many deferred capital

projects out of the files. These projects (new products, new factories, etc.) had been shelved because they couldn't be financed economically. Now, with lower interest rates, some of them will appear to be profitable. The corporations will spend money on capital equipment that they believe will make it less expensive eventually to produce their products. And so the capital goods industries enjoy a boom.

Through wages and profits, the money winds up in the pockets of individuals. Many people have more money than they did before the process began. In addition, if the monetary inflation causes their investments to increase in price, they'll feel even wealthier. And so they increase their purchases of consumer goods. The extra cash and easier credit give a special boost to the sales of more expensive durable goods—cars, appliances, and houses.

The boom has now progressed from the investment markets and banking system, through the capital goods industries, and into the consumer goods industries. Each businessman affected sees demand increasing for his products. So he enlarges his inventory, adds extra personnel, and buys new equipment to handle the bigger volume.

So far, so good. And if increased activity is all that matters, the monetary inflation is a success.

But while the government can create new money out of thin air, it can't create real goods and services. The government hasn't made people wealthier, it has only made them *feel* wealthier. Thus deluded, and equipped with paper dollars, they plan to buy more than actually exists. The result is that prices are bid upward—just as at an auction.

This happens because businessmen attempt to hire more workers and purchase more raw materials than exist. When the shortages become apparent, businesses bid up wages and prices in an effort to get what they need from the limited supplies available. They're sure these higher costs can be recouped by charging higher prices to the consumers who are now so eager to buy.

But the consumer hasn't expected prices to rise, or at least not by so much. He had good reason to believe that it was *he* who had more money, not everyone. He had no reason to believe that prices in general would rise so much. Now, as he sees higher prices, he begins to feel less wealthy. So he cuts back on his spending—especially the spending for durable goods, which can be postponed.

In addition he realizes that he's been spending some of his savings. At least he can see that, while the savings may have increased in dollars, they now cover fewer months' expenses than before.

The higher prices also cause interest rates to rise, as lenders insist on being compensated for the erosion of the money they're lending. The higher interest rates cause bond prices to decline, and stocks and other investments quickly follow.

And the higher interest rates abort the boom in capital projects. A project that was initiated when the interest rate was 6% must be abandoned as unprofitable when the interest rate rises to 9%. And so the capital goods industries head into a recession.

Meanwhile, with consumers spending less, the businessman's inventory doesn't sell as fast as it was expected to. And because interest rates have moved back up to more realistic levels, it becomes more and more expensive to finance these inventories. Orders for new goods are reduced, production is cut, and workers are laid off. The recession has spread through the whole economy.

The process of monetary inflation was undertaken in order to stimulate the economy. But while it created a flurry of activity, it added nothing to the nation's wealth. New wealth is created by saving something from present consumption and using that saving to finance more efficient ways of producing what consumers want.

Instead the monetary inflation encouraged those projects which are most favored by easy credit. As there was no actual increase in real savings, these projects were made at the expense of other projects that were more compatible with the normal pattern of consumer spending.

Employment was increased, but only because the new money made it possible to bid wages to higher levels than

workers were accustomed to. But when the capital projects
had to be abandoned, the newly employed had to be laid
off. In addition, many employees had been bid away from
their previous jobs to jobs that couldn't be sustained. Thus,
those who had been unemployed originally, as well as many
workers who did have jobs before, are now out of work. The
final result of the monetary inflation has been to increase
the total number of unemployed workers.

The recession that follows the inflationary boom is, in
effect, the economy's attempt to move back to the pattern
of activity that existed before the money supply expanded.
The jobs that are lost and the businessess that fail tend to
be in the areas that were artificially stimulated by the new
money.

Of course, the government that induced the monetary inflation won't give up. It responds to the readjustment process
with more monetary inflation—hoping to keep the boom
going.

However, the second dose of monetary inflation won't be
enough unless it is bigger than the first. Simply repeating
the first trick won't work. Consumers and businessmen must
be convinced that the situation really is different this time.

In addition, interest rates are now higher than they were
before the previous monetary inflation. Lenders require
higher interest rates to compensate them for the price inflation caused by the monetary inflation. To restore interest
rates to the levels that made the unrealistic capital projects
profitable will require a bigger dose of new money than
it did the first time.

This point is vital for an understanding of an inflationary
economy: *In order to keep an inflated economy going, the
rate of monetary inflation must be increased again and again.*

The rate must be consistent with the normal growth of
the economy; but, in addition, it must be increased to sustain
the unworkable investments of the past. If it isn't, those investments will fail—causing unemployment, business failures,
and other economic losses.

The money managers may not define their decisions in

this way. Instead, they may see only that interest rates continue to rise, in spite of a constant rate of monetary inflation. And so they step up the money-creating process, as necessary, to hold interest rates at a desired level.

THE CYCLE IN ACTION

We can see this process graphically in the chart on page 45. It shows the rate of monetary inflation, plotted monthly, from January 1960 to June 1978. The solid line indicates, at any given point, the amount by which the basic money supply (M_1) increased over the previous twelve months.[1]

For example, in January 1960, the money supply had increased by 0.8% since January 1959. In June 1978, the last month plotted, the money supply had increased by 8.8% since June 1977.

The rate goes up and down—but mostly up. As we've seen already, this isn't an accident; only a rising rate can keep the inflationary boom going.

The dilemma now facing the money managers is pictured on the chart by the upward channel (indicated by two broken lines). Whenever the monetary inflation rate has gone *above* the upper broken line, the economy has "heated up." Stock prices have soared upward, the unemployment rate has gone down, and business conditions have appeared to be quite good. But, a year or two later, the price inflation rate moved upward to levels that were considered dangerous at the time.

Whenever the monetary inflation has dropped *below* the lower broken line, the opposite has happened. Stock prices tumbled, unemployment rates went up, and the economy was officially declared to be in a recession. Price inflation declined afterward; but, by that time, the government was already neutralizing that benefit by stimulating the money supply again.

---

[1] M_1 is the amount of currency in circulation outside of banks, plus the amount of checking deposits at commercial banks. It is the nation's basic money supply.

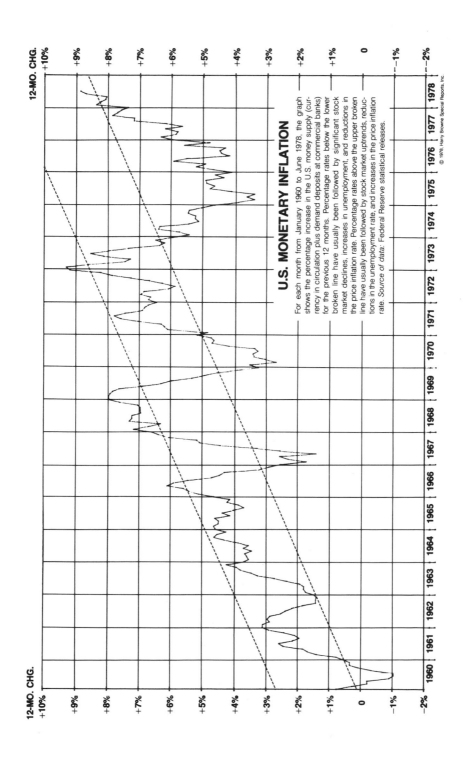

U.S. MONETARY INFLATION

For each month from January 1960 to June 1978, the graph shows the percentage increase in the U.S. money supply (currency in circulation plus demand deposits at commercial banks) for the previous 12 months. Percentage rates below the lower broken line have usually been followed by significant stock market declines, increases in unemployment, and reductions in the price inflation rate. Percentage rates above the upper broken line have usually been followed by stock market uptrends, reductions in the unemployment rate, and increases in the price inflation rate. *Source of data:* Federal Reserve statistical releases.

There is a time lag between a change in the rate of monetary inflation and its visible economic effects. The lag can be anywhere from three months to two years—depending upon the particular effect and upon surrounding economic conditions.

During the period when the monetary inflation rate stayed within the two broken lines, economic conditions were usually described as "normal." But the broken lines keep getting higher and higher—meaning that a "normal" condition can be sustained only by higher rates of monetary inflation.

In 1961, for example, a 2½% monetary inflation rate moved the stock market to an all-time *high*. But in 1974, a 5½% rate caused a twelve-year *low*. With the 2½% rate in 1961, unemployment was 5.6%; but the 5½% rate in 1974 pushed unemployment to 8.4% the following year. Thus, higher monetary rates produced smaller benefits.

In 1975 monetary inflation plunged further below the broken line than ever before. That caused what has been considered generally to be the worst recession (depression?) since the 1930s.

The sharp increase in the rate in early 1975 gave the stock market a nice boost. And another sharp increase a year later caused the stock market to go up again. But the monetary rates were still low enough to prevent the economy from recovering to a condition that would have been considered normal a few years before.

On the other hand, the rates weren't low enough to allow price inflation to go below 4.8% in 1976. It's easy to see why we now have high unemployment and high price inflation at the same time—even though the Keynesian economists assured us a few years ago that it wasn't possible.

As of June 1978 the monetary inflation rate had moved back up to the lower broken line. Because this book was going to press then, I can't give you a later report. At that time I expected the rate to drop again or level off because it was still above the Federal Reserve's targets for money supply growth. But the dropping rate would push interest rates up further and aggravate economic conditions. And so I anticipated that monetary inflation would be accelerated sometime near the end of 1978. That would provide the impetus for the next bull market in stocks.

SOFT LANDING

Pity the poor Federal Reserve governors. They're caught in a terrible dilemma. They set modest growth rates for the money supply—in the area of 4½% to 7% per year. But those rates are well below the lower broken line on the graph.

To keep interest rates from rising dramatically, they'll have to inject more new money into the economy than they've planned on. If they don't, the economy will plunge back into a recession that may be worse than the 1975 contraction.

On the other hand, if they let the monetary inflation rate rise to the necessary 10% or beyond, price inflation will undoubtedly increase beyond the 12% rate of 1974.

What are they to do? There's not much they can do. And the futility of the situation in which they're trapped makes it particularly dangerous for us to assume to know how such trapped individuals may react.

Some economists believe the economy can make a "soft landing" from these inflation rates. They believe that price inflation could be brought under control without disturbing the economy if the monetary inflation rate were reduced gradually—perhaps by ½% per year. In fact, this has been the Federal Reserve's announced policy since 1974.

I'm willing to be shown, but I don't see how it will happen. For one thing, the graph on page 45 shows that the Fed is still producing wide swings in the rate—even during the recent years of the supposed policy of gradualism.

In addition, my view of economics tells me that if the monetary inflation rate is kept constant, many companies will go under. Reducing it even gradually will produce effects that are worse.

Of course, monetary inflation will have to be reduced

sooner or later. And the sooner the mistakes of the past are paid for, the sooner the economy can begin with a clean slate. But I don't believe the money managers are willing to let that happen. If they were, the politicians would probably hire someone else.

RUNAWAY INFLATION

On the other hand, if the monetary inflation rate continues upward with the broken lines on the graph, there can be consequences of another kind.

At some point the price inflation rate will reach a level where everyone will realize that it isn't profitable to hold onto dollars while they depreciate. The rush to get rid of dollars, in exchange for anything of value, could cause price inflation to escalate to horrendous rates.

There's no way to know what level of price inflation would provide the takeoff point to runaway inflation. But there's no question that it's possible.

In some countries, the rate of monetary inflation has reached thousands of percent per year before the currency became worthless. But in the U.S. the currency could be destroyed totally at much lower rates. The U.S. has a credit system that makes it possible for people to get along with very little cash; consequently, they can be expected to spend the cash quickly whenever price inflation makes it too unprofitable to hold it. In other countries the need to hold cash is greater—even when the holder can feel it shrinking in his pocket.

An inflation rate of, say, 30% per year might lead to a flight from the dollar that would worsen the rise in prices. From then on, inflation would feed on itself—taking the U.S. into runaway inflation and, possibly, to a complete breakdown of the currency system.

A number of people have said that the U.S. could never suffer a runaway inflation like those of Latin America or of Germany in the 1920s or Hungary in the 1940s. As evidence they cite the differences in capital structure and other economic features that supposedly separate the U.S. from these other countries. The point that I believe is missed is that these foreign economies operate as they do *because* of inflation. If the U.S. economy suffered a similar inflation, it, too, would become more primitive.

In all my investment books I've warned that runaway inflation is a possibility that shouldn't be ignored. However, I don't believe that it's inevitable.

It's easy to believe that the politicians will do anything necessary to avoid a depression—even if it means inflating us right into runaway inflation. But that implies an economic acumen that they don't possess.

The politicians haven't succeeded in warding off recessions over the past thirty years—although every politician is against recessions. To prevent the 1975 recession, and later to get us out of it, the politicians could have inflated the money supply by 100%—but they didn't.

They can choose to accept inflation as the price of fighting unemployment. But that doesn't mean they know precisely how much monetary inflation will be necessary to win the battle. Nor does it mean that they'll even pay attention to. monetary inflation rates.

Certainly the politicians can be expected to promote various programs to fight unemployment—running large federal deficits to "stimulate" the economy. These deficits encourage monetary inflation because the Federal Reserve has to buy many of the government's new bonds in order to keep interest rates down. But the amount of monetary inflation that follows from a deficit is unpredictable.

The politicians can underestimate the amount of stimulation required at any time, as they did in 1973 and 1974. In that situation, by the time they reacted, it was too late to prevent the recession of 1974 and 1975.

And deflation can feed upon itself—just as runaway inflation can. The scenario is easy to visualize: If the monetary inflation rate is too small to sustain past mistakes, banks will have to call in loans from corporations. Many corporations won't have the cash, and some of the banks will go under. If enough banks fail, many people will feel safer with their cash at home, federal insurance or no federal insurance.

Runs on banks could occur—and the runs could easily exhaust the token resources of the Federal Deposit Insurance Corporation.

In 1974 it was Franklin National Bank that went under. The next time, it might be two or three big banks. And that might set off a frightening chain reaction—as other banks lose money kept at the banks that fail.[2]

A deliberate policy of deflating the money supply isn't necessary to touch off a deflation. Just by not increasing the money supply fast enough, the deflationary spark can be ignited.

DEFLATION, OR RUNAWAY INFLATION?

In my *Monetary Crisis* book, I said there was a 50% chance of runaway inflation by 1980. In light of what's happened since then (1973), I would reduce the chances to 15% or less by 1980. Over a longer period, say through 1988, I would rate the chance at 35%. In other words, there's about one chance in three that we'll have runaway inflation in the U.S. by 1988.

I believe there's about a 50% chance of a deflation by 1988. That leaves a 10% chance of a continuation of the present "stagflation" for another ten years. And, oh yes, I'll reserve the last 5% as the chance that the "soft landing" approach will succeed.

Although these estimates (guesses) are for the period through 1988, that doesn't mean that none of these things could happen sooner.

Deflation is the more present danger. It shouldn't happen during a period when the monetary inflation rate is rising

[2] Franklin National's ostensible problem was a loss suffered in foreign currency trading. Not surprisingly, however, big banks rarely go under except during periods of deflation (or a slowdown in the monetary inflation rate)—regardless of the ostensible problem. (The banking problem is examined further on page 168.)

(as shown on the graph on page 45). But anytime the monetary inflation rate is dropping, the danger exists.

A runaway inflation would take more time to develop. You would be forewarned by a period of steadily rising price inflation rates. And price inflation would have to exceed 20% before a runaway inflation could get started.

Until such time as a full-scale deflation occurs, we can expect continually high price inflation rates—high by the standards of the 1950s. It's very unlikely that the inflation rate will fall below 4% in the best of circumstances. And it may be many years before we'll see even 4% again.

THE SHORT TERM

Short-term forecasts must be taken with a grain of salt. I even gave up forecasting once. But forecasting is addictive; like smoking and drinking, you never really give it up "forever." And so I'll suggest the scenario I see for the next two years from the vantage point of June 1978.

As I indicated earlier, I expect the monetary inflation rate to drop during late 1978 (as the Federal Reserve struggles to get back within its growth-rate target range). Sometime around the end of 1978, interest rates should be too high and the economic problems too great; the Fed will have to respond with new monetary inflation.

Price inflation has been rising since 1976, due to the upsurge in monetary inflation from 1975 to 1978. Price inflation will probably continue to increase until at least the early part of 1979. The peak rate is unpredictable, but it could easily exceed 10%.

Sometime in 1979, the rate should begin to retreat— due to the lower monetary inflation rates of late 1978. We could see twelve to eighteen months of falling inflation rates, but the lowest twelve-month rate reached is unlikely to be less than 7%. If I'm correct in expecting monetary inflation to accelerate early in 1979, price inflation will probably start upward again in the second half of 1980.

The stock market should continue to suffer from the restraining monetary conditions through 1978. The next bull market should begin almost immediately with the speed-up in monetary inflation—probably during the first half of 1979.

I can't anticipate when the Federal Reserve will bring that round of monetary inflation to a halt. But, most likely, it won't be before late 1980. When it happens, the stock market will head into another bear market. And within a year or so afterward, another recession will be upon us. During 1981, we could see the surprise deflationary collapse I've spoken of.

The critical factor in all these estimates is the rate of monetary inflation. If the Federal Reserve changes its policies, I'll have to change my estimates.

Fortunately, it isn't necessary to know exactly how events will develop. I believe the investment strategy outlined in later chapters will protect you and probably provide a profit, whichever way the markets go.

The important thing to realize is that anything is possible. It isn't necessary to predict the future. But it *is* necessary to be prepared for all possibilities.

4

THE CRISES
TO COME

IN MY BOOK *How You Can Profit from the Coming Devaluation*, published in 1970, I said that a devaluation of the U.S. dollar was inevitable. I also said that we were in for higher price inflation and bad economic conditions generally.

Because these events did, in fact, occur, many people have attributed to me predictive powers that I certainly don't possess. It's one thing to understand that monetary inflation and government interference will create unfortunate consequences. It's another thing to know exactly when those consequences will show themselves—and exactly how they'll unfold.[1]

My investment suggestions have always asssumed a state of uncertainty; there's a great deal about the future we can't anticipate. It's dangerous to believe you know precisely what will happen next year—just because you understand what's happening this year.

To me the evidence is overwhelming that the crises will continue for several years to come. But I won't pretend that I know exactly what shape those crises will take.

Yet crises of the future must be planned for, even if they

---

[1] For example, the two devaluations of the dollar (in 1971 and 1973) turned out to be fairly small. The effects I had expected to follow from the devaluation occurred instead through the dollar's fall, and gold's rise, in the free market.

can't be predicted. You must somehow make your investment program immune from almost any surprise.

The potential investment crises are of two types: (1) future economic events that will result from the mistakes of the past and present; and (2) future actions of the government that might interfere with otherwise well-laid plans.

The first type of crisis was covered in the last chapter. I said that the general economic future will take the shape of: (1) a deflationary crash and panic; or (2) a runaway inflation, followed by a deflation; or (3) a fairly long-term continuation of the present "stagflation," followed by either number 1 or 2. I believe that the investment program I'll suggest can protect you against all three possibilities.

This chapter will discuss some of the programs the government may impose in trying to deal with any of the three economic scenarios. The discussion is intended to be suggestive, rather than all-inclusive. No matter how many possibilities I might think of, I'm sure the politicians can think of many more—since that's their business.

WAGE, PRICE AND PROFIT CONTROLS

An obvious possibility is that the government will attempt to outlaw price inflation with wage and price controls.

As any economics student knows, persistent and continuing price inflation can be caused only by monetary inflation—increases in the money supply. In the absence of monetary inflation, a large price increase in any product (such as oil) will not cause the general price level to go up. Consumers can spend only as much money as they have. If they spend more on oil, they must spend less on other products—causing the prices of the others to go down. So long as the money supply remains unchanged, the general price level has to remain unchanged—no matter what happens to any individual price.

But still the politicians believe that wage and price controls are the answer. With controls in force they feel free to inflate the money supply. But meanwhile the pressure for price increases builds up. And, eventually, the controls cause so much damage that the politicians are forced to remove them—and the price level soars upward. One reason that the price inflation rates of 1973–1975 were so jarring is that they incorporated price inflation that had been suppressed by controls during 1971 and 1972.

Yet the lessons of the past will have to be taught again and again. I believe that further price controls are an overwhelming probability for some time during the next few years.

Of course we should be aware that controls might be presented in a form that's different from what we're used to. For example, Dr. Henry Wallich, a governor of the Federal Reserve Board, has suggested a plan, which he calls an "incomes policy," that masquerades as a somewhat voluntary program.

With this plan a company is "free" to charge any price it believes its customers will pay, and to pay whatever wage rates it believes its employees will accept. However, if a company raises wages above the government's guidelines, it will have to pay a special tax. And if its profits exceed specified levels, the company will be subject to an "excess profits" tax. So, deterred from paying higher wages and prevented from earning higher net profits, the company will have no reason to raise prices.[2]

If this plan is adopted, we'll probably be told that it's less coercive and less bureaucratic than the old wage and price controls. But its object will be the same—to keep wages and prices from moving naturally in response to monetary inflation.

Dr. Wallich's plan has special consequences for investments—especially stock prices. Under normal wage and price controls, a company with superior management might be able to profit in spite of the controls. But if profit increases incur special taxes, what incentive has the company to prosper? And so a stock price could increase only because of expectations extending beyond the eventual end to the controls.

[2] London *Times,* February 21, 1978.

EXCHANGE CONTROLS

No government ever accepts the blame for its currency's falling. It finds someone else to blame and often responds to the crisis with exchange controls—restrictions against sending money out of the country.

Sometimes the restrictions are mild or easily avoided— such as the U.S. interest equalization tax that was imposed on foreign securities during the 1960s.

However, many governments currently prohibit all transfers of money out of the country except for approved purposes. Usually, money cannot be sent freely to a foreign country to purchase investments such as foreign currencies or foreign stocks and bonds.

Typically, the announcement of exchange controls is timed to prevent last-minute exports of investment money. The government slams the door shut without warning. Because there's no particular reason that the U.S. government won't impose exchange controls, it makes sense to have some capital outside the country at all times.

Exchange controls imposed by major governments usually exempt foreigners from the restrictions. Thus if you had money in a Swiss bank, your bank could make investments (in its name) in the U.S. and withdraw the money from the U.S. when the investments were sold.

REACTIONS TO FISCAL CRISES

The government's unrealistic welfare programs are leading it deeper into debt. This isn't news, but the way the government responds to its growing deficits may catch many people by surprise.

The possibilities, like the number of welfare programs, are endless. So I'll use the Social Security system as an example.

The Social Security program, although called an insurance plan, has never been insurance at all; it is simply a disguised form of welfare. If it were insurance, it would be voluntary, and the benefits it paid would not depend on the recipient's income.

However, by calling it an insurance program, the government is forced to conform to certain conventions. For one, benefits may be paid only from Social Security taxes—never from other revenues of the government. Also it's implied that the benefits an individual receives come from the tax money he once paid in—invested and nurtured by the Social Security system during the interim. They aren't, of course. Today's benefits are covered by the taxes that workers are currently paying—as in a chain letter scheme. There is no money put away for a rainy day—or for a sunny one either.

As the benefit obligations grow yearly, higher Social Security taxes must be imposed in order to pay them. But while some politicians are fighting to raise the taxes in order to keep Social Security from going broke, others are deploring the low benefits and seeking to increase them.

Through it all, the Social Security crisis is getting closer and closer. Whereas in 1947 the Social Security "trust fund" was equal to seventeen *years'* worth of benefits, by 1976 the fund was equal to only seven *months'* benefits.

There's much more to the Social Security story than we can cover here. But the main point is that many serious observers predict bankruptcy for Social Security. That won't happen—not unless the entire government goes under—but some drastic changes will be forced upon it.

Instead of a declaration of bankruptcy, it's likely that the government will continue to alter unilaterally the terms of the imaginary insurance contract you have with it. Here are some of the changes that might occur:

1. A wealth test will be added to the income test. Unless you can prove that you have no private insurance or other capital, you won't receive any benefits—no matter how much you've contributed.

2. The retirement age will be raised from sixty-five to some higher figure.

3. Persons *able* to work past the retirement age will be denied benefits, even if they choose not to work. (This and the previous possibility conflict with the efforts to fight unemployment, of course.)

4. The cost-of-living clause, which adjusts benefits for inflation, will be eliminated or weakened.

5. Social Security benefits will be made subject to income tax.

6. Other government revenues will be used to pay benefits.

7. The Social Security tax will be increased (a certainty).

8. Benefits will be reduced.

The last possibility is a virtual certainty; however, it's unlikely that the change will be called a reduction. More likely, one of the first five possibilities (or another I haven't thought of) will be used to disguise the reduction.

Of course, whatever step is taken, the default will occur without anyone's admitting that the entire system was a fraud from the start. The justification probably will be that some people are profiting unfairly from Social Security (by taking what they were promised) at the expense of the honest American worker. You won't hear any confessions that the system was simply a bad idea.

Social Security is only one example. Other government programs will be revised when it becomes impossible to sustain them in their present form. Among these might be the Federal Deposit Insurance Corporation (and other savings guaranty programs) and mortgage insurance programs (unless runaway inflation makes the mortgages worthless).

In some cases government obligations will continue to be honored—but perhaps with unmarketable federal bonds that don't mature for several years.

The simplest and most realistic way of looking at these programs is to expect nothing from them, to avoid contributing to them when possible, and to pay no attention to government guarantees of any kind.

OTHER CRISES

As I said earlier, the range of possible crises is endless. And to call attention to specific possibilities may be a disservice in that it could distract you from the full range of possibilities. A politician up a tree is a very imaginative creature.

The general concerns are these:

1. You may be prevented from sending money out of the country. This would limit your investment opportunities to those available in the U.S. And if the U.S. economy is depressed, you might find that there is no profitable way to invest your money. Even if you found a way of getting money out of the country then, it probably would be both expensive and dangerous.

2. Investments you hold could be damaged badly by government actions—such as price controls, profit limitations, or other new regulations.

3. Past profits could be wiped out. Surtaxes could be imposed on investment profits in general. Or surtaxes could be imposed on investments that are judged to be against the "public interest"—such as short sales in a declining stock market, or purchases of gold or foreign currencies. These taxes could be imposed after the fact—so that you wouldn't have known you were going to be subject to them at the time you made the investment.[3]

With these possibilities in mind, I see four general rules that should influence investment strategy for the coming years:

1. Have some of your capital outside the U.S. Later, if exchange controls are imposed, you can decide whether you'll comply. If you have no money outside the country, you'll have no choices.

---

[3] In San Francisco, for example, a movement developed in 1978 to confiscate profits made on the sale of a house. Although it probably won't succeed now, it may be just a few years ahead of its time.

2. Try to invest in ways that don't require that you expose your entire capital to government interference. For example, if you purchase an option instead of the underlying stock, you've exposed less of your capital. There's less to be confiscated and less to be lost if a new regulation ruins the investment. The strategy I'll suggest is more refined than that, but it relies on that principle.

3. Hedge against the unexpected. This is good policy at any time, but more so today. Hedging doesn't mean splitting your funds 50-50 in opposite directions. It means risking a small portion of your capital to buy insurance through an investment medium that's highly leveraged but has limited downside risk. In this way, a small investment will provide a big compensation if things go against you. I'll discuss these hedges in Part IV.

4. Whatever your present attitude, realize that any government is capable of carrying things to the point where the most scrupulous citizen will break the law without qualm. It's happened in many other countries; it could happen here.

You can reserve judgment on this if you hold some money in a form that doesn't leave records for the government to examine. So long as this money isn't used to earn more money (interest, dividends, *realized* capital gains), you aren't breaking the tax laws. By keeping some of your assets off the record, you avoid having to decide now what your attitude will be later. This gives you the *choice* later; but if everything is on the public record now, you leave yourself with no choice but to submit.

These four guidelines should be kept in mind when creating an investment strategy. Some of them may seem extreme. But some of the things I suggested in 1970 seemed extreme then.

5

THE CRISES
& HARD-MONEY
INVESTMENTS

THE PRESENT ERA OF CONTINUOUS CRISES ERUPTED AT THE beginning of the decade.

At about the same time, a particular class of investments began shooting upward in price. From 1970 to March 1978:

1. The price of gold rose from $35 to $180 per ounce—a gain of 414%.

2. The price of silver rose from $1.60 to $5.30 per ounce—a gain of 231%.

3. The price of the Swiss franc rose from 23 to 53 U.S. cents—a gain of 130%.

Gold and silver are often referred to as "hard-money" investments. The term is used because gold and silver are the most enduring forms of money, able to survive any political or economic disorder.

A currency rates the hard-money title, too, if its government will redeem it, on demand, for a fixed amount of gold or silver. And even though the Swiss franc (as with all currencies) is not actually redeemable in gold or silver, it is often called a "hard currency" or a "hard-money investment." The franc has this status because the Swiss government has been very restrained about increasing the supply of francs, just as it would be if it were actually on a gold or silver standard.

Because hard-money investments began soaring in price at about the time the crises erupted, it's easy to conclude that the crises caused the price increases. If so, a continuation of the crises should propel the investments still higher—and at the same rapid rate.

For example, if gold has increased by 414% so far, you might expect it to reach $900 within a few years—provided the crises continue.

But gold has risen for more reasons than just the events of the 1970s. It should continue to appreciate—but for different reasons, and at a slower rate, and in a different pattern. The same can be said of silver and the Swiss franc; there will be further rises, but the easy days are probably over.

This chapter will examine the causes of the past price increases. By understanding those increases, we can see why future rises will be different.

THE CAUSES

Why, then, did these investments appreciate so dramatically in the 1970s?

Each of the price increases was the inevitable consequence of a long period of price control. At the end of the control period, the price was certain to rise quickly—to make up for lost time.

When the price of a commodity is prevented from rising to a level that matches the resources of producers to the needs of consumers, a serious imbalance always follows. On the one hand, it will be unprofitable to produce the commodity; but on the other hand, demand for the commodity will be greater than it would have been at a higher price.

There are two methods by which a government can suppress a price. The first is simply to order that no sales occur at prices higher than the figure the government decrees. The government backs up its order with fines or imprisonment. This method is the more common and is always the basis for a program of general wage and price controls.

The second method is a little more subtle. It can be used only to suppress the price of an individual commodity and can work only when the government owns a large supply of the commodity. From its stockpile, the government sells enough of the product in the open market to keep the price from going up. If you (or your supplier) can purchase the product from the government at a given price, you won't pay a higher price to anyone else. So everyone does business at no more than the government's price.

The same principle can be reversed. If the government will purchase, at an announced price, all of a product that's offered to it, no one will sell at a lower price elsewhere. Thus the price is "supported" by the government's purchases, and the government accumulates a stockpile of the commodity.

The histories of gold and silver are histories of price control. First, the government bought to support prices. Later, it sold to suppress prices. Finally, when it stopped selling, prices rose—to the great benefit of the investors who had understood what was coming. Foreign currencies have gone through a similar history of price control.

These price control programs were described in detail in Chapters 11, 15, and 24–26 of my book *You Can Profit from a Monetary Crisis*. So here I'll provide only a brief summary.

GOLD

In 1792 the U.S. government promised to pay out a fixed quantity of gold for every U.S. dollar presented to it. With only brief interruptions, this commitment was honored until 1933. From then on, the government paid out gold for dollars only if the dollars were presented by other governments; U.S. citizens could no longer ask for gold. This arrangement continued until 1971, when the government ended the dollar's gold convertibility entirely.

Until 1933 the government was, in effect, selling gold for $20.67 to anyone who wanted it. Consequently, the price (in dollars) could go no higher. And because the government also agreed to purchase gold (from miners or anyone else) at $20.67, the price could go no lower.

Similar systems operated in many other countries, with the price of gold fixed in terms of the local currency. Indirectly this also fixed the price of one currency relative to another, since a unit of any currency was simply a receipt for a stated amount of gold. When a government changed its buying and selling price for gold, it automatically altered its currency's exchange rate.

And from time to time a government did change its buying and selling price for gold, usually by raising it. This came about because the government had increased the supply of its currency too much, reducing the currency's buying power. Because the currency's general buying power had shrunk, gold was the only thing still available at a low price, and a flow of requests to exchange currency for gold would reduce the government's gold reserves.

At that point the government would default on its promise to trade a fixed amount of gold in exchange for currency. It would make a new promise, offering less gold for each unit of currency and thereby raising the price of gold. This is the meaning of a devaluation.

On January 31, 1934, the U.S. government devalued the dollar—raising the price of gold from $20.67 to $35 per ounce. But this devaluation was abnormal. In the four preceding years, the currency had undergone a severe deflation, which had raised its purchasing power. Although this made a devaluation unnecessary, the devaluation nevertheless occurred.

As a result, the $35 gold price was much higher than the buying power of the dollar called for. And from 1934 to 1949, foreign governments chose to exchange gold for dollars; they valued the 35 dollars more than they valued one ounce of gold.[1]

---

[1] The foreign demand for dollars was further stimulated by World War II. Many foreign governments, fearing confiscation of gold by their enemies, traded gold to the U.S. government in exchange for dollars and then left the dollars in New York. But the basic trend of selling gold for dollars prevailed before and after the war.

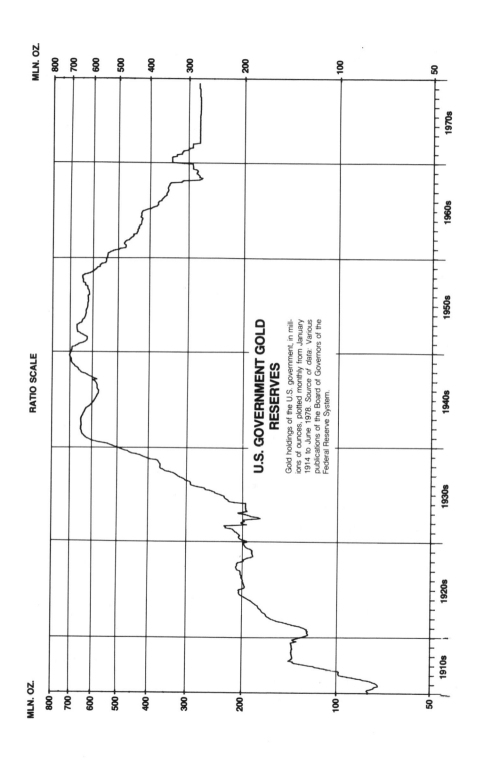

RATIO SCALE

MLN. OZ.

U.S. GOVERNMENT GOLD
RESERVES

Gold holdings of the U.S. government, in millions of ounces, plotted monthly from January 1914 to June 1978. *Source of data:* Various publications of the Board of Governors of the Federal Reserve System.

The U.S. government's gold stock increased from 1934 until 1949, when the trend changed. Thereafter other governments valued the gold more and began returning dollars to the U.S. Treasury in exchange for it.

From 1949 until 1971, as the price of everything else rose, the $35 price became progressively more unrealistic. But as long as the U.S. government would sell at $35, the price was effectively restrained.

Only governments could obtain gold from the U.S. Treasury, but individuals could trade gold in the free market. Although the free-market price fluctuated, it generally stayed close to $35 after 1952—probably due to the ever-present possibility of government sales in the free market.

But the cost of mining had risen considerably since 1934, and the supply available to the free market was shrinking. And so in 1961 the free-market price was poised to move to higher levels. Most governments wanted to hold it back, however, and so seven major governments formed the "Gold Pool." Led by the U.S. government, they bought and sold gold in the London market, as needed, to keep the price between $34.75 and $35.25.

By 1968 the Gold Pool had sold several hundred million ounces, and investors were buying so much gold that the remaining government supplies were threatened. On April 18, 1968, the Gold Pool gave up and went out of business. The price of gold was set free.

Governments continued to trade gold among themselves at the $35 price under an arrangement called the "two-tier" market—meaning one tier at $35 for governments and another at a fluctuating price for investors.

Many investors believed that with the Gold Pool out of business, the free-market price would rise dramatically. The need for massive government sales to hold the price at $35 was proof that $35 was too low. But the great quantities the government had sold were now in the hands of investors, many of whom were prepared to take their profits at prices not too far above $35.

This large private stockpile kept the market well supplied,

and so the price fluctuated mostly between $39 and $43 until late 1969. Then the price sank back to $35—probably because the expected rally hadn't developed, causing the supply from investors to increase.

But the fundamentals were still there; gold was greatly underpriced. And so in August 1970, with the supplies of impatient sellers apparently exhausted, gold began its ascent.

From 1970 to 1974, gold was searching for the realistic price that had been hidden since 1949. Nineteen years of price suppression (from 1949 to 1968) were offset in a dramatic four-year price rise—the inevitable aftermath of price controls.

It would be convenient to assume that the price rise should match the amount of inflation that had occurred during the price-control period. But prices don't go up and down in unison. To know where the price would finally settle, you could only wait and see.

The one thing that was certain in 1970 was that gold would have to be much higher than $35—and that it would reach that higher price soon.

As we'll see in Chapter 6, a bull market almost always goes too far. The gold rally was no exception. In the last stages, people who had never thought about gold were lined up in front of coin stores—trying to get on the bandwagon. Consequently, when gold reached $195, it was at an untenable level.

The price retreated and finally leveled off in mid-1975 at around $165. This was probably the natural level it had been seeking.

Later in 1975 the International Monetary Fund announced that it would auction off six million ounces of gold each year. This increased the available supply, and the price fell.

Just as the bull bandwagon had taken the price too high, the bear bandwagon took it too low. Gold dropped to $103, where it was underpriced once again, trading at a price below what was needed to keep supply and demand in balance. So a new bull market began. From August 1976 to March 1978, the price rose from $103 to $180 per ounce.

The bull market of 1970 to 1974 accomplished its purpose of offsetting the nineteen years of price control. Because the effects of price control have now been offset, we need to understand how present and future events will influence the price of gold.

My analysis of this will be given in Chapter 15.

THE SWISS FRANC

Currencies were price-controlled through a system of fixed exchange rates established in 1944. The ideal of the system was a world in which exchange rates never changed. But since governments were inflating their currencies at different speeds, every currency price was becoming unrealistic—some too high, others too low.

It was assumed that when a currency became overpriced, there would be a run on the gold supply that backed it. The decline in the government's gold holdings would force it to devalue and establish a new gold-to-currency rate.

As we've seen, the dollar became overpriced in terms of gold as early as 1949. But the enormous U.S. gold hoard seemed large enough to withstand any conceivable run. And so gold was left at $35, and U.S. holdings began to dwindle.

Just as the dollar was overpriced in terms of gold, it also was overpriced in terms of several other currencies. To sustain the unrealistic exchange rate, many governments regularly purchased dollars in the open market—paying with their own currencies.

Since the trend in these currencies was all in one direction, the support of the dollar made the exchange rates more and more unrealistic. Foreign governments were acquiring dollars at a progressively faster pace. Until 1968 they regularly exchanged these unwanted dollars for gold at the U.S. Treasury.

But in 1968 when the Gold Pool shut down, the U.S. government began rationing its gold. While continuing to quote a $35 price, it required foreign governments that wanted to buy gold to stand in line. And in 1971 the last pretense of gold convertibility was dropped; not even foreign governments could redeem dollars for gold.

Thereafter, a foreign government could hold its exchange rate steady only by buying and holding large quantities of dollars. And there was always the chance that the dollar might be devalued someday, automatically marking down the value of the foreign government's holdings.

Foreign governments that supported the dollar had another problem. The dollars were purchased with new issues of their own currencies, which inflated their own money supplies and distorted their own economies.

The situation was too disruptive to be permanent. Sooner or later the system would break down and currency prices would move to more realistic levels.

Finally, on January 23, 1973, the Swiss government threw in the towel. It reduced its purchases of dollars and announced that it would no longer maintain a fixed dollar-franc rate. Within a few weeks almost all the other major governments abandoned the fixed exchange-rate system.

Governments have continued to buy and sell dollars in the currency markets. However, they no longer announce fixed prices. Instead, a government will try to hold the price in a given range until it becomes too expensive to do so. Then it will back off and allow the price to move, after which the government will take a stand in a new price range.

As a result, currency prices don't move directly to their natural levels. They move up and back, influenced both by continuing government intervention and by speculative bandwagons. However, the tendency is for each currency to move eventually toward the level dictated by supply and demand.

During the fixed-price period, the Swiss franc became the most underpriced currency. And so it had further to rise when the fixed exchange-rate system collapsed. In addition, the Swiss government has intervened less since 1973 than the governments of other strong currencies. The Swiss attitude has been that it's better to let the franc rise than to risk inflation by buying too many dollars with too many newly created francs.

A government fights an increase in its currency's price in order to benefit export industries. If its currency rises, the country's products become more expensive for foreigners to buy—and therefore more difficult for producers to export.

But trade problems are really only symptoms of more fundamental disorders. If the pattern of industry is frozen by monetary inflation, government subsidies, and government-backed labor unions, it's difficult for the economy to adjust to changing conditions. But when government interference is relatively mild, the country can adapt fairly easily to new circumstances, including changes in exchange rates.

The labor market and trade in general are much freer in Switzerland than in most other countries. And so in 1976, even after the franc had appreciated 60% in three years, Switzerland recorded its first foreign trade *surplus* in twenty-five years. Meanwhile, other governments have been afraid they'll lose export sales if their currencies rise too much.

The franc's last rally ran from August 1977 to February 1978 and took the price to a high of 56 U.S. cents. I believe that this rally finally took the franc to a realistic level—and then past it. The years of price control have been more than compensated for.

How I estimated the natural price level, and what I believe the franc will do from here on, will be discussed in Chapter 16.

SILVER

Silver suffered the longest period of price control. And the controls were the most extreme in their effect upon supply and demand.

For most of the period from 1873 to the 1950s, the government *bought* silver to hold the price up. But thereafter it *sold* silver to keep the price down.

The government withdrew from the silver market gradually from 1967 to 1971. As with gold, the government had sold large quantities from its stockpile—in this case at $1.29

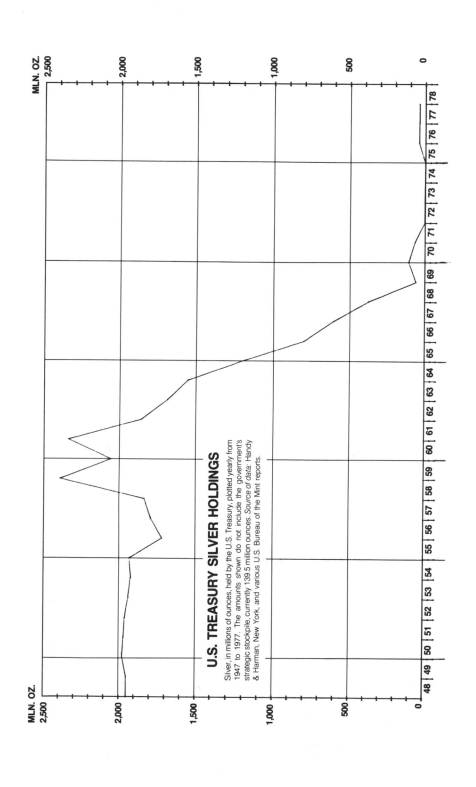

U.S. TREASURY SILVER HOLDINGS

Silver, in millions of ounces, held by the U.S. Treasury, plotted yearly from 1947 to 1977. The amounts shown do not include the government's strategic stockpile, currently 139.5 million ounces. *Source of data:* Handy & Harman, New York, and various U.S. Bureau of the Mint reports.

MLN. OZ.
2,500

2,000

1,500

1,000

500

0

MLN. OZ.
2,500

2,000

1,500

1,000

500

0

48 | 49 | 50 | 51 | 52 | 53 | 54 | 55 | 56 | 57 | 58 | 59 | 60 | 61 | 62 | 63 | 64 | 65 | 66 | 67 | 68 | 69 | 70 | 71 | 72 | 73 | 74 | 75 | 76 | 77 | 78

per ounce—and much of the silver had been bought by investors who expected the price to rise. These investors continued to supply the market after the government withdrew.

The price began to move upward from $1.29 in November 1971—and reached a high of $6.50 in February 1974. Then the price retreated and stabilized in the $4 to $5 range.

The statistics show that industrial consumption of silver far exceeds the production of silver. It's apparent that the difference has been offset by sales from the stockpiles held by investors. For four years, this supply has kept the price from moving much above $5.

Finally, in early 1978, there were signs that the market was running out of $5 sellers. Investors still held a great deal of silver, but too few of the hoarders were willing to sell at $5. And so as expected, in March the price moved through the $5 level to $5.50, retreated to $5, and then began its present rally.[2]

As with the other hard-money investments, the basis for silver's dramatic rise from 1971 to 1974 was the need to undo many years of price control. But unlike gold and the Swiss franc, that purpose hasn't yet been fully achieved.

Thanks to the years of price control, the worldwide consumption of silver still outruns production. The deficit is offset by investors who sell silver that was formerly part of the government's price-fixing stockpile. As the stockpile is gradually used up, the price will have to move higher to bring consumption and production into balance.

I'll discuss this further in Chapter 17.

SUMMARY

It is widely believed that the dramatic price increases of hard-money investments were a response to the crises of the early 1970s. But the pressures for price increases had been building up for many years. If these investments hadn't been

---

2 The advance indications of this price move are discussed in Chapter 17.

price-controlled for so long, the price increases of the early 1970s would have been milder.

The crises did trigger the increases, in that they finally made it impossible for the governments involved to continue controlling prices. But the increases would have come eventually; it was only a matter of time.

Also, the crises themselves added to the long-term potentials of these investments—in ways that we'll look at in Part III. But, mostly, the investments were simply making up for lost time.

With the exception of silver, these investments are now priced approximately at their fundamental values. But those fundamental values continue to increase—a phenomenon that's unique to hard-money investments during these years of crises. Consequently, hard-money investments still warrant special attention.

There will be further appreciation, but it will be for reasons occurring now and in the future. And since most investors don't understand the fundamentals of these investments, there are bound to be unjustified rallies—caused by misguided speculative opinion—followed by steep declines.

Thus, price movements will have to be watched more closely. We'll have to know when to buy, when to sell, and when to watch from the sidelines.

Even with silver, timing will be important. Although it hadn't completed its long-term rise in 1974, the price stalled for four years before moving upward again. That's too long to tie up one's capital without profit.

Except for investors who feel that they can't monitor their portfolios, hard-money investments should no longer be approached with a buy-and-hold attitude.

PART II

INVESTMENT
PHILOSOPHY

6

WHY THERE
ARE TRENDS

THIS PART OF THE BOOK DEALS WITH THE WAY INVESTMENT markets work, with common investment errors, and with the effect those errors can have on investment prices. We begin with a discussion of trends—why they exist, why they go too far, and why they end.

Investment prices often move in trends. Although a trend may not become apparent until it's well under way, trends aren't merely optical illusions that afflict chart watchers. Trends are real, despite the misleading notions many people have about them. An understanding of what is happening during a trend can help to put you on the right side of it— whether the trend is up or down.

INSIDE THE MARKET

Any liquid investment market includes a large number of participants. There are investors—some looking for current income, others looking for capital gains. There are market-makers—dealers who hold an inventory of the investment and quote prices at which they'll buy and sell. In a commodity market, users of the commodity will come to buy, and producers will come to sell. And in some markets, governments will participate by buying or selling to achieve a "public purpose."

Each of the participants has an influence, large or small, on prices. But each one acts from his own motives, with his own opinions, and in response to the information at his disposal.

These differences, especially differences of opinion, create something like a tug-of-war. Prices move as conflicting motivations pull against one another—exerting a net force in one direction or the other.

A trend occurs when there are *changes* in opinions over a period of time. To see what happens, let's follow a hypothetical trend.

Let's say that you invest in tin today at a price of $5 per pound because you believe it will go to $8 by next year. Your opinion about the price may be correct, but, obviously, not everyone in the tin market agrees with you.

How do we know that? If everyone agreed that tin would reach $8 next year, the price would be almost that high already. At any price under $7.25 or so, it would be profitable to buy tin now and hold it for a year, for resale at $8, just as you are doing. So any price lower than $7.25 is evidence that many people don't share your opinion of tin's future.

The current price could be called the collective judgment of the market—based upon today's knowledge and opinions. This idea is expressed in the investment maxim, "The market discounts everything that's known about the future," meaning that today's tin price already reflects what is known about tin.

But there's a danger that this maxim *about* the market will be taken too literally and prevent us from seeing what is happening *within* the market. It's too easy to infer that the collective judgment of the market is a unanimous judgment. It isn't.

Every price is a compromise of conflicting opinions. And like any other compromise, it represents no one's opinion precisely. In fact, each person trading in the market will see the price as either too high or too low—otherwise he'd have no reason to buy or sell at that price.

If investors were unanimous, the world would be quite different from the one we know. Everyone would have about the same portfolio, and trading volume would be nil because there would be no differences of opinion to motivate trades. But in the real world, portfolios differ greatly—because opinions and circumstances differ greatly. And trading is continuous, as some investors buy and others sell.

Whenever an event seems to remake an investment's future, whenever there's something large and new for the market to "know" about the investment's future, the price changes. But the price doesn't change in the way it would in a unanimous market.

The significance of a major event may seem obvious at first, but it isn't. Time is needed for investors to analyze the event and for the event to exert its full impact on producers and consumers. The implications aren't always simple, and there is plenty of room for differing opinions.

A major event will cause the price to move, but the new price is also a compromise. Eventually the price may reach a level consistent with your interpretation of the event. But it doesn't move there immediately, because not everyone agrees with you now. Even if you are correct, the price will move gradually, in steps that eventually add up to a trend—instead of moving in a sharp, straight line to the point you think is correct.

THE TREND BEGINS

Suppose the Bolivian government (which supplies about 12% of the world's tin) announces that it will withhold its tin production from the market next year. This may be what you had hoped for, and so you expect the price to begin its move to $8.

The price does rise, because most investors expect the

Bolivian policy to have the obvious effect. But they don't agree on how great the effect will be. Some think it will push the price to $10; others think $5.50 is about right. And so the price rises sharply the next day—but to $5.70, not to $8.

Is everyone buying at $5.70? Hardly. Not only are some people not buying, others are selling. Among the investors with an opinion different from yours are:

1. Those who anticipated the Bolivian announcement, and who felt that the $5 price already reflected its importance.

2. Those who are surprised by the announcement, but who believe the loss of Bolivian tin won't affect the price by the $3 you estimate.

3. Those who believe the Bolivian government won't stick to its announced policy. Some even see it as a public-relations trick to push prices up.

Investors with these and other relatively bearish opinions exert a restraining influence on the price.

As we can see, "the market" doesn't really "know" anything about tin. Only individuals know things. The market is where they meet to disagree. So no matter how obvious the future of tin or anything else seems to you, someone in the market will be willing to bet against you. Today's price isn't what "the market" sees; it is a compromise, the net result of conflicting judgments.

As time passes, purchases by tin users and sales by tin producers will pull the price in the direction it must go to keep supply and demand in balance. The true importance of the Bolivian announcement will become easier to see, and there will be less room for differences of opinion.

Those who have bet against the actual outcome will change their mind, close their bets, and take their losses.[1] Fewer new participants will bet against an outcome that each day seems more probable. The selling that restrained the price from going where it was destined will abate.

But the losing investors relent at different times, not all

---

1 However, the market isn't a "zero sum game"—in which each player's profit is matched by another player's loss. Each participant has his own reason for being in the market—to obtain capital gains, to earn income, to hedge, etc. It's quite possible for a buyer and a seller each to profit from their transaction—immediately and over a period of time.

on the same day. And so the price moves toward its ultimate level gradually—not in one leap.

As the price approaches $8, no one can know how much further it will go—not even those who correctly forecast a higher price when tin was $5. Some investors will sell their tin before it reaches $8—afraid that their profits may be lost in a sudden turnaround. But like the losing investors, each profit-taker will drop out at his own time.

Some of them may have chosen a specific price objective in advance—the price at which they'll take their profit. Often these objectives are round numbers—such as $6.00, $7.00, or $7.50. The tendency to sell at round numbers can cause the trend to stall or reverse temporarily at these points, as a number of profit-takers unload.

Others may have been holding tin for a long time. An investor may have bought two years ago—when the price was $6.60. He held on to his tin while the price dropped back to $5. Determined never to take a loss on an investment, he's hung on grimly—hoping for a rally that would save him from losing.

The Bolivian announcement was the answer to his dreams. Not only did it offer the hope that the price would return to $6.60, but it also gave him a chance to make a profit. However, as the price heads upward, it stalls here and there. And whenever the price drops a little, that terrible pain returns to his stomach. By the time the price does reach $6.60, the tension has become too great to endure. He sells with relief—happy to get out without a loss.

And so, despite the upward trend that you believe is so obvious, there are plenty of investors willing to sell along the way. As a result the price must labor toward its goal.

THE TREND GOES TOO FAR

When the price finally reaches $8, you're ready to sell and take your well-earned profit. But there are new buyers coming into the market—fortunately for you, since otherwise you'd have no one to sell to.

Why would anyone be buying now that the rally has completed its purpose?

For one thing, there will be people who are forecasting $9 or $10—just as there were others who forecast less than $8. In addition there are investors who have just heard about the Bolivian situation, several months late. They reason that if Bolivia isn't going to sell any tin, and if the price is already $8, then the price will have to go considerably higher. Of course that was *your* reasoning when the price was $5; but they don't realize that other investors have already allowed for the lack of Bolivian tin.

And there are new investors who have never heard of Bolivia. The price of tin is rising, and that's enough for them. The trend is obvious, and they want to get on the bandwagon. They're tired of holding investments that don't move, and tin is moving.

For these and other reasons, new investors will continue to come into the market—even while others are glad to sell and get out. The tug-of-war continues, but with new participants.

If $8 is the price that will match production to consumption, the market will most likely go beyond $8 temporarily. A moving bandwagon normally attracts less-perceptive investors (as well as traders who are counting on them), even if the bandwagon is close to running out of gas.

THE TREND IS OVER

So long as the bulls predominate, the upward trend will continue. But at some point they will be pushing the price *away* from the level dictated by supply-and-demand considerations, instead of toward it. From then on, the rally will become more and more fragile.

We can't know where the rally will finally end, but end it will. It can't go on forever—even if it has begun to seem perpetual. At some point, the forces of supply will outweigh the forces of demand and push the price downward.

Commercial users of tin will cut back on their purchases because they can't pass on the increased costs to their customers. Producers of tin will step up their output, because the higher prices warrant the higher costs of faster production.

And we've already seen that investors won't wait for the highest price to sell their tin. The price moves upward irregularly; and each time there's a slight dip, some investors fear that the rally is over and sell.

Others, even if they see still higher prices coming, will notice how greatly the tin they hold has grown in value. Tin will have become an excessively large percentage of each investment program. So they'll sell a little, merely to restore what they consider to be a prudent balance.

No matter how fast the price moves, no matter how bullish "everyone" is, there are always some people selling. Otherwise, who would supply the tin that the bulls want to buy?

More important yet and easily overlooked is the fact that the general bullishness can't, of itself, make the price go still higher. It may reduce the amount of tin offered for sale, but higher prices require more than just bulls holding tin. To make the price go higher, there must be *new* buyers and additional purchases by old buyers. A higher price requires a demand to buy (backed with money) that exceeds the supply being offered.

The extreme bullishness can be a warning. If most investors are bullish about tin, it may be that everyone who is going to buy has already done so. In that case the price can go no higher.

So one day there won't be enough bulls with enough money to buy all the tin that's offered for sale. Then the upward trend will be over.

DOWNTREND

The downward trend that follows will have the same general pattern as the upward trend. It, too, may pick up steam as it goes along—attracting short-sellers and convincing holders of tin to sell out. Just as the upward trend went above the $8 target, so will the downward trend probably go below it.

But the downward trend will end at some point, too. And it may not go beyond $8 by as much as the upward trend did. The meaning of the Bolivian policy is more widely understood and accepted now. And while the price level required to bring the use and production of tin into harmony can't be known exactly, the market's estimate of it is more accurate now.

If the fundamental basis for the price were to remain at $8, the price movements would become progressively less volatile—fluctuating around $8 in smaller and smaller swings.

But supply and demand conditions change constantly. The changes may be too small to be noticeable sometimes, but they occur. As a result, even a well-reasoned analysis of next year's tin price will be outmoded by the time next year arrives. Changing conditions will change the price objective. The new conditions may affect an investment only slightly— or they may call for a change in plans to avoid a loss.

The tin story has highlighted the effect that one large event can have upon the market. In practice, the market is affected by many events—large and small. Trends exist, as we've seen, because investors change their opinions as the future unfolds. In addition, new events cause new opinions to be registered, and sometimes a series of independent events all move the price in the same direction.

We can't know, in advance, all the events that might affect next year's price. Neither can we expect an analysis of today's conditions to be perfect. There's too much that we couldn't possibly know that might affect the outcome.

Therefore, I believe it's more useful to look for a few investments that may experience broad price movements continuing over a year or more—rather than to look for a series of investments that promise smaller, short-term movements. There are too many surprises waiting in the wings. The potential for profit should be great enough for the investment to absorb a few unwelcome surprises and still be successful.

SUMMARY

At any moment, each participant in an investment market will have his own goals; he'll be working with the knowledge available to him; he'll have his own opinion as to the implications of that knowledge; he'll have his own investment philosophy; he'll have his own resources and his own requirements for cash outside the investment market.

It's a semantic convenience to say that "the market" does this or has done that or will do something else. But we're really talking about what the *price* is doing. And the price results from the actions of diverse individuals, with differing opinions, motives, and resources. In other words, the market doesn't "know" anything; but the price reflects a consensus of what many different individuals believe.

The process isn't static. Every day new participants enter, and established participants alter their opinions and positions. These changes occur as the future becomes a little less uncertain, and as each individual's circumstances outside the investment market change.

Changes in investor opinion create what we see as trends. It isn't so much an event that causes a trend, as it is the gradual development of investor reactions to an event. As more and more investors begin to interpret the event in much the same way, the trend evolves.

Sometimes there is no trend—at least no trend that lasts long enough to catch our attention. The price of an investment may lounge in one price range for several months—or even several years. This is because no events have occurred that significantly affect the investment's value or investors' opinions of it.

When a trend begins, there's no way to know precisely how far it will go. So the investor who has expected the trend to emerge will be able to profit most from it. He believes he knows why the trend has started and, in general, the magnitude of change to expect from it.

However, an investor who does nothing but look for trends in price charts has no way to know how far any trend will go. The longer a trend lasts, the more compelling his belief that it will continue. But if he doesn't know what's causing the trend, he's only making an even-money bet that it will persist. Trend-watching, by itself, is not enough.

7

CYCLES

THE GRAPH ON PAGE 45 DEPICTS THE INSTABILITY OF U.S. monetary policy. There are two persistent features: (1) the monetary inflation rate swings up and down; and (2) the swings occur in progressively higher areas.

The swings occur because it's impossible for political decisions to manage an economy and its money effectively. As with other matters under political management, monetary policy doesn't respond to the requirements and resources of the economy; the money supply responds to centralized political decisions made outside the economy.

As a result, monetary decisions are almost always wrong. It's as though the Federal Reserve were trying to drive a car by remote control, without being able to see the road, and with a crowd of backseat drivers shouting directions.

The Fed speeds up the money supply until price inflation becomes a public scandal; then it slows down the money supply until the economy contracts. Though its judgment may be sensitive to politics, it is numb to economics. It lacks the market's subtle, gradual responsiveness to day-to-day changes in the abilities of producers and the desires of consumers. This car has only two speeds—very fast and very slow.

Hence there are wide swings in the rate of monetary inflation.

STOCK MARKET CYCLES

The stock market moves with these swings for two reasons:

1. The securities markets (bonds and stocks) are the first recipients of newly created money. Thus, they react sensitively to changes in monetary inflation.

2. Stock prices reflect company earnings, which depend upon general economic conditions, which in turn improve or worsen in response to monetary policy.

It's no surprise, then, that the stock market moves cyclically, like the economy, in a series of alternating bull and bear trends.

Each new cycle of monetary inflation touches off a new bull market in stocks—first by flooding the investment markets with cash, and later by boosting company earnings. This expansion eventually encourages an uncritical optimism, and many investors buy simply because the market has been going up.

But by that time, monetary inflation has gone too far and the Federal Reserve becomes restrictive. Its tighter policy drains money from the stock market and causes a bear trend to begin. After a while, company earnings decrease—adding more fuel to the bear trend. And finally the trend culminates in a wave of pessimism, with many investors believing that the market is definitely, absolutely, permanently dead.

So each trend (bull or bear) consists of three sections: (1) a reaction to the excesses of the last trend; (2) a continuation of the new trend based upon changing economic fundamentals; and (3) an overshooting of the level that's justified by the fundamentals.

Prices never move in a straight line; there are reactions to a trend along the way. And frequently the reactions cause the three sections of a trend to appear on a price graph as three distinct waves.

The first wave of a new bull market rises up from the pessimism of the preceding bear market. The bear trend has taken stocks below their fundamental values. Now, sponsored by the Fed's injection of new money, the first wave of the bull market takes stocks up to, and then past, their fundamental values.

Then a reaction sets in as the new money leaks out of the financial markets and into the rest of the economy. Without surplus cash to finance more purchases, stocks start slipping back toward their fundamental values, and part of the gain of the first wave is erased.

But soon company earnings begin increasing—raising the fundamental values of stocks. With values increasing, the market moves upward again. Because earnings don't increase visibly day by day, this second wave is usually the slowest of the three.

But after a while the growth in earnings creates an anticipation of even higher earnings to come. Optimism returns, and stock prices increase at a faster pace than earnings. The second wave ends when future earnings have been more than allowed for, and profit-taking by conservative investors temporarily outweighs new purchases by the bullish enthusiasts.

Stock prices retreat for a second time and continue to fall until the outflow of conservative investors has passed its peak. Then the third upward wave begins, and it attracts even those investors who swore off stocks when they sold them at the bottom of the last bear market. Enthusiasm becomes contagious. Because the third wave is largely irrational, it appears that no peak is beyond its reach; it is impossible to know where the trend will stop.

But of course it does stop. When a bull market in stocks comes to an end, the immediate cause is usually a tightening in monetary policy—which drains money from the market. But even without this, the trend would end for reasons we saw in the last chapter.

Usually the three waves of a bull trend are clearly visible on a graph, but not always. Although each bull market is propelled by three successive forces (the reaction to pessimism, the improvement in fundamentals, and the speculative excess), you won't always know when one force fades out and another takes hold. One wave may merge quietly into the next.

Each bull and bear market will have its own unique pattern. And it's a mistake to expect each trend to duplicate the one that preceded it.

For example, the 1974–1976 bull market displayed only two distinct waves—one beginning in December 1974 and the second in January 1976. When prices declined after the second wave, many investors waited patiently for the normal third wave to carry the Dow Jones Industrial Average past 1200.

But it never came. The decline that investors took to be the prelude to the third wave turned out to be the beginning of the next bear market.

The third wave may have failed to develop because the recovery from the 1975 recession never fulfilled its promise. Although corporate earnings improved, the improvement was weak compared to previous booms. With the recovery so feeble, it was difficult for anyone to become overly optimistic.

As the inflationary cycle continues, we're bound to see more irregularities in the investment markets. It would be an expensive error to expect cycles to repeat themselves in carbon-copy fashion.

SUPER-TRENDS

A look at longer periods will reveal that there are super-trends. From 1942 to 1965, for example, the stock market was in a super-bull trend that encompassed a number of normal bull and bear trends. Each bull trend took the market to a higher level, and the bottom of each bear trend was higher than the preceding bottom.

This super-bull trend finally ended in 1966. That a super-*bear* trend followed becomes apparent if the Dow Jones Industrial Average is adjusted to reflect changes in the purchasing power of the dollar (as it has been in the chart on page 16). Each normal bull trend ends at a lower peak than its predecessor, and each bear trend takes the market lower than the previous bear trend.

On a purchasing power basis, gold was in a super-bull trend from 1930 to 1945. The dollar price of gold was constant during the first four years of the trend, but a general deflation caused that unchanging dollar price to grow in purchasing power value. Then the devaluation of 1934 increased the dollar price of gold by 69%. Five years later, the turmoil of World War II caused the price to rise in free markets around the world.

Near the end of the war the gold price reached the equivalent of $70 per ounce in most of the markets that were still open. Then the price floated downward until it entered the $35 range in 1953.

Gold's super-bear trend lasted from 1945 to 1970. The super-bull trend that began in 1970 will probably last for many years to come, as a series of alternating bull and bear trends takes the price to higher and higher levels.

NUMBERS & CYCLES

It's tempting to look back through history, hoping to find a rhythmic pattern to the bull-bear cycles and super-cycles. How comforting it would be to know with certainty that every so many years a new bull market will begin.

Unfortunately, cycles don't keep calendars. Many people have tried to demonstrate that the cycles repeat themselves according to a predictable schedule, but their demonstrations always rest on a loose interpretation of the record.

If you sift through enough numbers, you can count on finding astounding coincidences. But they are only that—coincidences. Any large group of numbers will include some curious patterns. But if you can't find a fundamental reason for a pattern, an explanation based on the logic of human action, it is only a curiosity; it has no better than an even chance of continuing. If there *is* a fundamental reason for the pattern, you are safer watching the fundamentals than you are watching only the numbers.

Other curious forecasting techniques require only a little skepticism to reject.

Consider the "January barometer," for example. Its followers believe that the stock market's performance in January forecasts its performance for the whole year. And indeed, more often than not, a good January has been the start of a good year. And a bad January has been the start of a bad year.

What is overlooked is that the barometer is part of the event it's supposed to forecast. A good January *contributes* to a good year—and so part of the rise it "forecasts" for the year has already taken place.

Also we come back to the numbers game. January is only one of twelve possibilities. If you check the histories of each of the twelve months, there will *have* to be one with the best record of resembling the entire year. There will also be one month that runs contrary to the year's performance more often than other months.

In the same way, if you read through the telephone book, you'll find that one digit shows up more times than any other digit. And no doubt someone will be happy to attach a mystical significance to that number, and be the inventor, perhaps, of the "8 theory" of telephone numbers. But look through the telephone book of another city and you'll likely find that some other digit predominates.

I suspect that the January barometer was invented by someone who examined the records of all twelve months to discover which was "best." When it turned out to be the first month, it was a happy find.

Any cyclical scheme based solely upon a numerical pattern deserves your skepticism. It is true that there are constant relationships in the economic world, and discovering and exploiting them can be profitable. But if a given relationship can't be explained in terms of plausible human-action economics, if it can be asserted only because the numbers are there, then the relationship must be presumed to be coincidence.

Ludwig von Mises, the outstanding Austrian economist, once said that it's a pity most economists don't have a better understanding of mathematics; if they did, he said, they'd appreciate how little mathematics has to do with economics.[1]

[1] Ludwig von Mises, *The Ultimate Foundation of Economic Science*. New York: D. Van Nostrand Co., 1962, p. 4.

8

INVESTMENT
ANALYSIS

IF THE OLD PROVERB WERE LITERALLY TRUE—THAT THE CUR-
rent price of an investment already discounts the investment's future—you couldn't hope to make significant profits.
Investment analysis would be futile. Anything you might discover about an investment would be accounted for already
in the investment's price.[1]

The only task left would be to plan a program of diversification. Over time, you'd earn a return comparable to the
going rate of interest—probably a little more to compensate
for the risk you bear with even a diversified portfolio.

But as we've seen, while the market may "know" everything already, its participants interpret that knowledge in
different ways. And the differences of opinion present opportunities for profit.

In addition, investments are moved by general economic
conditions. It's easy to say that all economic factors are already known to the market, but it's difficult to find any
agreement about the meaning of those factors. The role of
the money supply and the effects of government spending
are just two examples of economic considerations that remain
controversial.

In a world without government, investment prices would

[1] Of course *someone* would have to be analyzing investments, or else the current
price wouldn't reflect the investment's future.

anticipate the future more accurately. Events would evolve naturally from what had gone before and would be easier to plan for.

But in the real world, governments touch everything. Because their policies are imposed upon the economy from without, they are a source of disturbance. And because the policies are changeable, they are a source of uncertainty. Most of history's surprise parties have been thrown by governments.

In such circumstances, the market "knows" less of the future than it would in a freer environment.

But while government policies are capricious, they aren't random. Like any mental disorder, government policies have a logic of their own—absurd, disturbing, and sometimes destructive, but not wholly unpredictable.

One predictable element in government policy is the monetary cycles. The monetary inflation rate swings up and down as part of the government's unreasonable attempt to fine-tune the economy. Because many investors don't understand the economic effects of the swings, investment prices don't fully reflect the eventual results of the changes in the monetary inflation rate.

These swings, as well as other government policies, can be a source of profit for investors who understand the cause-and-effect relationships. There will always be many investors who won't agree with your interpretation, so you'll have little trouble finding someone to bet against you.

If your viewpoint turns out to have been correct, you'll make a profit. And the extent of your profit will depend on the degree to which your interpretation conflicted with that of the majority.

If your opinion was close to that of the majority of participants, your profit won't be very great. The price at which you bought will have largely reflected that viewpoint already. But if you held a minority opinion that turned out to be right, you'll have purchased the investment at a bargain price, and your profit will be substantial.

In other words, the potential price movement you see in

an investment indicates the extent to which your opinion differs from the market's consensus. The more eccentric your viewpoint, the greater your profit will be—if you're correct.

This isn't the same as saying, "The majority is always wrong." The majority can be right *or* wrong. And while it pays to be skeptical of prevailing opinions, habitual non-conformity is no more profitable than habitual submission to fashion.

You must always make the best analysis you can—based upon your understanding of economics and current conditions. But having done so, the best investment opportunities occur when your analysis conflicts with the prevailing viewpoint. For then what you foresee will not yet be reflected in the price.

BARGAINS & LOSSES

The analysis is essential. It's fatal to buy an investment simply because it's moving. If you jump onto a trend without knowing what's propelling it, how will you know when to jump off?

On the other hand, the analysis can be both correct and unprofitable if you ignore current price trends. Many an investor has bought an investment because it seemed to be underpriced, only to see it become more and more underpriced.

The underpriced concept deserves a closer look. If an investment is underpriced by 20% today, it must have been underpriced by 5% on its way to becoming 20% underpriced. Someone bought it when it was down 5%, perhaps thinking it was a bargain—and he's already lost 15% of his money. Why wasn't the 5% underpricing a signal for the price to rise?

The very fact that an investment's price can be different from its fundamental value proves that estimating values is not the same as forecasting prices. There's no guarantee that an investment's price will ever reach the value you have estimated.

Obviously it's better to buy an underpriced investment than one that is overpriced. And if you're correct in your valuation, you'll tend to profit; a well-thought-out analysis loads the odds in your favor.

But if you ignore current trends you will often buy bargains that become bigger bargains before they finally turn around. There are many investors who believe that waiting out such a drop is evidence of their patience or sophistication. But there are several drawbacks to waiting for an eventual turnaround:

1. You can't know everything about an investment; you're always working with limited knowledge. Something you can't see may prevent the price from reaching the objective you're waiting for. And while you're waiting in vain, your losses are increasing.

2. All analysis is subjective. There are no mathematical formulas that reveal an investment's future price. You may have placed too much weight on one factor and too little on another. You don't have to give up analyzing investments just because you can't hope for absolute precision, but you should be skeptical about holding doggedly to a losing position.

3. The further a price moves away from its target, the longer it will take to reach its target once it begins moving in the right direction. Meanwhile, the ingredients of your analysis could change. By the time the investment turns upward, a lower price objective might be warranted. Even if you wait it out, you may be waiting only for your loss to get smaller.

4. And even if the original target is reached eventually, the investment may prove to have been a poor use of your money's time. Inflation is constantly changing the meaning of the numbers you see, and other investments may be going up while yours is going down. If after five years an investment that was underpriced by 30% finally reaches its target, how much have you really profited?

A few years back I said that timing wasn't important. Then it wasn't. In the hard-money investment era the potentials were so great, and the effort they required was so little, that for most people it was simpler and safer to buy the hard-money investments and sit on them. The fundamentals were so strong that they couldn't weaken enough in a year or two to make the investments unprofitable.

That era is over. It's going to require more effort now to do as well—or even to do half as well. Timing is more important now, because there are no broad, long-term opportunities that other investors are determined to ignore.

Like it or not, we have to pay attention to trends. Buy underpriced investments, yes; but buy only when you believe the expected trend has begun, or when you have good reason to believe that it's about to begin. In the latter case, be prepared to sell if the market decides to follow its own schedule rather than yours.

OTHER INVESTORS

Because investment prices can diverge from investment values by so much and for so long, it's easy to believe that prices move only as a result of what other investors believe. In fact, another investment proverb says, "It isn't what's true, it's what investors believe to be true, that counts."

According to the proverb, you should try to determine what other investors will be willing to pay for an investment next month or next year. And taken very strictly, there's nothing wrong with the proverb; obviously, if an investment is to be profitable, what other investors come to think of it will be very important.

But this idea is sometimes stretched into what is called the "Greater Fool Theory." If the opinions of other investors are all that matter, don't worry about fundamental values; just try to outguess the market. Look for an investment that is likely to capture the fancy of other investors, no matter how fanciful the investment might be or how high its current price.

The message of this theory is that other investors are stupid.

But in the real world, most people aren't stupid, and even the stupid ones aren't reliable about it.

Investors who are foolish enough to buy an overpriced investment can't be counted on to buy the one you own. Nor can they be counted on always to be unreasonably optimistic; tomorrow they may be unreasonably pessimistic.

Foolish bets are sometimes won. But you'll win more often when you bet on your interpretation of the fundamentals, instead of trying to outguess the follies of others.

FUNDAMENTAL VS. TECHNICAL ANALYSIS

Any attempt to estimate value is an example of *fundamental analysis*. It is a forecast of the future price based upon supply and demand conditions. *Technical analysis* forecasts investment prices by referring only to the record of prices; it is an attempt to read the future in the past.

Arguments between fundamentalists and technicians are sometimes as emotional and unyielding as those between one-button and two-button Baptists. Neither sees any point to the other's attitude.

The technicians believe that the fundamentalists are wasting their time looking at data on the money supply or company earnings, since all relevant data have already been processed by the market and are reflected in the price. The fundamentalists see the mysterious interest in price patterns as nothing more than voodoo for capitalists.

Each can recite the drawbacks of the other's art. And since I've already warned of some of the drawbacks of pure fundamental analysis, I should call attention to some of the drawbacks of technical analysis.

It's easy to look at a graph of past prices and see clearly defined trends. You can also see many of the patterns technicians consider to be significant (head-and-shoulders formations, wedges, pennants, etc.). And you can imagine how decisively you would have acted upon these signals, and how well you would have profited.

But making an investment *during* a trend isn't the same as looking at a trend after it's over. A trend may last anywhere from one day to two years or more. If the price retreats today, is that the end of the trend or merely a pause? And few actual chart patterns adhere precisely to the classic examples. Will the pattern that seems to be developing today turn into something else tomorrow?

What you see *during* a fluctuating price movement is quite different from the picture of last year's completed movement. The past is always obvious, but it wasn't obvious while it was happening. That's why useful books on technical analysis usually suggest that you play the market on paper for a while before investing real money. By doing so, you can learn what it's like to make decisions during a price movement, when you don't yet know how the movement will end.

A number of academic studies have tested purely technical trading systems. The tests were made by programming a computer to apply a trading system's rules to a long history of actual prices. Every study has concluded that the systems don't work. That is, they work no more often than would be expected from the laws of chance, or they don't work well enough to make a profit after paying commissions.[2]

These studies have done a great deal to discredit mechanical trading systems, but I believe that in some ways they may have missed the point. There are two considerations that the studies didn't test—and, in fact, couldn't test.

One is the intuitive skill of an experienced trader. Intuition is the unconscious processing of knowledge and experience. You drive a car by intuition, in that you don't consciously think about each move you make while driving.

In the same way, a trader with long experience can react intuitively to price movements. His experience can tell him that a particular movement has significance, although he may not be able to explain that significance to you. In fact, very

2 Some of these studies are reported in *A Random Walk Down Wall Street* by Burton G. Malkiel (Norton, 1973); *The Stock Market: Theories and Evidence* by James H. Lorie and Mary T. Hamilton (Irwin, 1973); and *Modern Developments in Investment Management*, edited by James Lorie and Richard Brealey (Praeger, 1972).

few successful people in *any* field can explain their "secrets of success." The trader's skill can't be distilled into hard-and-fast rules, and so it can't be tested by a computer. It can be tested only by his profit-and-loss statement.

The second consideration is that while technical analysis might be useless by itself, it still might be very useful in conjunction with fundamental analysis. Using both, you wouldn't act upon a technical buy or sell signal just because it was there. Nor would you buy an investment just because you thought it was underpriced.

But you would act upon a technical signal if you had determined already, through fundamental analysis, that there was a good reason for the price to move. The fundamentals would tell you what to trade, and technical analysis would tell you when to trade.

This dual approach can't be tested by computer because the results will be only as good as the system of fundamental analysis used *and* the technical system used. You can't test either independently.

At one time I used only fundamental analysis. But as timing has become more important, I've had to employ additional tools. In studying technical analysis, I've accepted only the guidelines that can be explained by the nature of human action in the marketplace.

That means I put no store in a method that comes with no explanation other than "the pattern always works this way." Such patterns don't "always work this way," although a case (usually with numerous exceptions) can be made to show that almost any relationship exists.

Also, to make use of technical analysis, you don't have to believe that insiders or conspirators are manipulating the markets. The common errors of investors are sufficient to explain why some price movements can be anticipated.

I'm not going to suggest that you become a full-time technical analyst. Like anything else, technical analysis is a skill that some people are suited to learn and others aren't.

Instead, I've created a strategy that I believe most investors can put into practice. It uses fundamental analysis to place your investments in harmony with the broad trends created by general economic conditions. A few, relatively simple, tools of technical analysis are used to identify only the beginning and end of each broad trend. And a few tactical rules are employed to hedge against mistakes.

I'll also suggest simpler strategies for those who find even this too ambitious. When you've finished the book, you can decide for yourself which tools are appropriate for you. Your investment program must allow for your own limitations of time, talent, and interest.

9

THE BIG-LOSSES,
SMALL-PROFITS
DISEASE

A DISEASE IS SOMETHING THAT EVERYONE IS AGAINST, BUT WHICH continues to afflict the population. And while all investors are in favor of big profits and small losses, most of them usually settle for the opposite.

Almost all investors have heard the proverb, "Cut your losses short and let your profits run." In other words, be ready to sell with a small loss as soon as you see that your investment isn't going the way you expected. And when you catch a winner, don't take your profit too quickly; give it every chance to grow.

An investor who practices this rule should have a few small losses, each limited to 5% or so, with an occasional large gain of perhaps 50% or 100% or more. Each large gain will not only offset several small losses, but will leave him with a healthy overall profit.

Unfortunately, agreeing with the rule isn't the same as practicing it. Most investors (even those who praise the rule) will hang on to an investment while the losses pile up—hoping against hope that it will turn around. And the same investors will often cash in an investment as soon as it shows a 10% profit. Somehow, the rule gets left behind when investors shift from talking about strategy to carrying it out.

103

The purpose of this chapter is to discover why this happens, and to create an approach that makes it easier to apply the big-profits, small-losses rule in practice.

WHY LOSSES RUN

First, let's look at the loss side.

An investor buys a stock for $30 per share because he has some reason to believe it will go up. But, instead, it begins to drop almost immediately. When the price reaches $27, his loss is already 10%. The investment has clearly moved contrary to his expectations. According to the rule, he should "cut his loss" right there.

But he doesn't. He hangs on. Why?

For one thing, there's no way to know what the price will be tomorrow. It might drop further—but it might start moving upward. If he sold today and the price rose tomorrow, he'd kick himself for his lack of patience.

On any given day, the price could go either way—no matter what the principal trend might be. And so the investor's indecision can continue day by day until his loss is 50% or more. Clearly, there's something missing in his investment approach—something that might eliminate this expensive procrastination. We'll come back to it a little later.

Meanwhile, let's recognize that there's another possible reason for his not selling. It may be that to sell at a loss would conflict with some nonfinancial consideration—such as protecting his ego.

Perhaps he made the investment in spite of warnings from his family. He'd hate to have to admit now that the investment was a mistake—his mistake. Or his pride might be on the line if he's boasted to his friends about making a shrewd investment.

In fact, his ego can be involved even if no one else is aware of the investment. *He* knows—and perhaps his opinion of himself isn't high enough to allow for another mistake.

If he doesn't sell now, he may be able to convince himself

or others that he hasn't lost a dime—that "paper" profits and losses don't mean anything, that real losses occur only when an investment is actually sold.

In truth, "paper" profits and losses mean everything. The value of an investment is what you can sell it for today. What you paid for it is meaningless once it no longer can be sold at that price. Making light of a loss as "paper" is only a device for sidestepping the truth.

The big-profits, small-losses rule fails to guide an investor in practice because it doesn't consider all the factors that will bear down upon him at a critical moment. He is affected by hope, fear, threats to his self-esteem, and all the energies of self-deception these factors can summon. These and other considerations may be financially irrelevant, but they're emotionally important.

And at the moment of truth, the investor might feel that the pain of acknowledging a mistake outweighs every other consideration. And so he'll hang on to his investment—in order to delay paying that price, and in the hope of somehow avoiding it entirely.

When an individual makes his first investment, he may have specific financial goals in mind. But investing can turn into something else—a test of his personal value. His original ends are lost, and his purpose becomes solely that of avoiding losses. Consciously or unconsciously, his only rule becomes *never take a loss.*

SMALL PROFITS

Little wonder, then, that when an investment does make a profit, he sells quickly. Any profit—10%, 5%, or 2%—is sufficient to represent a victory. He can say, "Yes, I made a little money on IBM last week."

Why should he hold on and "let his profits run" when the market can turn around at any moment and take this precious little triumph away from him?

Of course, it doesn't matter to him that he may have held

on for several years before he took his tiny profit. He's won a trophy—and that outweighs the fact that he could have done better with his money in a savings account.

No wonder that so many investors sell out quickly—once the price is above the original purchase price.

THE CURE

The first step in curing the big-losses, small-profits disease is to be realistic about the job of investing.

The first principle of investing is: *you can't know everything*. You're working with incomplete information and you're bound to make mistakes.

No one is right about every investment. The skilled investor doesn't expect to be. He doesn't hope for the impossible; he deals only with the possible and probable. He weighs all the possibilities and chooses those that are probable and which offer a worthwhile reward.

Since he can't expect to be right all the time, *he expects to have losses*. And because he knows that having some losses is unavoidable, he doesn't insist that his *next* investment *must* show a profit.

Once you accept this principle, you won't approach your next investment with a sense of desperation—a feeling that it's all or nothing. The next investment is merely a stepping-stone to where you're going—which is a profitable position when you consider the total of *all* your investments.

Naturally, you'll select your next investment as wisely as you can. And you'll pay attention to it. And you'll *hope* that it will be a winner. But you shouldn't feel that your financial future or your self-esteem demand that it be a winner. If you feel those demands *are* being made, perhaps you shouldn't be investing.

OBJECTIVES

There are two judgments you should make *before* an investment is purchased:

1. The maximum loss you're willing to accept.

2. The potential profit the investment offers.

Obviously, the potential profit should be a good deal more than the loss you're willing to tolerate.

In Chapter 30, I'll discuss methods for timing investment purchases and for determining how great a loss to accept before changing your appraisal of an investment. If you find these methods useful, the maximum-loss question will be answered almost automatically.

But if you don't use these methods, there are others. If you have reason to believe that the timing is right for your purchase, almost any significant price decline will be a signal that you were wrong—if not about the investment itself, at least in the timing of the purchase. In that case, you can set the maximum loss at somewhere between 5% and 10%.

If you aren't assuming that your timing is precise, you still have one method left to you. Simply determine the price level at which you could no longer afford to let your capital shrink. If that point is reached, you must sell.

There is a concrete step you can take to put this into practice. Enter a stop-loss order for the price that represents the maximum loss you'll accept.[1]

Some investors have the discipline to sell on their own initiative if the maximum-loss point is reached. Most of us aren't that disciplined—at least not until we've worked at it for some time. So it's far safer to issue the stop-loss order when you buy the investment—which will take the decision out of your hands if the critical moment comes.

And that's very important. If the price drops *below* the cutoff point and you haven't sold, it becomes harder and harder to do so. The problem is like that of an alcoholic who can resist a first drink, but who has no hope of resisting a second. Once you've broken your resolution, you're on your way to accumulating another large loss.

Once the stop-loss is placed, it should never be lowered. You're very unlikely to have a good reason for increasing

---

[1] A stop-loss order is an instruction given to your bank or broker, telling him to sell your investment automatically if its price falls to a predetermined level.

the maximum loss once you've decided what it should be.

Realize that you don't necessarily abandon an investment forever when you cut your loss. If the price begins moving upward, and if you think your original reasons for buying the investment are still valid, you can buy back in.

Buying the investment again means that you'll lose a little in commissions. But that extra cost is offset by the benefit you derive from looking at the buy-back decision as an outsider. An investment has a different appearance when you don't own it—different from the way it looks when you own a lot of it and the price is dropping.

And you might have the good fortune to buy it the second time at a price far below what you sold it for. Some investors like to "average down" when a price is dropping. They buy at $30, buy some more at $25, more at $20, and more at $15. But if you must start out with a loss, it is far better to buy at $30, sell at $27, and then buy again at $15.

If you establish in advance the maximum loss you'll take, and if you make your decision concrete by placing a stop-loss order, you're on your way to cutting your losses short.

PROFIT OBJECTIVE

The second decision to be made in advance concerns the investment's potential.

It isn't easy to determine how high a price should go. With stocks, your interest in an investment may be based on an idea of how earnings will grow and what price-earnings ratio will materialize. This will imply a potential price. But with commodities, it's much more difficult. You may believe that a shortage of a commodity will occur next year but have no notion how high the shortage will drive the price.

The important thing is to determine that the profit potential is substantial. Because you'll have losses at various times, you can't afford to invest when there is nothing more to hope for than a gain of 10% or 15%. You need larger profits than that in order to offset the occasional losses and still show a healthy overall profit.

You might imagine that investment success can be built upon gains of 10% here and 15% there—perhaps making several investments of this kind each year. But it usually doesn't work out. Some of those investments show small losses; others don't move much at all. And so the winners that do come along have little left for you after they've offset the poor results of the other investments.

Even if you can't know how high the price is capable of going, you should at least know that it has the potential to go quite high—50%, 100%, or more. There's no magic number, of course; just be sure that the investment promises a return you believe is significant.

There are two reasons for attempting to identify a profit potential in advance:

1. The effort can prevent you from jumping on a bandwagon just because it's moving. If you have no idea of the price the investment should reach, you'll be less tempted to join the crowd on a bandwagon with an unknown destination.

2. If you buy the investment and it begins to move up, you'll be less likely to settle for a 10% profit. You'll know there's a lot more to be made.

Although you should never lower a stop-loss order on a losing investment, you should raise it on a winning investment. Chapter 30 will include tactics for picking the prices for stop-loss orders. Here I'll mention only one general rule.

The stop-loss should be just under the purchase price (5% to 10% below it) when you buy. But when the price is moving upward, you should place the stop-loss order much further below the current price.

This may not seem sensible at first. One Wall Street proverb says, "Never hold a stock you wouldn't buy"—meaning that if you didn't own it and you wouldn't buy it, you shouldn't keep it. It might seem that my stop-loss suggestion is a violation of this proverb—in that I'm saying you should be *more* tolerant of an investment you already own than you would be of one you're about to buy.

But if you've purchased the investment with good reason, and if an upward price movement has vindicated your judgment, you're dealing with a different situation now.

Before your purchase, you believed that there were fundamental reasons for the investment to appreciate. However, you knew that those fundamental reasons might not exert themselves immediately. An "undervalued" investment can become more undervalued—as we saw in the last chapter. And you don't want to hold the investment through a downtrend *before* it begins to fulfill its fundamental promise.

And so you place a stop-loss order slightly below your purchase price. If it turns out that the time hasn't come for the investment to begin moving, you will want to get out and wait on the sidelines.

But once the price starts moving upward, once a clear uptrend is established, the situation is different. Now you know that the fundamentals have begun to work—and you want to be sure you don't sell until the investment has had every chance to demonstrate how far it can go.

The difference between the two situations is not whether you own the investment, but whether the investment has already proven that its time has come. Until it proves that the time is now, you'll be cautious. Once it's proven that the time *is* now, you'll allow it plenty of room to fluctuate.

The original price isn't significant because you bought there; it's significant because it's in the area where the price broke out of its previous pattern.

EXAMPLE

To put the big-profits, small-losses rule to a test, let's go back to the tin investment you made in Chapter 6.

That story had a happy ending (as well as a happy beginning and middle), since the price went up soon after you bought in. But this time we'll leave out the Bolivian government and the assurance that one event could make your investment a winner.

Your analysis has indicated that tin should go up from its present $5 price. You're not sure how far it will go, but you can see that $8 or more is a reasonable objective. You've been watching the price for a while, waiting for a sign that tin is about to fulfill its promise.

Finally, one week the price moves up three days in a row and reaches $5.20. This is higher than it has been in many months; it has moved out of the range in which it had been fluctuating. And so you call your broker and place your order.

You also tell your broker to enter a stop-loss order at $4.85, based on considerations we'll discuss in Chapter 30. The next day, the tin is purchased at $5.25.

A day or two after you buy, the price retreats to $5.10, stays there a few days, and then moves up again. Over the next few weeks, the price fluctuates between $5.10 and $5.45. But you don't sell and you don't raise your stop-loss order.

There are two different endings to this story, and I'll tell them both. First, ending number 1.

After the price has fluctuated in this range for the next few weeks, it resumes its upward movement. After a few days, it stalls at $5.75, retreats to around $5.50, fluctuates between $5.50 and $5.75 for a week or so, and then heads upward again.

At this point, you raise your stop-loss order to $5.35. And, to keep the story brief, we'll assume that the same general pattern is repeated several times. That is, the price backs off, fluctuates in a fairly narrow range for a while, moves to a new high, and you increase your stop-loss price—always keeping the stop-loss well below the current price.

If the stop-loss is far below the current price, does it serve any purpose? Yes; it accomplishes two things: (1) it protects you against any sudden events that could send the price moving downward rapidly; and (2) if the price should drift downward, you've already established the price at which you'll sell; you won't have to reopen the question every day during the downtrend.

Finally, the price reaches $8 and exceeds it. In fact, the uptrend has picked up speed. This is exciting, but it's also dangerous. You're quite sure that the rapid movement is the result of uninformed speculation. And you know that this bandwagon could run out of gas at any time; when it does, the reaction might be sudden and swift.

According to your analysis, there's no sound reason for the price to go higher. So you place your stop-loss much closer to the current price—perhaps only 5% or less below today's price. And as the price continues upward, you keep raising the stop-loss, always staying close to the current price.

One day the price reaches $9.10, reverses, and drops far enough to trigger your stop-loss at $8.70. Your investment is completed, and you've done very well.

On the way up, there were several price reactions that made other investors wonder if the rally was over. But, until the last few days, you allowed the price plenty of room to fluctuate. So your stop-loss wasn't activated until you intentionally placed it close to the current price, and only when you felt the rally had probably gone too far.

Now let's look at ending number 2.

When we branched off to the first ending, the price was fluctuating between $5.10 and $5.45, and your stop-loss was still placed at $4.85.

The second ending takes less time to tell. After fluctuating for a while, the price drifts downward, leveling off at $5.00. Then it drops again, finally activating your stop-loss at $4.85.

Your investment is completed and you lost 8%. As you look back, you notice that you could have sold when the price was $5.45. Had you done so, you would have had a 4% profit instead of an 8% loss. Should you be upset with yourself for letting that profit get away from you?

I don't think so. The 4% profit would have made very little difference in your life. You didn't make the investment in order to obtain a 4% profit; you made it because you saw the possibility of a profit of 60% or more.

When the price was $5.45, you had no way of knowing which way the price would go from there. But you felt that there was a good chance that it could go considerably higher. To sell then would have been to give up the hope of a higher profit.

As it turned out, you had an 8% loss. That's a prudent risk to take (for most people) against a potential gain of 60% or more. Your strategy was based on the assumption that it's better to take an 8% loss than to miss out on a 60% profit.

LAW OF AVERAGES?

The small-losses, big-profits approach isn't based on the law of averages. It doesn't assume that any investment has an equal chance of dropping slightly or showing a spectacular gain. If that were true, you could pick any five investments at random; four might show 5% losses and the fifth would earn a 100% profit.

But that isn't the way markets work; only a small minority of investments rise by spectacular amounts. So the maxim "let your profits run" is useless by itself.

The strategy assumes that you'll apply your best judgment to the selection of investments. It assumes that you'll be disappointed part of the time—perhaps even frequently—but that each investment is selected for good reason.

By applying good judgment to your investment selections, you load the odds in your favor—provided you cut your loss as soon as you know that either the timing or the selection was wrong.

But it isn't enough to cut your losses quickly. You must have big profits occasionally. Only with an occasional large profit can you offset the inevitable small losses and show a healthy profit overall.

And to get big profits you have to let a small profit evaporate sometimes. You have to be willing to give your investment every opportunity to realize its potential—once it has demonstrated that its time has come.

The big-losses, small-profits disease can be cured by:

1. recognizing that the result for any given investment is far less important than the result for your overall investment program;

2. making investments only when you can see a large profit potential;

3. placing a stop-loss order 5% to 10% under the purchase price when you buy; and

4. making sure your stop-loss is well under the current price once the price moves into an uptrend.

These rules are valuable tools for the strategy I'll suggest in Part IV. We'll be dealing with broad trends whose beginnings are often uncertain. The small-losses rule will help you cope with the uncertainty. And the big-profits rule will help you exploit a broad trend once it's begun.

These tactics weren't important during the buy-and-hold era of 1970 to 1974. They're very important now. But I know that some investors won't be prepared to manage their investments in the aggressive way I've described in this chapter. For them, other suggestions will be made in Parts IV and V.

10

CHASING
INTEREST RATES

It's natural to think of an investment in terms of the dividends or interest it yields. The allure of cash income has led many investors to search for stocks that pay the highest dividends, and for bonds and bank accounts that pay the highest interest rates. Unfortunately, in searching for high yields it's very easy to lose sight of considerations that are more important.

In the consumer markets an old axiom says, "You get what you pay for." In the investment markets, the axiom might be, "You are paid for what you get," meaning that the yield you receive is an indication of an investment's other characteristics.

Interest rates and dividend yields are established, as are other prices, through the interplay of supply and demand—in this case the supply of and demand for investment assets. The interest or dividend rate you are promised on an investment reflects the market's consensus regarding three principal characteristics: (1) risk, (2) depreciation, and (3) liquidity.

We'll examine each of these.

RISK

Risk refers to the possibility that the money you expect to receive from your investment might not actually be forthcoming—either because the investment's market price might fall or because a debtor might default.

The safest debt investments pay the lowest interest, other things being equal. Thus, since the U.S. government is likely to break every other promise before it breaks its promise to make good on Treasury bills, T-bills pay very low interest rates. In contrast, if you buy the bonds of a new company, you can expect a much higher return—perhaps twice what you'd receive on Treasury bills.

The higher rate is your compensation for bearing the risk that the company might not repay its debts. You can't expect to earn the high rate unless you're willing to accept the possibility that the entire capital could be lost.

The same principle applies to dividends. For example, it is not by accident that the dividend yields on South African gold stocks are exceptionally high. Investors in general are afraid that any money risked on a gold stock might be lost if the South African government should collapse. Consequently they are willing to buy a South African stock only at a price that is low compared to its dividend. So the dividend, as a percentage yield, is high.[1]

On the other hand, the stock of a company with very stable earnings and dividends will trade at a price that is high compared to the dividend. The percentage yield is low because the capital is considered to be relatively safe.

The first component of the interest rate is the risk that your money might not be returned to you. The more risk you're willing to take, the greater reward the market will promise—because the promise might be broken.

DEPRECIATION

While risk considers the possibility that you might not get your capital back, depreciation considers the *expected* decline in the value of what you'll get back.

---

[1] Another reason for the high yield is discussed on the next page.

In March 1977, for example, banks in Argentina were offering a 98% interest rate on time deposits. That's a very tempting yield, but let's look a little closer.

You could have invested $1,000, exchanging the dollars (at the rate of 320.50 pesos per dollar) for 320,500 Argentinian pesos. After one year, the interest would have increased your account to 634,590 pesos. But unfortunately the exchange rate had deteriorated to 698.13 pesos per dollar. If you divide 698.13 into 634,590, you find that the value of the deposit had declined to $908.99—a net loss of 9%.

I've used an extreme example intentionally, in order to make a point: You could have let your $1,000 earn 0% in a safe-deposit box and come out better than by earning 98% in Argentina.

Or, for another example, you could have placed the $1,000 in a Swiss bank account in March 1977, earning the indecently low rate of 3%. As the exchange rate was 2.56 francs per dollar, the $1,000 would have been deposited as 2,560 francs. A year later, your account would have increased to only 2,636.80 francs.

But by then the exchange rate had improved to 1.90 francs per dollar. When you divide 1.90 into 2,636.80, you find that you get back $1,387.79—a return of 38.8%. In other words, the Swiss interest rate is low partly because the franc isn't expected to depreciate; in fact, as we've seen, it may increase in value.

Interest rates in any currency reflect the rate of price inflation (depreciation in purchasing power) that is expected for the currency. Within any category of risk, interest rates will rise and fall as the expected inflation rate rises and falls. Thus the anticipated *real* interest rate (the return after allowing for the depreciation from inflation) changes very little from year to year.

Physical depreciation can also be a reason for high yields. A second reason for the high yield on a South African gold stock is that it isn't possible for the company to continue paying dividends indefinitely. A gold-mining company depreciates physically as it uses up the ore that is its main asset.

Thus someday the company will exhaust its resources and no longer pay any dividends at all. By the same token, companies that are accumulating resources, rather than using them up, will tend to pay low dividends.

LIQUIDITY

The third component of an interest rate is *liquidity*—the ability to know what your investment is worth at any time and to sell quickly without paying a penalty for haste.

For example, a savings account earns a lower rate of interest than a time deposit that can't be withdrawn on demand. A bank can attract savings deposits at the lower interest rate because customers value the freedom to withdraw their funds without waiting.

In the same way, a stock that is seldom traded, and therefore can't be sold quickly at a favorable price, will ordinarily be priced (on the occasions when it is traded) to yield a high dividend rate—higher than you can receive on a stock with a larger, more liquid market.

IMPORTANCE

That high interest rates reflect unfavorable risk, depreciation, or lack of liquidity may seem obvious. But I'm constantly amazed at how easily investors ignore the fact. Chasing interest rates has become a habit for many investors, and it's difficult to convince them that there's far more to an investment than its nominal yield.

High yields can be a characteristic of fool's gold even in normal times, but today each of the three components of an interest rate has a special meaning.

When you invest funds with U.S. banks or corporations, you take on the risk that an unexpected deflation will make it difficult or impossible for the borrower to repay you.

When you make any kind of loan or deposit, you have to

expect the value of the principal to shrink at the rate of price inflation for the currency in which the loan is being made. You also take on the risk that the inflation rate will accelerate, making the money you receive worth even less than you expect it to be.

And when you buy an investment that can't be liquidated easily, you may find yourself unable to move quickly the next time the government decides to change the rules or when you foresee a change in the investment's prospects.

In other words, you should take your eyes off yields and pay more attention to capital.

When making an investment, there are a series of questions to ask:

1. What is the risk of losing the money you invest—through bank failure, corporate failure, loan default, or government intervention?

2. How liquid is the investment? Can you change your mind at any time and get out? If not, how long will your money be immobilized? Could conditions change significantly during that time?

3. If the investment has a fluctuating price (such as a bond, stock, foreign currency, or commodity), how much of a loss could you tolerate before being forced to sell?

4. How much should you expect to lose from price inflation, exchange rate changes, or other types of depreciation during the time you hold the investment?

5. How much could the investment increase in value?

6. If the answers to the first five questions make two investments seem equally attractive, does one of them pay a higher yield?

A high yield doesn't guarantee that an investment is risky, illiquid, or likely to depreciate. The high yield does reflect the market's consensus on the question—but the market (other investors) can be wrong. So if you believe that other investors have overestimated the problems of a particular investment, don't let the high yield scare you off.

But until you make your own appraisal, take the high yield as a danger sign.

CAPITAL AND INCOME

If you are living on the income your investments earn, would forsaking high yields force you to dip into your capital?

In one sense you're *always* dipping into your capital—if you spend any money at all from your investments. Once an interest payment or dividend has been received, it is part of your capital; if you spend it, your capital is less than it would have been if you hadn't spent it.

At first this may seem to be an exercise in semantics. It's not. The point is that the distinction between income and capital is fictitious; your capital is, in fact, a single fund of money. Interest, dividends, or other income you receive are not separate from the whole. So anything you withdraw from the fund causes it to be less than it would have been without the withdrawal—whether or not the amount withdrawn is matched by income.

Suppose for example that you divide your capital among a collection of high-yielding investments—low-grade bonds earning 12%, gold stocks earning 15%, and Brazilian cruzeiro deposits earning 40%. Overall, the portfolio yields 20%. Being thrifty by nature, you decide to live off only one-fourth of the income—5% of the capital. So it appears that you're increasing your capital by 15% per year.

But of course you're actually living beyond your means. The gold stocks are shrinking in value year by year as the mines use up their ore; the cruzeiros are depreciating at 45% per year; and it will be a stroke of luck if all your low-grade bonds are repaid. All in all, your capital is shrinking 5% to 10% per year.

Now suppose that you put your money into investments that earn no income at all, but which appreciate in value 20% per year. You can withdraw and spend 5% and still your capital will grow by 15% each year.

What your investments appear to be "earning" isn't significant by itself. What does matter is the value of what's left at the end of each year. If that's growing, you're not eating into your capital; if it's shrinking, you're spending more than you can afford to. Income, or the lack of it, won't change the matter.

INCOME PLAN

There are safer ways to arrange for a spendable income than by relying on investments that are illiquid, overly risky, or subject to depreciation.

Imagine that in 1968 you invested all your funds in gold bullion. Gold pays no interest (as financial advisors are so fond of telling us). How then could the investment produce a spendable income?

Suppose you had told the bank or broker holding the gold to sell, each year, 5% of the ounces in the account—and to send you the proceeds. To simplify the example we'll assume you invested $1,000 and that you received the payments once every three months.

The table on page 122 shows that you would have received $46.84 in 1969—equal to 4.7% of your investment. Every year from 1972 onward, your payment would have exceeded $50.00 (5% of your original investment), moving upward to $119.40 (or 11.9%) in 1977.

For the ten-year period through 1978, the average annual payment would have been 8.9% of your original investment— much more than the 5% you'd expected. And what has happened to the capital?

Only 60% of the ounces you purchased are left. But each ounce is now worth 348% more in dollars than it was in 1968. Thus, the value of the gold remaining is $2,706, or almost three times what you started with, even though you have been "depleting your capital."

Adjusting these dollar figures for price inflation of 87.5% since 1968, we find that the average annual payment to yourself was 4.8%, measured in purchasing power. And the value

GOLD INCOME PLAN

	Price	Ounces Sold	Payment To You	Ounces Left	Value
June 30, 1968	With $1,000 purchase 24.45 ounces @ $40.90/ounce				
Sept. 30, 1968	$ 39.60	.31	$12.10	24.14	$ 956.12
Dec. 31, 1968	41.90	.30	12.65	23.84	999.00
March 31, 1969	42.90	.30	12.79	23.54	1,010.06
June 30, 1969	41.20	.29	12.13	23.25	957.91
Sept. 30, 1969	40.68	.29	11.82	22.96	934.00
Dec. 31, 1969	35.20	.29	10.10	22.67	798.00
March 31, 1970	35.30	.28	10.00	22.39	790.34
June 30, 1970	35.49	.28	9.93	22.11	784.66
Sept. 30, 1970	36.40	.28	10.06	21.83	794.72
Dec. 31, 1970	37.38	.27	10.20	21.56	805.81
March 31, 1971	38.88	.27	10.48	21.29	827.67
June 30, 1971	40.10	.27	10.67	21.02	843.08
Sept. 30, 1971	42.60	.26	11.20	20.76	884.44
Dec. 31, 1971	43.63	.26	11.32	20.50	894.40
March 31, 1972	48.38	.26	12.40	20.25	979.49
June 30, 1972	64.65	.25	16.36	19.99	1,292.53
Sept. 30, 1972	64.20	.25	16.04	19.74	1,267.49
Dec. 31, 1972	64.90	.25	16.02	19.50	1,265.29
March 31, 1973	90.00	.24	21.93	19.25	1,732.71
June 30, 1973	123.25	.24	29.66	19.01	2,343.19
Sept. 30, 1973	100.00	.24	23.76	18.77	1,877.41
Dec. 31, 1973	112.25	.23	26.34	18.54	2,081.05
March 31, 1974	173.00	.23	40.09	18.31	3,167.22
June 30, 1974	144.25	.23	33.01	18.08	2,607.87
Sept. 30, 1974	151.25	.23	34.18	17.85	2,700.24
Dec. 31, 1974	186.50	.22	41.62	17.63	3,287.93
March 31, 1975	177.25	.22	39.06	17.41	3,085.79
June 30, 1975	166.25	.22	36.18	17.19	2,858.11
Sept. 30, 1975	141.25	.21	30.35	16.98	2,397.97
Dec. 31, 1975	140.25	.21	29.76	16.76	2,351.23
March 31, 1976	129.60	.21	27.16	16.55	2,145.53
June 30, 1976	123.80	.21	25.62	16.35	2,023.89
Sept. 30, 1976	116.00	.20	23.70	16.14	1,872.67
Dec. 31, 1976	134.50	.20	27.14	15.94	2,144.19
March 31, 1977	148.90	.20	29.67	15.74	2,344.08
June 30, 1977	143.00	.20	28.14	15.55	2,223.06
Sept. 30, 1977	154.05	.19	29.94	15.35	2,364.90
Dec. 31, 1977	164.95	.19	31.65	15.16	2,500.58
March 31, 1978	181.60	.19	34.41	14.97	2,718.58
June 30, 1978	183.05	.19	34.25	14.78	2,706.03

Average quarterly payment: $22.35, equal to an average yearly income of 8.94% on an investment of $1,000.

Net capital gain: 170.60%.

of the capital remaining is $1,443 in 1968 values. Thus, your capital showed a *real* increase of 44.3% while it paid you a *real* dividend of 4.8% per year.

Again I've taken an extreme example. There are very few investments that have appreciated by 348% in the past ten years. And I've already pointed out that you shouldn't count on gold continuing to rise as it has.

But the example may make it easier to understand the principles at work. The high dividends or interest you receive may be earned at the cost of imprudent risks, depreciation, and illiquidity. The value of your capital can shrink, even though you are spending only the income. On the other hand, you can live off an investment that pays no interest or dividends at all. To do so, you must nurture the capital as a whole—rather than isolate interest and dividends.

I have mentioned gold only as an example, not as a suggestion. To use gold as the sole source of your income would be as imprudent as to tie up all of your capital in an illiquid time deposit. And so, in Chapter 26, I'll suggest a more balanced portfolio for providing spendable income—without accepting high risk, illiquidity, or depreciation.

11

THINGS
THAT AREN'T SO

No one can keep in touch with the investment world and not encounter certain clichés that circulate without criticism. I think it's important to examine some of these clichés.

MISERY LOVES PROFIT

One popular cliché is, "You're profiting from other people's misery." This taunt is usually aimed at the speculator who sells food or any other commodity at an unusually high price during a shortage. In fact, the charge is often made by the very person who caused the shortage—the politician.

Shortages are frequently caused by political actions—by price controls that discourage production, by regulations that make production unprofitable, and by political programs that squander resources on "social" schemes. The saviour in these situations is the individual who buys the commodity that is being squandered or regulated, sets it aside, and later makes it available when it is most needed—perhaps just after price controls have been removed. It isn't realistic to say that if he hadn't bought the commodity, someone else would have. Without him *all* the resource might have been squandered.

The speculator who provides a commodity when the community's need is greatest is no different from the doctor who cures an otherwise fatal disease. It isn't his fault that the disease exists; he deserves your thanks, not your complaint, for providing a cure.

There are people who enjoy doing "good works." But the world can't depend for its salvation on these few people. If a difficult, lifesaving service isn't allowed to earn a high profit, the world will soon find that there is no one prepared to perform the service.

And anyone who complains that the lifesaver has charged too much for the service is invited to try performing the same service at a lower price. He might find that the job is not as simple as he'd imagined.

SPECULATION

Another cliché says, "Speculation causes prices to fluctuate irrationally." The assumption is that markets without speculators would be calm and orderly.

The first step in examining this idea is to determine what a speculator is. And no matter how you try to distinguish "speculators" from "investors," you'll probably return to the basic definition that *speculation is the purchase of an investment with the hope of selling it at a higher price.* Thus the only investment activity that escapes the speculative label is the purchase of an investment solely for the interest or dividends it yields.[1]

An investor who purchases a blue-chip stock for "solid" long-term growth is just as much a speculator as the man who buys soybean futures in the hope of doubling his money in a year. The only difference between them is in the degree of risk they're willing to tolerate.

Let's suppose that the government outlawed all speculation

[1] We'll bypass the question of the investor who must "speculate" on future price inflation rates, etc., affecting the value of fixed-interest investments. It wouldn't add anything to the discussion at hand.

in commodities. The only lawful traders would be producers and users of the commodity.

Now let's suppose that you raise cattle tails. On Tuesday you bring a load of cattle tails to market, but there are no buyers around. You ask the janitor if he's seen any buyers recently, and he says, "Oh, I think there were a couple here yesterday, but there wasn't anybody selling. So they went home. I think one of 'em said he'd be back Thursday."

So you come back on Thursday. The buyer is there, but so are three other sellers. As the buyer relaxes with a drink in his hand, you and the three other sellers bid the price of cattle tails down to a third of what you had hoped to receive. You make the sale, but you're not sure how you're going to stay in business.

As you're leaving you speak to the janitor again. He says, "You shoulda' been here yesterday. There were five buyers and only one seller. I think the guy finally sold his tails for about four times what you got."

Of course no free market would remain that inefficient for long. You'd probably hire a representative to watch the market and let you know when buyers arrived. Or the janitor would do a little brokering on the side. Or the market's participants would agree to meet on a scheduled day each month.

But even then there could be critical imbalances between supply and demand on market days. Prices might be much higher one month, then much lower the next month, and so on.

The reason prices don't fluctuate in this way is that people from outside an industry are allowed to participate. Speculators cushion the swings. If prices are unusually low one day, speculators will buy in anticipation of a higher price tomorrow. Through their buying, they will prevent the price from going as low as it would go without them. Later, when they sell, any price rise will be dampened.

In this sense speculators are no more than middlemen or time straddlers. They buy the overproduction of one month and make it available in a later month when production is lower. Often a speculator is merely an individual who is willing to buy something no one else wants, and later make it available when others want it very much—in order to make a profit.

I've mentioned that speculative excess will usually carry a price beyond its fundamental objective. If you focus on that alone, you can easily conclude that speculation causes price swings to be exaggerated. But the distortions caused by speculation are minor compared with the wide price swings that would occur in markets without speculators.

Because it's impossible to know the future precisely, prices will always zigzag. But as long as speculators offer insurance against the uncertainties of the future, price movements will be less disorderly.

Some observers like to divide investment markets into those in which speculators are helpful and those in which speculators are parasites. But the division is false. In every investment market, speculators provide liquidity—a reduction in erratic price movements—enabling other participants to buy or sell at any time without having to pay a penalty for acting quickly.

THE BETTER MOUSE TRAP

Another cliché says, "Unless kept secret, a successful trading system would attract enough users to become self-defeating."

There are many reasons that a workable trading system might be available to the public and still go unused:

1. Each person has his own ideas about the way the markets (and the rest of the world) work. These ideas, right or wrong, can keep him from adopting an approach that would be profitable. For some people, it's an article of faith that gold is a bad investment; they wouldn't buy a KrugerRand if it came with a Good Housekeeping Seal of Approval. Others will not buy a stock priced under $10, or invest in a company that's "part of the establishment."

2. Many trading systems, despite the claims of their ad-

herents, aren't successful. People know this, so naturally they're skeptical of any new idea they encounter. Thus, it's easy for a good idea to get lost in the crowd.

3. Not every idea is simple; some are very complicated—either in concept or in application. A sound idea may be too difficult for everyone to understand or to employ.

4. No successful trading system produces a profit on every transaction. Thus, it can't reassure the user by proving itself every hour. This provides room for doubt by people who don't like the idea, who don't understand it, who believe no system is possible, or who think that a good system should be riskless.

One way or another, we don't have to worry that all investors are going to adopt the same trading system.

And my own experience with investors tells me that the cliché is false. I've made a fair amount of money in the investment markets, but it's easy to find people who disagree with me. In some cases, investors have greater confidence in programs of their own; in other cases, the reason may be that the price of accepting my suggestions is to give up the idea that government is a friendly giant.

SELF-FULFILLING PROPHECIES

A popular cliché is, "If enough people believe a prediction, the prophecy will be self-fulfilling"—that is, the actions of the believers will cause the prophecy to come true. For example, "If enough people believe that banks are going to fail, they will all try to withdraw their money, and the banks will fail. *Ergo*, the prophecy will be self-fulfilling."

The cliché is untrue, at least in financial matters. If a bank is properly run and makes only the promises it can keep, then it can survive any false rumor. The rumors won't be good for business, of course, but they won't cause insolvency. So if a prediction of a bank failure comes true, the prophecy wasn't self-fulfilling, it was correct.

Politicians often try to "talk up" the economy with rosy

predictions, but self-fulfillment doesn't seem to work for them. In 1929, the consensus of soothsayers called for a permanent boom, but the magic failed. On the other hand, a depression was widely expected following World War II, but somehow prosperity couldn't be avoided.

People act on their opinions, and their opinions are influenced by what they hear. But people are also influenced and restrained by what they're able to do. There's a limit to how much of an investment anyone can buy or sell, regardless of what he believes. And no business shuts down in anticipation of a depression; it waits until a depression actually affects it.

The "self-fulfilling prophecy" cliché is usually trotted out by someone who is afraid that others will believe the prophecy and act on it. But people respond to the same statement in different ways.

UNANIMITY

A similar irrelevancy is the rhetorical question, "What if everyone were to do what you're suggesting?" But, of course, the question is as meaningless as "What if everyone became a doctor?"

There isn't anything that everyone is going to do.

INVESTMENT PRICES

Another variation of the self-fulfilling prophecy cliché says, "If investors expect prices to go up, prices will go up." Not only is this one not true, it is usually the opposite of the truth.

An investor who expects a price to rise has probably already acted on his expectation—unless the idea has come to him just this moment. He's already bought, and his expectation has *already* influenced the price. Unless he becomes even more bullish (and buys more of the investment), the market won't hear from him again until he sells.

His bullishness affects the price only in that he won't *sell* his investment today; otherwise he can't influence the price in any way. He can stand in the gallery and cheer for his investment, but that won't push its price up.

And as we saw in Chapter 6, if "everyone" is bullish and has already acted on his bullishness, who is left to bid the price up further? The first time anyone tries to sell, the price will break. Widespread bullishness should alert you to the possibility that the price will be dropping soon.

PHILOSOPHY

The past six chapters have discussed investment philosophy—general guidelines concerning the way investment markets work and what to expect from them.

It's always more profitable to look at the markets realistically. But in a time when so many people are trying to explain the crises away, it is especially important to have a well-founded understanding of the way the world actually works.

PART III

INVESTMENT
SURVEY

12

THE U.S. STOCK
MARKET

THE CHAPTERS IN PART III SURVEY INDIVIDUAL INVESTMENT markets. We will look at the opportunities and risks to be found in each market, in preparation for the discussion of investment strategy in Part IV.

STOCKS AND MONETARY POLICY

Investors have long thought of the stock market in terms of cycles, but it is only recently that they have attributed the cycles to disturbances in the money supply. The stock market is cyclical because the government's monetary policy is cyclical; up-and-down swings in the growth rate of the money supply cause up-and-down swings in stock prices.

Although news about the money supply is now a common part of reports on the stock market, the nature of the relationship is not well understood. Investors seem to know that the money supply has an effect upon stocks, but they are not sure just what it is.

For many years many people believed that stocks could protect an investor from price inflation; stock prices were expected to rise along with all other prices. The investors who understood that price inflation results from monetary inflation would interpret a faster expansion of the money supply as bullish for stocks—since the increased monetary inflation would lead to price inflation.

The "inflation hedge" idea was demolished once and for all by the events of 1973 and 1974. As price inflation reached rates of 8.8% and 12.2%, the stock market suffered its greatest losses since the crash of 1929.

This led to an opposite, and equally wrong, theory—that price inflation is bad for the stock market. In truth, there is no *direct* link between price inflation and stock prices. Both are results of a third factor, monetary inflation.[1]

As we saw in Chapter 3, the stock market is one of the first recipients of newly created paper money. As a result, stock prices are highly sensitive to changes in monetary policy. When monetary inflation is increased, stock prices go up; when monetary inflation is curtailed, stock prices go down.

Those who believe that price inflation is bad for the stock market see the relationship upside down. When the money supply is increased abnormally, they anticipate price inflation, which they see as bearish for stocks. But by the time the price inflation actually occurs, stock prices will have already gone up.

It takes time for new money to work its way through the economy. At some point well after the new money has affected the investment markets and the banking system, price inflation will follow. The time lag isn't predictable with any precision, but price inflation usually peaks about two years after the peak in monetary inflation.

TYPICAL CYCLE

This time lag is the reason most investors don't understand the relationship between money and stocks. To see how it works, let's take a hypothetical example.

---

1 Real values of stocks are affected by price inflation. But we're discussing here the factors that *move* stock prices, not the fact that inflation causes a stock's real value to be other than what it seems to be.

In January 1979, the Federal Reserve System surveys the economic situation. It sees that for nearly two years the money supply has grown at a slow pace. As a result, interest rates are at high levels, the stock market is suffering through a bear trend, and the economy is sliding deeper into a recession. Also, the restrained rate of monetary inflation is *just now* beginning to bring the price inflation rate downward.

The Fed feels that it's both necessary and safe to step up the growth of the money supply. This will bring interest rates down and help to cure the recession. In addition, the "unused capacity" theory holds that monetary inflation during a recession won't aggravate price inflation.[2]

And so in January 1979, the Fed enters the bond market as an eager buyer, paying for its purchases with new paper money. The new money goes through the bond market and into the stock market almost immediately—and a new bull market is underway.

As stock prices rise, the press reports, "Investors, encouraged by news of slower price inflation, bought heavily today and pushed stock prices broadly higher." Of course, the writer is expected to provide a reason for the stock rally, and any analyst will be glad to tell him that waning price inflation is the cause. But the cause has been misunderstood. Stock prices are rising because of *new* monetary inflation, while price inflation is easing because of the *previous* period of monetary restraint.

The new monetary uptrend continues for nearly two years —to, let's say, October 1980. By that time the stock market is at a new high, and the economic "recovery" is widely acknowledged. But price inflation, which had been dropping for almost two years, is now beginning to move upward.

Because price inflation is rising, the Fed decides it's necessary to restrain the growth of the money supply—and does so. Interest rates rise, money is drained out of the investment

[2] The "unused capacity" theory states that an economy with a high unemployment rate and unused plant facilities can be stimulated without risking high price inflation, because the new money won't bid up the price of labor or other underused resources. The theory hasn't been confirmed by the experience of the past several years, but that hasn't injured its popularity.

markets, and a new bear trend in stocks is underway.

As stock prices fall, the press reports, "Investors, discouraged by reports of higher inflation rates, sold heavily today and pushed stocks broadly lower." Again, the analysis is mistaken.

The Fed usually enters a period of restraint at about the time that its previous period of monetary stimulation begins to reflect itself in higher price inflation. So one could use the price inflation rate as an indicator of the stock market's future. When the trend in price inflation changes, expect monetary policy to change, which will cause the stock market to change course.

But this is a roundabout and imprecise method. Fed policy isn't consistent; we have no guarantee that it will respond at precisely the time the trend in price inflation changes. Other political considerations could be more important, and so it's far better to look to the basic cause of stock market trends—monetary inflation.

MONEY WATCHING

But this, too, has its problems. There are insignificant short-term fluctuations in the money supply, just as there are brief fluctuations in almost everything else. A big jump in the money supply one week doesn't signal the start of an uptrend.

The week-to-week disturbances reveal only the Fed's imprecision—not its intentions. When the Federal Reserve creates new money, it doesn't know exactly how the money will be used. It might be held dollar for dollar in the form of currency, or it might be multiplied by commercial banks that use it as reserves upon which to create a larger quantity of deposits. Because the Fed can't control the way the money will be used, it can't know precisely how its actions will affect the money supply.

Adding to the uncertainty is a delay in learning the results. The money supply data the Fed receives from commercial banks are always at least one week old. (The figures announced each Thursday refer to the week ending eight days earlier.) So the Fed often acts during one week to counteract the errors of one to two weeks earlier.

The fact of the Fed's imprecision has inspired some investors to use a reverse form of money watching. If the weekly money supply shows a large increase, these investors turn bearish—because they expect the Fed to restrain the money supply during the coming week, in reaction to the figures just released.

This, too, is a chancy investment policy. Since monetary control is imprecise, the Fed may intend to restrict the money supply next week but not succeed. And even if the desired monetary result is achieved, the stock market may not be affected so quickly.

If this short-term money-watching system did work, it would be appropriate only for investors who trade rapidly in and out of the stock market. Stocks would be bought and sold from week to week.

For an investor trying to spot long-term changes in monetary policy, short-term movements in the money supply are meaningless. The graph on page 138 shows the rates of change for one-month, three-month, and six-month intervals. As you can see, compared with the twelve-month chart on page 45, this chart reveals no trends that could be used in making investment decisions.

Because week-to-week changes are not significant, you will be able to discern a change in the trend of monetary policy only some time after it has occurred. But, as we'll see in Chapter 28, that delay need not stop us; there are signals that show up soon enough to be used profitably.

For now the main points are:

1. The stock market responds sensitively to changes in the monetary policy of the Federal Reserve. A more stimulative policy causes a bull market; a restrictive policy causes a bear market. Major changes in monetary policy occur only every couple of years, so there are long-lasting trends in stock prices.

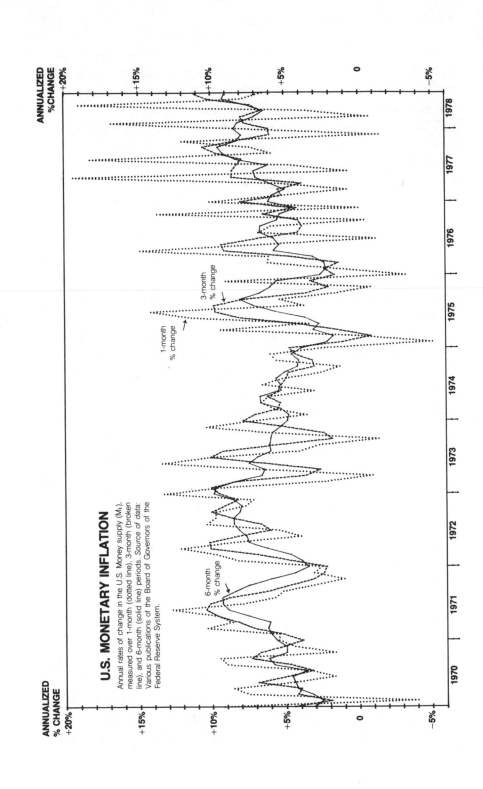

U.S. MONETARY INFLATION

Annual rates of change in the U.S. Money supply (M₁), measured over 1-month (dotted line), 3-month (broken line), and 6-month (solid line) periods. *Source of data:* Various publications of the Board of Governors of the Federal Reserve System.

ANNUALIZED % CHANGE

+20%
+15%
+10%
+5%
0
−5%

1-month % change

3-month % change

6-month % change

1970 1971 1972 1973 1974 1975 1976 1977 1978

2. The price inflation rate also is affected by monetary inflation, with a time lag of roughly two years. As a result, price inflation can appear to affect the stock market; but it's a misleading indicator.

3. Since there will inevitably be another expansion in monetary inflation, the stock market will see another bull trend. And the trend will probably begin when it seems least likely—when the present bear trend seems permanent.

STOCK MARKET INVESTMENTS

There are no perfect forecasting techniques—although there are successful ones. You shouldn't expect to identify the absolute top or bottom of a trend until sometime after the event.

As with any investment, it's a mistake to bet all your capital as though you know precisely what lies ahead. A developing bull market can be sidetracked by a change in monetary policy, by new forms of government interference, by many things. For this reason I believe it's best to invest in the stock market in a way that limits your potential loss.

Stock options are one way to limit risk. But a stock option expires within nine months at the most. That doesn't allow much tolerance for inexact timing. If you buy four months before an uptrend actually begins, the underlying stock may drop for four months, rise for four months, and end the nine-month option period unchanged. And if you buy the option only after you're convinced that a new uptrend has started, the cost of the option will be higher than if you had purchased during a quiet or falling market.

WARRANTS

Stock warrants are a more suitable medium for the investor who wants to catch a broad uptrend.

A warrant is like an option; it is the right to purchase a

share of stock at a specified price. And, like an option, a warrant is good for a specified period of time.

Unlike an option, a warrant is issued by the company whose stock is involved. And while an option is usually good for no more than nine months, a warrant may have a life of many years.

Here's a hypothetical example:

In 1964 the Ajax Company sold a new issue of bonds in order to raise money. It offered an interest rate ½% less than would be normal, given the company's credit rating. To make the bonds attractive at this rate, the company included one warrant with each $1,000 bond.

Each warrant gave its holder the right to purchase, from Ajax, one share of Ajax stock at a price of $25—which, at the time, was approximately the market price of the stock. The right to buy the stock at $25 continues until November 1, 1994.

The bondholder is free to sell the warrant in the open market, like any other investment. Whoever happens to own the warrant can "exercise" it by returning it to Ajax, together with $25, in exchange for one share of Ajax stock.

Let's assume that you own one of the Ajax warrants and that the price of Ajax stock is now $33. Obviously, the warrant has an immediate *exercise value* of $8. With the warrant and $25 (its *exercise price*), you can purchase a share of Ajax stock that could be resold immediately for $33. Thus, the warrant is worth at least $8.

The warrant has an additional value beyond its immediate exercise value. Since it doesn't expire until 1994, owning it has certain advantages compared with owning the stock directly. So the warrant might trade for, say, $12.

What are the advantages? Suppose I buy the warrant from you for $12 instead of paying $33 to buy the stock. If the price of the stock increases by, say, $10, the warrant's exercise value will increase by $10 also. The warrant's market price will increase by a similar but somewhat smaller amount —by, say, $9.

In that case I would have made a $9 profit on a $12 investment (75%) instead of a $10 profit on a $33 investment (30%).

Also, if the Ajax stock should tumble, I could lose $10, $15, or $20 or more on the stock. But I can't possibly lose more on the warrant than I've paid for it—in this case $12.

And since I have until 1994 to enjoy these privileges, they are worth something to me. Thus, if you own the warrant, I'll pay more than its immediate exercise value of $8 to buy it from you.

The amount by which the warrant sells above $8 is its *premium*. The premium reflects: the advantage of investing with a cash outlay that is less than the price of the stock; the leverage that results from the lower outlay; the limitation of potential loss; and the amount of time remaining before the warrant expires. Since the Ajax warrant currently sells for $12 and has an exercise value of $8, its premium is $4.

If the stock price doesn't change at all, the warrant's premium will tend to decrease as the expiration date comes closer. On the day the warrant expires, the premium will be zero. The warrant can be worth no more than its exercise value on the last day, because by then all its other features will have disappeared. On the day after the warrant expires, it will be worthless.

Before then, if the stock is selling for less than the warrant's exercise price, there will still be a premium—even though the warrant has no exercise value at all. The amount of the premium will depend upon the length of time remaining until the expiration date, how far the current stock price is below the exercise price, and the current trend of the stock.

At the beginning of a bull market you can expect most warrants to be "out of the money"—which means that the price of the underlying stock is below the warrant's exercise price. Each warrant's market price will be all premium, with no exercise value.

The table on page 142 shows some examples from March 1975, just after the stock market had begun a new bull trend. All these warrants were out of the money. So, for each one, the entire price was a premium.

SELECTED WARRANT & STOCK PRICES, MARCH 1975

Name	Stock Price	Warrant Expiration Date	Exercise Price	Warrant Price	Of Which — Exercise Value	Premium
Allegheny Airlines	$ 4.25	April, 1987	$17.31	$2.00	$0.00	$2.00
Financial Gen. Bankshares	5.25	June, 1978	6.65	2.13	0.00	2.13
Budget Industries	3.75	Nov., 1983	20.00	.75	0.00	.75
Gould	20.38	June, 1976	36.67	2.75	0.00	2.75
Phoenix Steel	6.63	Dec., 1979	7.80	2.00	0.00	2.00
Hospital Mortgage Group	5.00	Feb., 1977	25.00	1.00	0.00	1.00
Atlas	2.13	Perpetual	6.25	1.00	0.00	1.00
Indian Head	19.50	May, 1990	40.00	1.25	0.00	1.25

The exercise price for the Allegheny warrant was $17.31, but the stock was selling for only $4.25. Yet the warrant still had twelve years to run, and so there was hope. As a result, the warrant sold for $2.

The Gould warrant had only fifteen months left. And the stock's price of $20.38 was below the warrant's exercise price of $36.67. Yet, the warrant sold for $2.75. The stock price would have had to increase by 80% in fifteen months in order to give the warrant an exercise value. Still, at the time, the warrant was worth $2.75 to someone.

MECHANICS

There are 12 warrants traded on the New York Stock Exchange and 39 traded on the American Stock Exchange. Hundreds more are traded over-the-counter by dealers, though many of them are very small issues.

Usually, one warrant entitles its owner to purchase one share of stock. But sometimes a warrant entitles the owner to purchase an odd number of shares—such as 1.32 or .87 shares. This happens when a warrant has been adjusted for stock dividends and splits—so that the warrant's relationship to the stock it covers will be unchanged. And there are other ways in which a particular warrant can differ from the standard form I've given here.

Like stocks, warrants are traded in round lots of 100. When you hold a warrant, you receive no dividends from the company.[3]

WARRANT STRATEGY

A warrant contains built-in leverage. If Ajax stock (in the hypothetical example) fell to $20, its warrant would probably sell for around $2.00. If the stock then rose to $30, the war-

---

[3] A detailed explanation of the warrant market is given in *Using Warrants* by Terry Coxon (listed in the *Suggested Reading* on page 448).

rant would probably rise to about $6. Thus, a 50% increase in the stock price would cause a 200% increase in the warrant price.

In this situation the warrant offers 4-to-1 leverage—meaning a given percentage increase in the stock will cause a percentage increase four times as large in the warrant. (The 4-to-1 figure is only an example; the amount of leverage will vary from warrant to warrant.)

Many investors buy warrants in order to obtain this leverage. For example, if you have $10,000 to invest in Ajax, you can purchase 500 shares of stock at $20 or 5,000 warrants at $2.00.

By putting the whole budget into warrants, you give up the limitation on loss that warrants offer, however. A warrant price can drop to zero, just as stock prices can. In fact, if the stock falls, the warrant's leverage will cause it to fall faster than the stock.

But you can put warrants to work in a different way. From the $10,000 budget (which could purchase 500 shares of stock), purchase 1,200 warrants—costing $2,400. You'll have tied up only 24% of the available funds, you'll have limited your potential loss to 24% of the funds (against 100% if you purchase the stock), and you'll be able to gain from increases in the stock's price on close to a dollar-for-dollar basis.

If you're concerned about potential exchange controls or other government interference, only $2,400 will be exposed in the U.S. stock market. The remaining $7,600 could be sitting in a Swiss bank and could be used, perhaps, for another investment.

And if your timing turns out to be bad, or your stock selections poor, you've limited the amount that your error can cost.

Because the costs of trading warrants (commissions, spreads, etc.) are a higher percentage of your investment than the costs of trading stocks, you can't easily move in and out of the warrant market. As I see it, there are two purposes for which warrants are appropriate:

1. You can purchase an assortment of warrants when you

believe a new bull stock market is beginning. By buying the warrants of twenty or more different companies, you'll be betting on the bull market itself, not on individual stocks. And the warrant investment should require only about 15% to 25% of the investment required for the stocks of those companies.

2. At other times, you might keep 10% or so of your investment capital in warrants. This would provide a hedge against the possibility that future events could catch you by surprise.

For example, suppose that 80% of your funds are invested in gold, silver, and currencies during a bull trend in those investments. Suddenly the investments reverse and drop quickly. By the time the trend is confirmed, you might have lost 15% to 25% of your capital (if you don't have stop-loss protection).

But such a turnaround would probably be accompanied by a new bull market in stocks (as it was in 1975). If you had 10% of your capital in warrants, the profit on the warrants might offset most of the loss suffered on the other investments. On the other hand, if your original investments continue to appreciate, your maximum loss in the warrants would be 10% of your capital.

So the warrants can be used both to speculate on a bull trend in stocks and as an inexpensive hedge at other times.

DRAWBACKS

The principal drawback of warrant investments is the small size of the warrant market. As of May 1978, only 57 companies had warrants that were actively traded and whose expiration dates were far enough away to be useful. To create a diversified investment, you should use at least twenty of them.

In addition, warrants tend to be issued by smaller companies; there are only a few blue-chip stocks for which warrants are available. So you can't duplicate the Dow Jones

Industrial Average with warrants. But you should be able to create a portfolio that will approximate the general movement of the stock market.

We'll return to the subject of warrants in Chapter 31—and I'll include a method for choosing among them. I'll also offer suggestions for selecting other types of stock-market investments.

STOCK MARKET PROSPECTS

Although it might not seem likely at the time you read this, the stock market will rise again. It always does.

The stock market provides an opportunity for profit during the periods when gold is declining. And so the stock market will play a part in the strategy to be suggested in Part IV.

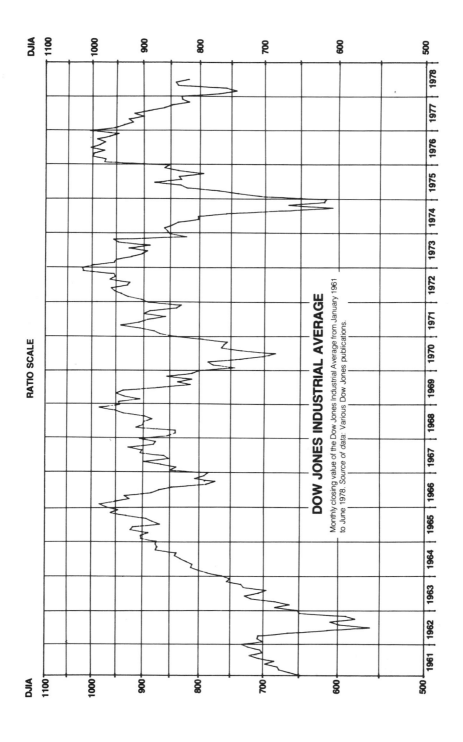

RATIO SCALE

DOW JONES INDUSTRIAL AVERAGE

Monthly closing value of the Dow Jones Industrial Average from January 1961
to June 1978. Source of data: Various Dow Jones publications.

13

REAL ESTATE

MANY INVESTORS HAVE STRONG FEELINGS ABOUT REAL ESTATE—
either for or against. And neither a rising nor a declining
market will shake those feelings.

I should tell you at the outset that I'm not enthusiastic
about real estate, and I haven't been for the past ten years.
During that time, U.S. real estate prices have generally risen,
and in some areas they've risen substantially. But the rise
has done nothing to make real estate seem more attractive,
nor has it left me with any feeling of regret for the profits I
haven't made.

In the first place, I don't feel that I must participate in
every uptrend. I want to stay only in those markets that are
liquid, that are easy for me to understand and deal with, and
that offer an attractive compromise between risk and reward.

In the real world you have to pay a price for safety and
liquidity. And you'll have something new to regret everyday
if you don't recognize that you can't know everything. The
rational investor understands this and ignores what "might
have been" had he invested in Main Street properties fifteen
years ago, bought coffee futures in 1976, or sold short in
1929.[1]

---

[1] Unless, of course, these were areas of his expertise, and he failed to act on his
own judgment.

For some reason many investors like to tell me how well their real estate investments have been doing. Assuming that the appreciation they cite can actually be realized when the property is sold, the figures still are impressive only in comparison with the performance of the stock market or some other victim of the monetary crises.

In comparison with hard-money investments, real estate's performance hasn't been so impressive. An investment so simple and liquid as a bank account in Swiss francs has appreciated by 100% during the last ten years; a simple, liquid investment in silver has grown by over 200%, and an investment in gold has grown by over 400%. None of these investments has incurred property taxes or required the cost of maintenance or the trouble of management.

The status of hard-money investments has changed, however, so I have had to reconsider my appraisal of real estate. I've come to the same conclusion as before—but with one significant difference. Added to the perennial drawback of illiquidity is the possibility that the real estate boom is in its final days.

I can't tell you when the boom will end. In fact, it won't end at the same time everywhere, so no simple prediction could possibly be correct. But there is good reason to believe that the general boom in real estate is living on borrowed time.

In this chapter, I'll discuss real estate values and what has happened to them. And I'll examine the two most quoted arguments in favor of investing in real estate: (1) the supply of land is limited, and so a rising population will force land prices upward; and (2) real estate is a hedge against inflation.

PRICES

Any investment can be overpriced—no matter how great its fundamental value or how secure its prospects.

In the absence of a more thorough analysis, it's reasonable to suspect that investments in a market that has been rising for a long time are overpriced. In itself that guideline isn't a signal to sell; it is a signal to make a closer examination.

It's understandable that investments in a long-rising market would be overpriced. The longer an uptrend continues, the more investors become convinced that it will continue forever. They gladly pay a premium over the investment's current value—confident that the fundamental value will continue to increase and hoping that the premium itself will rise.

This is comparable to the "growth stock" that sells for forty times its annual earnings when the average stock sells for twenty times earnings. Because the growth stock's earnings have risen in the past, investors assume that future earnings will be even greater and will catch up with the price.

However, there's no reason that the fundamental value of a stock or a piece of real estate must continue to rise. In fact, although it's clear that real estate prices have been rising, it isn't clear that real estate *values* have risen by as much. Property can sell above its fundamental value because the value has been overestimated—or even ignored—or because of the thoughtless assumption that the value will always rise.

REAL ESTATE VALUES

What is the fundamental value of a piece of real estate?

The value of any tangible asset is its value to the person who uses it. A driver pays $5,000 for a car *not* because that's the cost of manufacturing the car or because that's the price at which it can be resold. He's willing to pay $5,000 only because $5,000 is the value to him of the services the car will provide—compared with other uses of the money. If the price is higher than the value to him, he'll buy something else instead.

The fundamental value of a house is its value in use to someone who would live in it. The house is no more than a package of housing services (the shelter and comfort that it provides each day), and the house itself is worth as much as those services are worth—no more, no less.

But because a house lasts so many years, much of the service won't be consumed until far in the future. So it's difficult to estimate just what the service will be worth later and hence what the house is worth right now. Although it may be difficult to apply the principle of use value, the principle is clear: The value of a house depends upon the value of the services it provides.

The principal indication of the use value of a house is the *rent* it can earn. The rent is the price that people are willing to pay to use the services the house produces. This is true even if a property isn't being held for rental, as in the case of an owner-occupied house. A homeowner pays himself rent, whether or not he thinks of his ownership in that way. Any house can be made available to renters, and any homeowner can sell his house and rent somewhere else, or even rent from his buyer.

The value of a house, then, is reflected in the rental income that it can produce. A long-established rule of thumb is that a property is worth 100 times its monthly rental. After allowing for operating expenses (upkeep, depreciation, taxes, management costs, etc.), the rule usually implies a net return of 3% to 6% per year.

The rule of thumb obviously isn't very precise; operating costs vary from property to property and from area to area. With lower operating costs, a property can sell for more than 100 times its monthly rent and still produce a net return in the 3% to 6% range.

However, one subtle feature of the rule is that it should apply even at high rates of inflation. The dollar value of a property will continue to rise as long as the rent it earns can be adjusted upward. If inflation causes the property value and the rent to increase at the same rate, then the net return in dollars will increase, too. So the relationship between property value and rental income needn't be upset by inflation; if 100 times rental income is a satisfactory price when inflation is 1%, it will be satisfactory when inflation is 20%.

Also, we should recognize that a property· will be affected by local rental values, even if the land is barren and undeveloped. The land's only value rests in the possibility that it *might* someday be put to use—and the return it might produce is indicated by the rent earned by developed property in the same area.

Starting from the idea of use value, we can establish a method for analyzing what has happened to the **real estate** market.

1. The value of a property will have an unchanging relationship to the rent the property produces. Whatever the correct multiple (100 times rental income, 200 times, etc.), that multiple should not change. So property *values* will appreciate or depreciate as rents increase or decrease. If you know how rental values are moving, you'll know how property values are moving—even if you don't know the appropriate multiple.

2. The values of *all* properties, developed and undeveloped, in a given area will rise or fall as rental incomes rise or fall.

3. If you know how much rental values have changed, you know how much fundamental property values have changed. And by comparing the change in property values with the change in prices, you can determine if property has become overpriced or underpriced.

The tip-off that real estate is now generally overpriced is that the prices of single-family houses have risen much faster than rents. According to the U.S. government's figures, since 1967 housing prices have risen by 122.2% while rents have increased by only 58.0%.[2]

Of course the figures are only averages, but the difference between 122.2% and 58.0% is great enough to raise an eyebrow. It means that prices have been increasing about twice as fast as fundamental values.

These indices cover the entire United States; the situation

2 U.S. Department of Commerce: *Price Index of New One-Family Houses Sold,* Fourth Quarter 1977; and U.S. Department of Labor: *CPI Detailed Report,* February 1978.

in any particular location might be different. However, the statistics reported for all individual regions of the country are consistent with the general conclusion. The table on page 154 shows four trends—rents, prices of single-family houses, costs of home ownership, and general living costs—for each of eight cities.

Again, these are averages. But the situation is the same in all eight areas: Housing prices have increased faster than the rate of inflation and *much* faster than rents.

It isn't enough to say that land is in short supply or that there's a housing shortage. If those were the reasons for the real estate boom, rents would have risen comparably. But they haven't.

The disparity means that the investment yield on real estate is dropping. The drop means that real estate is no longer competitive with other forms of investment.

Why then do investors pay these prices for real estate? Obviously, because they expect real estate prices to rise, and to do so steadily and rapidly. But is there a fundamental basis for the expectation? We should look at the inflation-hedge and population arguments to determine that.

INFLATION HEDGE

An inflation hedge is an investment that is affected directly by inflation, and so can be expected to compensate an investor for changes in the general price level.

Real estate doesn't fit this definition, because there's no automatic correlation between inflation rates and real estate prices. As the table on page 154 shows, rents have not kept up with price inflation, which means that fundamental real estate values have lagged behind inflation.

If your real estate holdings have done well, it isn't because of inflation. It is simply that you have managed to profit from an investment during a time of inflation—which is something quite different from owning an inflation hedge. And the

REAL ESTATE PRICES, RENTS, & COSTS
Increases from 1967 to 1977

Area	Price Inflation	Housing Prices	Rents	Ownership Costs
Atlanta	84.4%	92.7%	38.1%	112.9%
Chicago	80.1%	94.0%	46.8%	93.7%
Detroit	84.3%	94.0%	55.2%	99.3%
Kansas City	82.7%	94.0%	35.4%	115.5%
Los Angeles	84.5%	133.9%	65.0%	120.8%
New York	88.7%	103.9%	74.9%	107.0%
Philadelphia	86.9%	103.9%	71.1%	106.7%
San Francisco	87.3%	133.9%	71.1%	129.6%
All U.S.A.	**86.2%**	**122.2%**	**58.0%**	**133.0%**

Price Inflation, Rent, & Ownership Costs are taken from "CPI Detailed Report," February 1978, published by the Bureau of Labor Statistics, U.S. Department of Labor. For the U.S. as a whole, *Ownership Costs* are a weighted average of financing, taxes, and insurance, together with maintenance and repairs. For the individual cities, *Ownership Costs* are distorted slightly as the only category published includes these items plus home purchase prices.

Housing Prices are taken from "Price Index of New One-Family Houses Sold; Fourth Quarter 1977," March 2, 1978, published by the Bureau of the Census, U.S. Department of Commerce. The Bureau publishes a national average index, plus indices for the four principal U.S. regions; the figures shown above are the figures for the regions in which these cities are located and, hence, are not precise.

Changes in housing prices are from the 1967 average to the fourth quarter of 1977. All other figures are changes from the 1967 average to December 1977.

difference means that you can't count on inflation to boost the value of your holdings in the future.

No matter what may happen to inflation, some properties will appreciate, others will depreciate, and others will change very little. Property has the least chance of continuing to appreciate in areas where real estate prices have already surpassed use values.

Even if you're convinced that real estate is an inflation hedge, this doesn't mean that real estate will be a good investment. A continuing theme of this book is that an unintentional deflation is a real possibility.

THE POPULATION

When examined closely, the population argument isn't very impressive. What would you estimate is the average annual increase in the U.S. population: 5%? 10%? 2%?

From 1970 to 1977, the population increased at an average yearly rate of 0.8% (8/10 of 1%). And the rate has been slowing. In the 1950s, the annual rate was 1.7%; in the 1960s, it was 1.3%; and now it is 0.8%.[3]

The growth rate is higher in some areas than in others. But, generally, population has been growing faster in areas where cities have room to expand, thus moderating the pressure on property prices.

TRENDS AGAIN

The population and inflation-hedge arguments are weak, widespread, and misleading. But they aren't the real reasons most people invest in real estate; they are only the outward justifications.

Most real estate investors are more impressed by the apparent price uptrend than by anything else. They believe

3 Bureau of the Census: *The Statistical Abstract of the U.S., 1976,* Table no. 1; International Monetary Fund: *International Financial Statistics,* May 1978.

that prices will continue to rise simply because they *have* been rising.

But the trend will end, just as all trends must eventually end. And the end will probably come fairly soon.

As prices rise faster than rents, the purchases will have to come more and more from part-time speculators. Real estate professionals will find the yields less and less attractive, and anyone who simply wants a place to live will find it cheaper to rent than to buy.

With rents so low compared with prices, investment properties are becoming a burden to their owners. Notice in the table on page 154 that ownership costs have risen faster than the general rate of price inflation, far faster than rental income, and even faster than the increase in housing prices.

If a house sells for 200 times its rent, the landlord may be spending all his rental income on the costs of owning the house. With a zero return on his investment, his only incentive is the hope of a rising price. Any sign that the price rise may be over will motivate him to sell out.

ILLIQUIDITY

Unfortunately, one can't just sell out and take a profit when the game appears to be over. It may be six months or more before a property is sold, because the real estate market isn't liquid. There are few market-makers in the real estate world— dealers who will offer to buy on the spot—and you can't expect to receive a good price even if you find one.

So unless you're willing to accept a low price for a quick sale to a dealer, you can only put the property on the market and hope for the best. Even then you won't know what the property is worth; everything is conjecture until someone makes a written offer.

Real estate brokers can give you their opinions about the current market—but their opinions will be based on limited information and on an abundance of wishful thinking. You won't even know whether the general market is in a bull or bear trend until it has become so obvious that everyone's talking about it. By that time, the trend may be over.

With real estate you never really know the state of the market. Nor do you even know the market value of your own holdings. All you know is what "everyone knows," and such information is usually more public than reliable.

It's hard to stay out of a market when everyone is talking about the phenomenal boom. To steel yourself against the excitement, always remember that, in the real world, no investment goes up every year, year after year.

Whenever I'm told about the boom in the local real estate market, whenever I hear that "prices have doubled in just the last two years," my thought is always, "Sounds like a good time to sell."

REAL ESTATE

By now you must be expecting me to urge you to sell your real estate holdings tomorrow morning.

Not at all. Every investment has risks and drawbacks. The important thing is to recognize them, to be aware of what can happen to your investments, and to make sure you aren't exposed to risks you can't afford.

I find the illiquidity of real estate too much of a burden, especially now. But the reason for the illiquidity is that every property is different. This variety means that some properties may be underpriced even though the average property is overpriced. So if you have a skill for identifying bargains, my skepticism shouldn't discourage you from using it, and I know that it won't.

With or without that skill, the illiquidity can be much more tolerable if your real estate holdings don't represent a large portion of your total assets. If only 10% or 20% of your net worth is in real estate (perhaps just the home you live in), you don't have to panic. Even if the worst happens, it won't be catastrophic for you.

But if 75% of your net worth is tied up in real estate, I believe you have a lot of thinking to do.

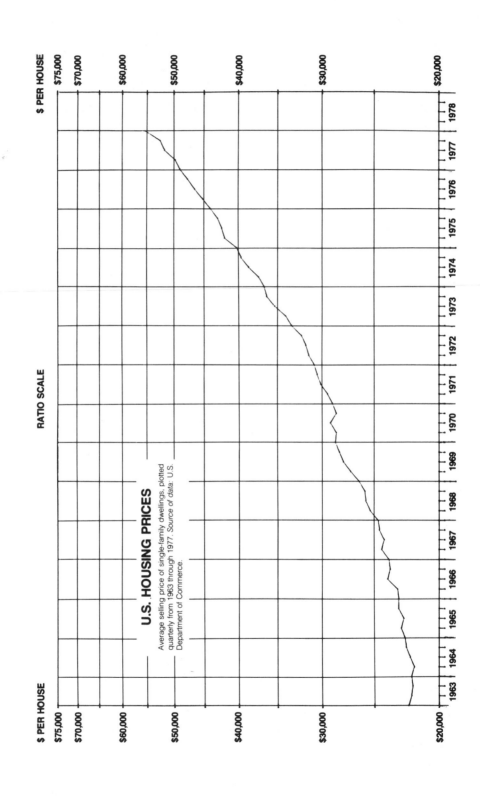

$ PER HOUSE

RATIO SCALE

$ PER HOUSE

U.S. HOUSING PRICES

Average selling price of single-family dwellings, plotted quarterly from 1963 through 1977. Source of data: U.S. Department of Commerce.

14

FIXED-INTEREST
INVESTMENTS

MUCH HAS BEEN SAID AND WRITTEN ABOUT THE POOR PER-
formance of fixed-interest investments during times of price
inflation.

The simpler, less-risky, short-term investments (such as
Treasury bills and savings accounts) generally fail to keep
up with inflation—providing a net loss of purchasing power.
Higher-paying investments (long-term corporate or government bonds) produce a net return, after inflation, of only 1%
to 3%—despite the risks inherent in those investments.

And of course you're taxed on the full amount of the interest, not just the net after inflation. So if you pay income
tax at all, you're almost sure to wind up with a loss in purchasing power, unless you buy the riskiest fixed-interest investments available. The table on page 160 records the recent
performance of these investments.

None of this is news. Most people know what's going to
happen to their money when they put it into a savings account. Why, then, do they invest in a sure loser?

The answer is that many people see no simple alternatives.
Hard-money investments are volatile; the poor performance
of stocks is obvious to the most casual observer; and so-called
"collectibles" (numismatics and other rarities) are too exotic,
too illiquid, and don't pay interest.

REAL RETURN ON INTEREST-BEARING INVESTMENTS, 1970-1977

Investment	Average Annual Yield	Net Yield after Inflation	Net Annual Yield After Taxes & Inflation	
			25% Bracket[2]	50% Bracket[2]
Baa long-term corporate bonds	9.1%	+ 2.6%	+ 0.4%	− 1.9%
Aaa long-term corporate bonds	8.0%	+ 1.5%	− 0.5%	− 2.5%
90-day bank CDs	6.6%	+ 0.2%	− 1.5%	− 3.1%
Commercial paper (4-6 months)	6.6%	+ 0.2%	− 1.5%	− 3.1%
Long-term U.S. govt. bonds	6.5%	+ 0.1%	− 1.6%	− 3.2%
U.S. Treasury bills, one year	6.0%	− 0.4%	− 1.9%	− 3.4%
State & local government bonds	6.0%	− 0.4%	− 0.4%[1]	− 0.4%[1]
Savings & loan passbook account	5.8%	− 0.7%	− 2.1%	− 3.6%
Commercial bank savings account	4.8%	− 1.7%	− 2.9%	− 4.0%

All yields are effective rates, except for commercial bank savings accounts which are based upon maximum legally allowable rates.

State and local taxes are not included in after-tax yields.

Period covered: January 1, 1970, to December 31, 1977, during which the average effective price inflation rate was 6.4%.

Figures may not agree because of rounding.

[1] Free of federal income tax.   [2] Investor's tax bracket.

Sources of data: *Federal Reserve Bulletin* and *Federal Home Loan Bank Board Journal.*

Thus, for many investors, it seems better to lose a little every year than to risk losing a lot.

That attitude may change, however, if the losses grow. As the graph on page 164 shows, price inflation is in a super-bull trend, and the trend is bound to inspire some people to take more chances.

Although our objective isn't to find ways to lose a little every year, I believe there are good reasons to examine fixed-interest investments such as bonds and bank accounts. Like stocks, bonds move in normal bull and bear trends, providing occasional opportunities for profit. And the stability of the banking system would be an important question even if you didn't want the convenience of a bank account.

BONDS

Interest rates move up and down in cycles because monetary inflation is cyclical. Bond prices are also cyclical, moving opposite to the direction of interest rates.

A bond that pays interest equal to 5% of its face value will have to be priced below face value when other bonds are paying more than 5%—so that the dollar amount of the interest, as a percentage of the price of the bond, will be competitive.

If new, ten-year bonds are paying 7%, then an existing 5% bond that matures in ten years will be priced around 86. If interest rates rise to 8%, the price of the 5% bond will fall to around 80. If interest rates drop to 6%, the bond's price will rise to about 93.[1]

Long-term bonds have been in a super-bear trend since 1946 (after a super-bull trend that began in 1921). The trends in bonds and interest rates are shown graphically on pages 162 and 163.

As with stocks, the super-bear trend in bonds argues against

---

[1] Although most corporate bonds have a face value of $1,000, bond prices are quoted as if the face value were 100. Thus, a price of 80 really means 80% of face value.

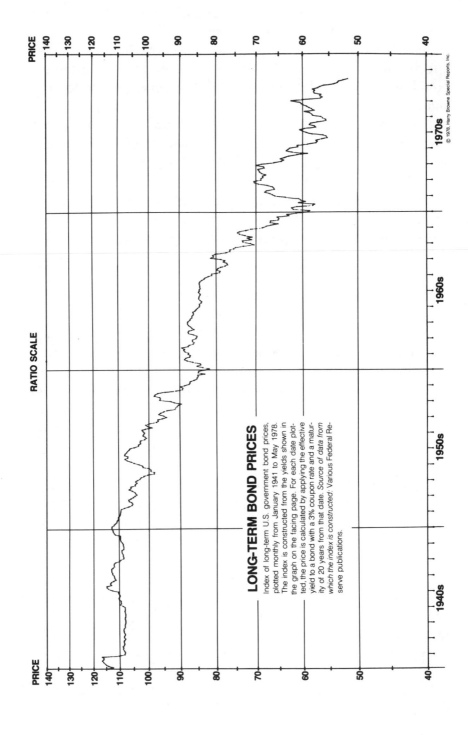

PRICE

RATIO SCALE

PRICE

LONG-TERM BOND PRICES

Index of long-term U.S. government bond prices,
plotted monthly from January 1941 to May 1978.
The index is constructed from the yields shown in
the graph on the facing page. For each date plotted, the price is calculated by applying the effective
yield to a bond with a 3% coupon rate and a maturity of 20 years from that date. *Source of data from
which the index is constructed:* Various Federal Reserve publications.

140
130
120
110
100
90
80
70
60
50
40

1940s   1950s   1960s   1970s

© 1978 Harry Browne Special Reports, Inc.

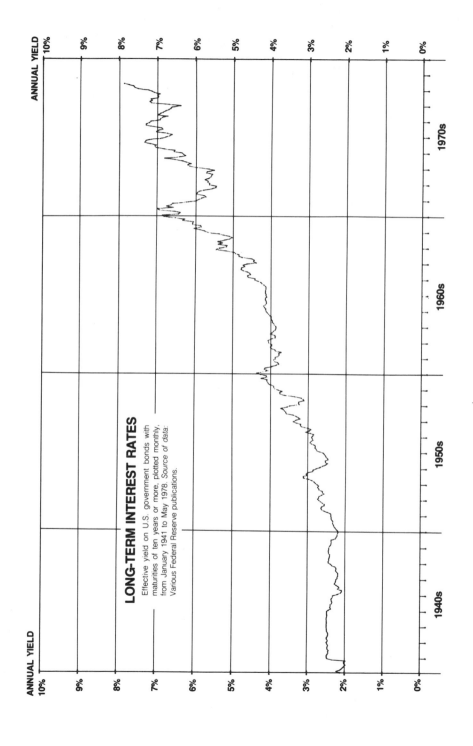

ANNUAL YIELD

LONG-TERM INTEREST RATES

Effective yield on U.S. government bonds with maturities of ten years or more, plotted monthly, from January 1941 to May 1978. Source of data: Various Federal Reserve publications.

1940s   1950s   1960s   1970s

ANNUAL YIELD

10% 9% 8% 7% 6% 5% 4% 3% 2% 1% 0%

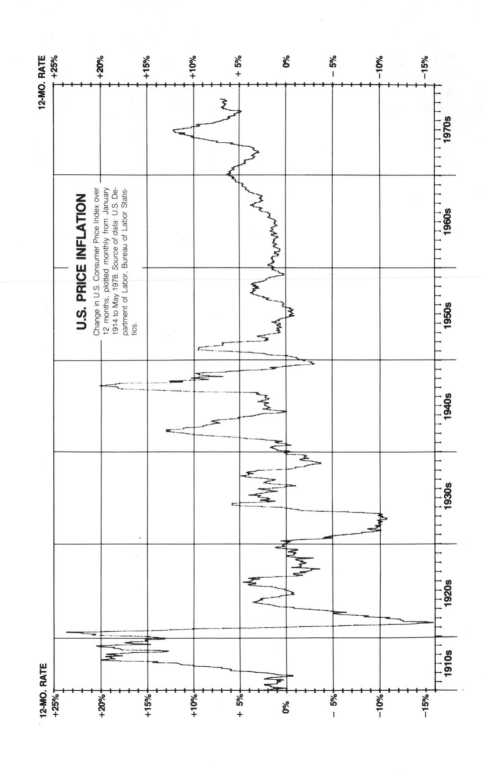

12-MO. RATE

U.S. PRICE INFLATION

Change in U.S. Consumer Price Index over
12 months, plotted monthly from January
1914 to May 1978. *Source of data:* U.S. Department of Labor, Bureau of Labor Statistics.

a buy-and-hold approach. However, again as with stocks, the long-term decline is interrupted from time to time by bull markets that can be profitable for investors who understand that the uptrends are temporary.

Interest rates began their latest uptrend in late 1976. My best guess is that the uptrend will end near the beginning of 1979, initiating a new bull market in bonds. I believe it makes sense to consider taking advantage of that bull market.

Stocks and bonds almost always move together, but it can be a good idea to hold both. For one thing, selecting a specific bond is much easier than selecting a stock. Most bonds (and all government bonds) move with the general trend, but an individual stock often goes its own way.

A bond can move a considerable distance during a single bull or bear market. The distance will depend upon the bond's remaining life and upon the bond's coupon rate (the interest it pays as a percentage of its face value).

The longer the life of the bond, and the lower its coupon rate, the more its price will move in response to a change in interest rates. For example, a bond with twenty years remaining to maturity will fluctuate in price more than a ten-year bond. And, to a lesser extent, a bond paying 3% will fluctuate more than a bond paying 5%.

During a major downtrend in interest rates (lasting perhaps two or three years), the price of a long-term, low-coupon bond can rise substantially. A twenty-year bond paying 4% can rise by 20% to 50%.

To illustrate this, the table on page 166 shows the 1974–75 lows and the 1976–77 highs for a variety of bonds, together with the percentage gain each bond achieved. Although you can't expect to buy at the bottom and sell at the top, the record does show that there's money to be made in bonds when interest rates are in a downtrend.

And if the appreciation shown isn't enough for you, bonds can be purchased on thin margin—with cash requirements ranging from 10% to 50%—which multiplies the volatility of your investment.

BOND PRICE VOLATILITY

Bond Issuer, Coupon Rate & Maturity Year	1974-75 Low	1976-77 High	% Change
Best Grade Corporate[1]			
Illinois Bell, 2¾%, 1981	67.75	89	+ 31.4%
U.S. Steel, 4½%, 1986	58.5	85.5	+ 46.2%
Am. Tel. & Tel., 3⅞%, 1990	53	73.5	+ 38.7%
Union Pacific, 2½%, 1991	41	56.125	+ 36.9%
Ches. & Ohio, 4½%, 1992	49.25	71	+ 44.2%
Atchison T&SF, 4%, 1995	46.5	64.25	+ 38.2%
Consumer Power, 5⅞%, 1996	48	76	+ 58.3%
Norfolk & West., 4%, 1996	44	63	+ 43.2%
Exxon, 6%, 1997	66.5	89.875	+ 35.2%
General Electric, 8½%, 2004	93	111	+ 19.4%
Intermediate Corporate[1]			
Ford Motor, 8⅛%, 1990	88.5	104.5	+ 18.1%
Louis Nash, 7⅜%, 1993	69	89	+ 29.0%
St. Louis SF, 4%, 1997	43.125	60	+ 39.1%
Bethlehem Steel, 6⅞%, 1999	73	95.125	+ 16.6%
Detroit Edison, 9%, 1999	69.5	102.5	+ 47.5%
Phila. Electric, 7⅜%, 2001	65	90.375	+ 39.0%
Alabama Power, 9¾%, 2004	89.125	108.25	+ 21.5%
Pacific Gas & Elec., 7¾%, 2005	78	96.25	+ 23.4%
Missouri Pacific, 4¼%, 2005	37	56	+ 51.4%
Second Grade Rails[2]			
Northern Pacific, 4%, 1984	74	83.5	+ 12.8%
Minneapolis & St. L., 6%, 1985	58	88	+ 51.7%
Chicago Gt. West., 4%, 1988	35.5	57	+ 60.6%
Chi. Mil. St., 4%, 1994	27	39.5	+ 46.3%
U.S. Government			
4%, Feb. 1988-93	69.9375	86.6875	+ 23.9%
7½%, Aug. 1988-93	75.625	104.25	+ 37.9%
4⅛%, May 1989-94	69.8125	86.5625	+ 24.0%
3½%, Feb. 1990	69.75	86	+ 23.3%
6¾%, Feb. 1993	82.5625	98.6875	+ 19.5%
3%, Feb. 1995	69.75	102.28	+ 47.5%
3½%, Nov. 1998	69.75	86.0625	+ 23.4%

[1] As defined in *Barron's* Confidence Index.
[2] As defined in the Dow Jones Bond Averages.
Source of data: The *Dow Jones Investor's Handbook*, 1975-1978.

In addition, you'll earn interest on the bonds while you hold them, but that won't be the primary reason for buying.

Risks

The era of economic chaos hasn't ended; in fact, it will continue to worsen for many years. We will continue to see the collapse of corporations, banks, and possibly even the financial collapse of governments. I'd prefer that such events cause you to feel sympathy rather than personal loss.

If you invest in bonds at what appears to be the beginning of an interest-rate downtrend, there are three major risks:

1. The interest rate downtrend usually begins near the start of an economic recession. Some companies will make it through the difficult time and others won't. Also, if the monetary stimulus that aids the interest rate downtrend isn't sufficient, there could be a deflationary panic that would affect even more companies. The risk of a bond default is always present.

2. In addition, such a deflation would cause interest rates to shoot up temporarily, sending bond prices down.

3. Even if a deflationary crisis doesn't materialize, you may have simply miscalculated. After a brief fall, interest rates might resume their uptrend.

Guidelines

To lessen these risks I have two suggestions:

1. Invest only in U.S. government bonds. Governments are notorious for breaking promises, but, historically, a government will injure its credit only as a last resort. A government survives on credit (to finance its deficits) and must protect its reputation for repayment.

State and municipal issues aren't as secure as debts of the U.S. government. Local governments don't have the Federal Reserve standing ready to buy their bonds and assure that older bonds are repaid when due—as New York City's problems have demonstrated.

2. As with other investments, place a stop-loss to have your bonds sold automatically if the market should prove you wrong. The stop-loss won't protect against every possible adversity, but it will allow you to get out gracefully if the trend in interest rates changes unexpectedly. If your broker doesn't accept stop-loss orders for bonds, watch the price more closely, and resolve to sell at a predetermined "stop-loss" level.

Bonds can be purchased through securities dealers in the U.S. and through Swiss banks. American banks sell government bonds only. We'll return to the use of bonds in Parts IV and V.

THE BANKING SYSTEM

For one reason or another, you're going to want to keep some money in dollars—as a form of liquid capital. The amount you keep in banks will depend upon how secure you feel the banking system is. Other investments depend on the health of the banking system as well, so its stability is a major concern.

Liquidity

Most U.S. banks have chosen operating policies that make them illiquid. A bank receives a deposit from a customer, some or all of which is withdrawable on demand. But the bank invests the money in an auto loan or other loan that isn't collectible on short notice.

Or a bank receives money in the form of ninety-day Certificates of Deposit (CDs) and buys long-term bonds in order to earn higher interest rates. The bank hopes that when its CDs must be repaid, it will be able to sell new CDs to replace them. And it hopes that the interest rate it will have to pay on the new CDs will still be less than it is earning on its long-term bond holdings.

In a world without inflation, this policy of mismatching assets and liabilities might do little damage. But in our world, the damage has been great—although the extent of the damage is hard to measure. It's impossible to know the liquidity position of a U.S. bank because, typically, the balance sheet it publishes does not include the information necessary to judge the bank's condition.

For example, banks list the depreciated long-term bonds they own at the bonds' original cost. Valued in this way, the securities amount to 23.7% of the assets of the nation's banks.[2]

Apparently the banks accept, or expect others to accept, the fallacy embraced by the big-losses, small-profits investor of Chapter 9—that a loss isn't real until a losing investment is actually sold. Banks insist that market values are unimportant on the grounds that they can hold a depreciated bond to maturity and then collect its face value. But in the meantime, while a bank is trying to outwait reality, it is forced to pay higher and higher interest rates on its CDs—to finance the ownership of a bond with a fixed interest rate.

And a bank's bond portfolio is supposed to be its *liquid* assets. If the bonds must be held to maturity to be worth what they're claimed to be worth, how can they be considered liquid?

The most liquid investments banks can hold are Treasury bills and other short-term government securities. These assets can normally be sold at a moment's notice and with little likelihood of depreciation from the purchase price. A bank often makes a point of highlighting these short-term assets in its financial statement to show how strong and liquid it is.

Banks undoubtedly have the short-term securities they claim (at least I have no reason to believe otherwise), but in many cases the implication of liquidity is highly misleading. Too often, the bank has *pledged* these assets as collateral,

---

[2] *Federal Reserve Bulletin*, April 1978, page A18. Total assets are $1,066.8 billion; securities are listed at $253.1 billion.

which means that they can't be sold. They are pledged as security so that the bank may accept deposits from a trust account or from a government agency. The assets must be available to guarantee the specific deposit against loss. Too, banks regularly pledge these assets in repurchase agreements. One way or another, the supposed liquid assets just aren't available to be liquidated, should the bank need to raise cash.

One large California bank, for example, has reported that 8.4% of its assets are in short-term government securities. But a footnote to the report shows that virtually none of those assets was held free and clear; most of them were pledged and unavailable for sale.

These accounting practices are amazing if you understand how strict the government is about financial reports from other, nonbank, corporations. If the managers of a mutual fund tried to ignore the market value of the fund's investments, they could be thrown in jail. Investor protection can be very selective. For most corporations, the legally enforced accounting standard is "full disclosure"; but for banks, half full is full enough.

U.S. banks generally don't attempt to match their assets and liabilities in a conservative way. The banking system operates on two assumptions: (1) that interest rates won't rise so fast that banks must pay more for short-term deposits than they earn on the long-term investments they are committed to; and (2) that no more than a few depositors will try to withdraw their funds at the same time.

As long as withdrawal demands don't increase significantly, banks won't have to try to call uncallable loans, and they won't have to reveal the true value of their assets.

Deposit Insurance

By conventional thinking, the principal assurance against a bank run comes from the Federal Deposit Insurance Corporation. Presumably, the FDIC has legislated bank runs out of existence, because, even during a crisis, depositors will not fear for the safety of their funds.

Unfortunately, the FDIC's reputation isn't deserved. It's true that the FDIC can handle the failure of a small bank— as it often has in recent years. Depositors are usually reimbursed promptly, although administrative problems sometimes cause brief delays.

But the FDIC couldn't handle the failure of a major U.S. bank or an epidemic of bank failures. Even if it had enough money, the FDIC couldn't deal with the administrative problems of liquidating a large number of failed banks at once. Depositors might be kept waiting for months.

But the administrative problems are the least of its difficulties. The FDIC simply doesn't have the money to deal with a nationwide banking crisis. As of December 31, 1976, bank deposits insured by the FDIC totaled $628.3 billion. The FDIC's reserves totaled $7.3 billion, only 1.2% of the total deposits. Obviously, such a reserve wouldn't last long in a banking panic.[3]

In fact, *no* insurance company could have the funds necessary to insure against a widespread banking crisis; it would require insurance premiums so large that banking would be an uneconomic enterprise. Thus a banking crisis is an uninsurable risk.

Actually the FDIC isn't an insurance company at all. Like Social Security, it's a welfare agency. If the FDIC were an insurance company, there wouldn't be a maximum insurable deposit ($40,000)—and the maximum wouldn't be a matter for Congress to decide.

A true insurance company would protect against a bank failure, and so it might place a limit on its coverage of any one bank. But it wouldn't care about the size of individual accounts.

The FDIC is a welfare agency, and the benefits it pays are determined by political considerations. As such, FDIC benefits shouldn't be taken too seriously as protection against a de-

[3] *Annual Report of the Federal Deposit Insurance Corporation,* 1976.

pression. During a depression, deposit insurance will be just one more form of welfare the government may be forced to cut back.

Lender of Last Resort

The stability of the U.S. banking system depends more upon the Federal Reserve System—the so-called "lender of last resort"—than it does on the FDIC. If a bank gets into trouble, it will appeal to the Fed for a loan. If the bank has acceptable collateral, the Fed will lend it all the money it needs.

If the bank doesn't have sufficient collateral and its survival isn't considered important to the banking system, the Fed will let the bank fail—bringing the FDIC into the picture. But if the bank is considered important, the Fed will lower its standards. In that case, the Fed might accept office desks, adding machines, or anything else as collateral.

A bank's importance to the Fed depends in large part upon the bank's relationship to other banks. A large bank ordinarily holds deposits from many smaller banks. If the large bank were to fail, the smaller banks might lose so much money that they, too, would fail. The possibility of such a chain reaction is a dominant consideration when the Fed decides how far it will go to keep a bank afloat.

The Fed has to be selective because the cost of keeping a troubled bank alive can be far greater than simply paying for its immediate problems. For example, the weakness of Franklin National Bank was first noticed in 1974, when the bank revealed losses of about $150 million from securities and foreign currency trading. It borrowed from the Fed to tide it over, but as news of the problem spread, the crisis grew. By the time the Fed finally let the bank die, Franklin had borrowed $1.8 *billion*—twelve times its losses.[4]

4 *Federal Reserve Bulletin*, October 1974, page 740.

The news of Franklin's problems had inspired many of its customers to withdraw their money. To cover withdrawals, the bank tried to sell assets from its portfolio, but many of these assets weren't worth the amounts stated in the bank's balance sheet. The bank was unable to meet the run.

During the run, other banks, which had been making uninsured overnight loans to Franklin National, were the most eager to withdraw their money. In addition, many holders of the bank's CDs, which were only partly insured, understandably chose not to renew them when they came due. But what is most telling is that numerous withdrawals were made from accounts that were fully insured by the FDIC. Apparently, the insurance sticker in the bank's window didn't reassure many depositors.

When a bank failure occurs, the *post mortem* usually points to a specific error—such as Franklin's foreign currency dealings. But the real problem is the lack of liquidity. A bank customer believes his deposit is a liquid asset, not a share in a speculative venture that juggles assets in the air. But most banks aren't liquid, and so are vulnerable to any small problem that might upset the juggling act. When Franklin failed, there must have been a number of bankers thinking, "There but for the grace of God . . ."

Crisis Conditions

It is assumed that the Fed can and will do whatever is necessary to save the nation's banks. There are no legal limits on the amount of currency it can print, and there is no limit to the financial assistance that it can extend to banks. But the lack of legal limits on the Fed's rescue power doesn't mean that there can't be a banking crisis.

For one thing, the Fed must act slowly and calmly so that its own actions don't contribute to the state of panic—like a spectator shouting "Fire!" in the proverbial theater.

Second, a simultaneous run on all banks could be met only

by giving depositors currency in exchange for their deposits. If the troubles of a few large banks made people suspicious of all banks, there would be a massive logistics problem in printing and distributing the currency that depositors would demand. It would have to be printed and shipped overnight.

To be successful, the rescue operation would have to be executed perfectly in every detail. The slightest hitch (such as a printing press running out of ink or a currency-laden plane not arriving on schedule or a traffic jam slowing up an armored truck) might be enough to leave a bank without currency while lines of depositors waited to make withdrawals.

Once that happened, the entire system of banking safeguards —the Federal Reserve, the FDIC, and the other regulatory agencies—would be discredited. The demand for currency would be universal, and the panic would be out of control.

At some point the whole government would have to be marshaled against the crisis. But what would the government do?

I've given a great deal of thought to the subject, but I can think of only one substantial measure the government could take. After the fireside chats and the reminders about deposit insurance had failed to accomplish anything, the President would probably declare a banking holiday—and all the banks would be closed.

For a week or so, the authorities would go through the motions of liquidating some banks and declaring others to be sound. When the banks reopened, the public would be reassured that all remaining banks were solvent. And in case the public didn't believe it, the banks would be well stocked with fresh cash for the reopenings.

The FDIC wouldn't have the assets to cover all deposits in the failed banks. So Congress would appropriate more money quickly, but the $40,000 deposit limit might be cut in half so that people who weren't "in need" couldn't "raid" the Federal treasury.

It's strange how, after years of "enlightened" legislation and new safeguards, we could wind up back in 1933.

Uncertainty

Many people consider the idea of a banking crisis a fairy tale. They may be right in thinking that a crisis will not occur. I don't know that there's going to be a banking crisis this year or any other year, and I don't believe anyone else can be sure that there will be—or that there won't. All we know is that the safeguards people speak of include such things as allowing banks to report assets they don't have, allowing banks to operate without liquid assets, and allowing the Federal Reserve to print all the money it wants.

We've seen that the U.S. government's three regulatory agencies didn't save Franklin National Bank, though they tried. We've seen that the mystique of the FDIC didn't stop depositors from demanding their funds back from Franklin. And we know that the FDIC doesn't have the resources to cover the deposits that could be lost in a widespread banking crisis.

And we haven't discussed the $40 billion in loans to "third world" governments held by the 119 largest U.S. banks—or the $117 billion in real estate loans—almost none of which can be collected to meet deposit withdrawal requests.[5]

To say that there couldn't be a banking crisis is to believe that it doesn't matter what banks do with their assets, that any degree of illiquidity is tolerable, that no event could make depositors fear for the safety of their money. No matter what safeguards have been built into the system, there is a point at which irresponsibility will overwhelm them.

We can't know precisely where that point is, because we can't know at what point people will be afraid to keep their money in banks. And perhaps that's the whole point: Without liquidity, the system rests upon an unstable base of public confidence. It could fall at any time.

[5] The loans to third-world governments are reported in the Federal Reserve System's "Currency Exposure Report," issued January 16, 1978; the real estate loans are listed in the *Federal Reserve Bulletin,* April 1978, page A18.

Deposit insurance is a government scheme to protect the banking system by fooling the public into believing that no danger exists. But the scheme may have fooled the banks more than the public, leaving banks with the impression that depositors will never be so rude as to ask for their money back.

In sum, we can't know that the system won't survive, but it would be foolish to believe that nothing can go wrong. Nor can we know just what would happen if a crisis occurred. We can expect emergency legislation, a lot of announcements and reassurances; we can be sure that Congress will investigate and tell us who the scapegoats are; but, mostly, we can expect a lot of surprises. Beyond that, the situation is unpredictable.

Other Savings Institutions

Savings and loan associations, mutual savings banks, credit unions, and non-Fed-member commercial banks are in worlds of their own.

The Federal Home Loan Bank system performs the same function for the savings and loans as the Federal Reserve does for commercial banks. However, the FHLB does not have the ability to create deposits out of thin air. To help a savings and loan in trouble, it must sell assets from its portfolio of cash and bonds. As of December 1977, it held $3.9 billion in this portfolio, while U.S. savings and loan associations owed their customers $386.9 billion in deposits. In other words, the FHLB system has an emergency portfolio equivalent to 1.0% of the deposit liabilities of the savings and loans.[6]

Savings and loan deposits, up to $40,000 each, are insured by the Federal Savings and Loan Insurance Corporation, in the same way that the FDIC insures bank accounts. At the close of 1977, the FSLIC insured $378.9 billion in deposits and held a reserve fund of $4.9 billion—or 1.3%.[7]

---

6 Federal Home Loan Bank Board *Journal,* April 1978, pages 72 and 74.
7 Federal Home Loan Bank Board *Journal,* April 1978, page 31.

Alternatives Needed

While the banking system may survive the next ten years intact, it doesn't offer the safety and reliability that are the usual reasons for holding cash. Each of us may have his own opinion about banks, but if you have any doubts at all, you should look for a way to protect yourself.

It would be troublesome to do without a bank account, but today one cost of using a bank account is the element of risk you have to accept. The answer to the dilemma, I think, is to limit your exposure to banks to the minimum necessary for convenience (perhaps one month's expenses in a checking account), and find other depositories for the balance of your liquid funds.

TREASURY BILLS

One alternative is U.S. Treasury bills. A T-bill is a short-term debt of the U.S. government, issued for a period of one year or less.

T-bills trade in a large, liquid market and can be bought or sold at any time through a commercial bank, securities broker, or Swiss bank. Newly issued T-bills can be bought through any Federal Reserve bank.

A T-bill is issued at a discount from its face value; at the end of its life (three, six, or twelve months later), it is redeemed at face value. The interest you earn is the difference between the issuing price and the redemption price. In early 1978, the interest rate was around 7%. The short life-span of a T-bill means that its market value can change very little, even if interest rates are changing rapidly.

For the past several years, the interest rate on T-bills has been roughly equivalent to the rate of price inflation. So you wouldn't buy T-bills primarily for the interest they earn, but as a liquid way to hold dollars. They are the safest medium available, outside of bank notes.

As you've gathered by now, I don't have much confidence in the schemes and promises of governments. But Treasury bills are the safest debt instrument you can buy from a stranger. T-bills are issued every week of the year, the government relies upon them for short-term financing, and the bills couldn't be sold at such low interest rates if there was ever a default.

T-bills are no longer represented by certificates. Ownership is simply registered in the records of a Federal Reserve bank. Your bank or broker is listed in the Federal Reserve's computer as the nominal owner of the T-bill, and you receive a receipt from your bank or broker showing that you're the beneficial owner.

The minimum Treasury bill denomination is $10,000, and T-bills generally trade in round lots of at least $100,000.[8]

If you're confident that you'll hold a T-bill until its maturity, the round-lot minimum will be irrelevant. If not, or if you have less than $10,000 to hold in dollars, another medium may be more appropriate.

MONEY MARKET FUNDS

The other medium is the money market fund. It is similar to a mutual fund—in that it issues and redeems shares and invests its shareholders' money for them.

However, while a conventional mutual fund invests mostly in stocks or bonds, a money market fund invests in short-term debt instruments—Treasury bills, Certificates of Deposit, bankers' acceptances, commercial paper, bond repurchase agreements, floating-rate notes, and Euro-deposits.

These are all fixed-interest securities with effective lives of less than one year. The object of the fund isn't to buy assets with rising prices, but rather to earn interest on assets with stable prices.

Most funds pay dividends daily, to keep the price of a

---

8 A round lot is the smallest transaction to which the best price and lowest commission rate apply.

share fixed at $1. Each day's small dividend is automatically reinvested in new shares. When you withdraw your money from the fund, you'll have more $1 shares than when you began; the difference will be the income the fund has earned for you.

To withdraw your money, you can write, wire, or telephone the fund. It will send you a check or wire the money to your bank, as you request. Most funds even allow you to redeem shares by writing a check on the fund's bank account. You can use the check to pay a bill, or you can deposit it into your own bank account.

Thus a money market fund is only slightly less accessible than a conventional bank. A fund account earns interest (in the range of current price inflation rates or a little less), there are no commissions, and your money is withdrawable upon demand.

There are about fifty money market funds in the U.S. Most of them compete to pay the highest interest rate. The competition has led many of them to invest in the riskier kinds of short-term debt instruments. A fund that invests heavily in bank Certificates of Deposit is really just another part of the banking system.

Each fund issues a prospectus and periodic reports, from which you can determine the kinds of investments it holds. The funds that are heaviest in Treasury bills pay the lowest interest but, in my opinion, they are the safest. Funds that pay the highest interest, especially those that invest in CDs, would be the most vulnerable during a general financial crisis.

The minimum investment varies from fund to fund, but $1,000 is common. Four funds with rather conservative portfolios are listed in Chapter 32.

INVESTMENT POSSIBILITIES

Liquidity and safety of capital are essential ingredients of an investment plan. Most fixed-interest investments not only pay interest rates that are misleading during an inflationary period, but are also dangerously vulnerable to a general crisis.

However, there are four reasons why you might want to keep a part of your portfolio in fixed-interest dollar investments:

1. Because no investment seems more attractive at the moment;

2. Because you're trading in foreign currencies and, at a given time, you believe the dollar will generally appreciate against other currencies;

3. Because you want to keep some money in dollars at all times for diversification; or

4. Because you believe interest rates are in a downtrend, causing bond prices to rise.

For the last reason, the best medium is long-term U.S. government bonds. For any of the first three reasons, I believe Treasury bills or a conservative money market fund would be best.[9]

In none of these cases should interest income be the motivation. Whatever interest you receive should be treated as a bonus, not as an objective. The motivation should be safety and liquidity and, in the case of reason number 4, capital appreciation.

[9] In Chapter 21, I'll explain why I don't believe a U.S. dollar account in a Swiss bank is suitable.

15

GOLD

In Chapter 5 I gave my explanation for the 1970–1974 uptrend in the price of gold. I believe that gold now has risen enough to undo the nineteen years (1949–1968) of government price control.

That doesn't mean gold has had its day and should be forgotten. But to know what to expect from it, we need to understand gold's place in the world.

GOLD AS MONEY

For most of the world's history, gold has been the principal money. Even when it coexisted with paper money, most people accepted the paper only as a convenient proxy for gold. Paper money was handier to use in day-to-day exchange, but the paper was valuable only so long as the holder knew it could be exchanged for gold, at a fixed rate, at any time.

Occasionally a government would dishonor its promise to repay gold for the paper it had issued. But the failure was always considered temporary. It was understood that sooner or later the government would return to the gold standard. And sooner or later the government did.

We are in one of those periods today. No government of

181

the world offers anything as security for the paper money it issues; as before, the gold standard has been suspended.

But there's a difference between the current situation and the suspensions of the past. In each of the previous cases, the suspension was part of a temporary national emergency. As often happens with a problem a government touches, the emergency would turn out to be less temporary than advertised. But throughout the crisis, the government continued to promise a return to the gold standard.[1]

Today no government is promising a return to the gold standard. As far as the politicians are concerned, gold is dead, and a new era has been born.

Because gold is more reliable than government paper as a long-term store of value, gold is usually bid up above its official price during times of gold suspension. Although the rise took longer this time, we have seen once again the world's evaluation of the difference between gold and paper.

I have little doubt that the gold standard will return someday—and probably before the end of this century. There's nothing ideological in my expectation; it's simply that the world hasn't yet invented a money system as in keeping with the nature of human action as gold is.

In the meantime, however, we must approach gold as an investment, not as a medium of exchange. It must be treated as just one more free market commodity—like wheat, silver, steel, etc. In short, we must look at the fundamentals—supply and demand.

SUPPLY AND DEMAND

Approximately half the gold produced each year comes from South Africa, another 25% from the Soviet Union, and the remaining 25% in small amounts from around the world (about 2% comes from the United States).

The one difference between gold and other commodities

---

[1] This was true in the U.S. and, as far as I know, in the other countries of the world.

is that each year's production is such a small part of the available supply. Very little gold is actually consumed; most of it is simply hoarded, or stockpiled.

The existing stock of gold is analyzed in the table on page 184. Governments outside the communist bloc acknowledge holdings of 1.17 billion ounces, and the communist bloc holdings are estimated at 225 million ounces. The supply in private hands is estimated at 784 million ounces, bringing the total to 2.18 billion ounces. At a price of $200 per ounce, the existing stock of gold is worth about $436 billion.

New production is small compared with the existing supply. Production fluctuates from year to year but averages around 50 million ounces. So there's a hoard equivalent to forty years' production being held by governments and private investors.

Industrial consumption of gold uses up around 40 million ounces per year, although consumption dropped to as low as 16 million ounces in 1974. The difference between production and consumption, which can vary from 5 to 30 million ounces, goes mostly into additional investor stockpiles, with small amounts being added to government reserves. Of the amounts going into investor stockpiles, about 5 million ounces first passes through the hands of governments and is minted into new coins, such as KrugerRands.

WHY GOLD?

I can understand how difficult it is for many people to comprehend the demand for gold. It's easy to believe that the rise in gold prices is simply a case of a "self-fulfilling prophecy," that it isn't based upon any fundamental demand— only upon a bullish wish that must spread to other investors to be fulfilled.

Other investments produce interest or dividends. Or as with commodities, there is a recognized demand for them from consumers. Gold produces no income, and little of the metal is consumed; it merely sits in vaults and gathers dust.

WORLD GOLD HOLDINGS
(March 1978 — Millions of Ounces)

Non-communist Governments

United States	278
International Monetary Fund	129
West Germany	118
France	102
Switzerland	83
Italy	83
Netherlands	55
Belgium	42
Portugal	32
Japan	24
Great Britain	22
Canada	22
Austria	21
Spain	14
Venezuela	11
South Africa	10
Bank for International Settlements	10
Lebanon	9
Australia	8
India	7
Sweden	6
Other non-communist governments	86

Total Non-Communist Governments	**1,172**
Communist Governments	**225**
Total for All Governments	**1,397**
Private Holdings	**784**
TOTAL WORLD GOLD STOCK	**2,181 million ounces**

Sources: Non-communist government holdings are from International Monetary Fund *International Financial Statistics*, June 1978. Communist government holdings are estimated from annual gold market reports of Consolidated Gold Fields Ltd., London. Private holdings are estimated by Franz Pick in *Pick's Currency Yearbook*, 1976-1977, and updated with figures from *Gold 1978*, Consolidated Gold Fields Ltd.

Figures may not agree because of rounding.

THE WORLD GOLD MARKET, 1968-1977
(millions of troy ounces)

SUPPLIES TO THE MARKET

	1977	1976	1975	1972	1970	1968
New Gold Produced	**45.9**	**46.0**	**44.5**	**50.8**	**52.7**	**50.4**
South Africa	22.5	22.9	22.9	29.2	32.2	31.2
Soviet Union	14.3	14.3	13.1	12.2	11.1	9.8
Canada/U.S.A.	2.7	2.7	2.6	3.6	4.1	4.2
All other nations	6.4	6.0	5.8	5.9	5.2	5.3
Net Government Sales[1]	**20.8**	**9.0**	**1.9**	**15.6**	**38.7**	**44.7**
United States	—	—	1.3	15.6	22.5	33.5
South Africa[2]	2.9	5.1	.5	—	12.8	—
IMF	17.9	3.9	—	—	—	11.3
All others	—	—	—	—	3.4	—
Net Investor Sales[3]	**—**	**—**	**—**	**4.6**	**11.9**	**—**
TOTAL MARKET SUPPLY	**66.7**	**55.0**	**46.4**	**71.1**	**103.2**	**95.1**

MARKET DEMAND

	1977	1976	1975	1972	1970	1968
Industrial Consumption	**42.2**	**40.0**	**24.9**	**43.0**	**43.8**	**38.1**
Jewelry	31.5	30.1	16.4	32.0	34.2	29.4
All other	10.7	9.9	8.5	11.0	9.6	8.7
Coinage by Governments	**4.4**	**5.7**	**7.8**	**2.0**	**1.5**	**2.2**
South Africa	2.9	2.9	5.6	.7	.2	—
All others	1.5	2.8	2.2	1.5	1.3	2.2
Net Government Purchases[1]	**15.1**	**2.2**	**7.3**	**26.0**	**58.0**	**33.5**
United States	2.8					
South Africa[2]	—	—	—	6.2	—	18.9
IMF	—	—	—	18.2	58.0	—
All others	12.3	2.2	7.3	1.6	—	14.6
Net Investor Purchases[3]	**5.0**	**7.1**	**6.2**	**—**	**—**	**21.4**
TOTAL MARKET DEMAND	**66.7**	**55.0**	**46.4**	**71.1**	**103.2**	**95.1**

WORLD MARKET SUMMARY

	1977	1976	1975	1972	1970	1968
Net Purchases or (Sales) by all Governments	(5.7)	(6.8)	5.6	10.4	19.3	(11.3)
Net Purchases or (Sales) by all Investors	5.0	7.1	6.2	(4.6)	(11.9)	21.4
Net Industrial Consumption & Coinage vs. (Production)	.7	(.3)	(11.8)	(5.8)	(7.4)	(10.1)
Yearly Prices						
Average	$147.72	124.79	160.41	59.09	35.99	39.26
High	$167.95	140.35	185.25	70.00	39.19	42.60
Low	$129.75	103.05	146.25	43.73	34.75	35.14

[1] If a government listed here sells more than it buys during a given year, the net difference is shown for that year under "Sales by Governments." If it buys more than it sells, the difference is shown under "Purchases by Governments."

[2] If the South African government sells to the world more than was produced in South Africa, this is considered to be a sale from the government's reserves. When less is sold than was produced, it is considered to be a purchase by the government.

[3] If investors, as a total unit, buy more than they sell during a given year, the net difference is shown under "Net Investor Purchases." If sales exceed purchases, the net difference is shown under "Net Investor Sales."

Sources: Figures for production, industrial consumption, and government coinage are from Consolidated Gold Fields Ltd. Data for government purchases and sales are from the International Monetary Fund. Investor purchases or sales are the net differences from all other figures. Prices are for London morning and afternoon gold fixings. All data has been rearranged to fit this format.

Figures may not agree due to rounding.

To understand the demand for gold, you have to see the world through the eyes of other people. Just as you might never in your life use a computer, but still might see the sense in purchasing IBM stock, you have to understand the special role that gold plays in the lives of so many people.

In other parts of the world, there are millions of people for whom gold is still *the* store of value. To them, it serves the same purpose that you might see in Certificates of Deposit, bank accounts, stock certificates, bonds, a private business, or an annuity.

Gold is like an insurance policy. It can't be spent in stores; it won't make one's car run better, and it can't be eaten. But it's there when it's needed.

No one can know in advance how much his gold will be worth to him when he needs it. But no one knows what his fire or life insurance policy will actually be worth either. What an insurance buyer does know is that if the policy is ever needed, having it will be far better than not having it —no matter what its purchasing power.

But why would an individual ever need gold? Because it is the only insurance policy that does not depend on any insurance company; because it is the only insurance policy that can't be canceled by any government, and because it's the only insurance policy that's recognized and respected worldwide.

Gold is a hedge against financial, political, and social destruction. It's bribe money. It's getaway money. It's money that can be buried. It's money that can be smuggled easily and spent anywhere.

Few Americans can appreciate these values. But in the rest of the world they're primary concerns. It's hard to remember that half the present governments of the world didn't exist ten years ago. Revolutions are a way of life for many people; currencies come and go; wars destroy societies; governments rise and fall; communities are at peace, and then good neighbors go bad. But gold can see an individual through the worst of it.

There are many other commodities that *could* provide this

insurance but are far less effective. Gold has three basic attributes that make it the premier store of value:

1. It's virtually imperishable. It can be stored for thousands of years without being degraded in any way.

2. It's a highly compact form of value. One ounce of gold (about the size of a silver dollar) is worth as much as sixty bushels of wheat. Thus, you can store a great deal of value in a very small space.

The relationship between value and size derives ultimately from gold's commercial uses. It is called a "precious metal" not merely because the supply is small, but because the metal has so many unique properties. Today, the properties most in demand are its low resistance to electric current, its durability in tiny, thin shapes, and its chemical stability in uses such as dental work. Throughout history, one or another of gold's special properties has kept it in demand, apart from its use as money.

Without those special properties, the demand for gold would be only a passing fashion; it would be no more stable than the demand for paper money. Gold is valuable not simply because people use it as money; it is used as money *because* it's so valuable.

3. Gold is a consistent, homogeneous material that is easily recognized and evaluated. Once an ounce of gold has been assayed and its fineness (purity) determined, it has the same value as any other ounce of gold.

A gold coin doesn't have to be appraised; its weight tells its value. And, in most transactions, a bar of gold with the hallmark of a known refiner doesn't have to be assayed. Unlike other commodities, gold is recognized immediately for what it is.

There are other features of gold that have contributed to its development as the world's primary store of value, such as its divisibility and its portability. But these derive from its status as a durable, compact, recognizable commodity.

Gold's compactness can be appreciated, perhaps, by comparing gold with what is currently the most talked-about commodity—oil. It seems that nothing in the world is more sought-after than oil. And yet, a barrel of oil sells for around $12. That same barrel could hold 63,040 one-ounce gold coins—worth about $11,000,000 at a market price of $175 per ounce. No wonder that few people bury barrels of oil in the backyard or ask their Swiss bank to store it for them.

Still, it can seem that the demand for gold is purely psychological—that it rests upon the continued favor of investors. The demand *is* psychological in that it rests on a desire for material security. But the demand isn't a matter of whim or emotion. The need for a store of value that is independent of government is real, and gold has the properties—divisibility, portability, marketability—that satisfy the need.

The demand for gold is totally independent of gold standards and government policies. No, that's not true. I mean to say that governments can't legislate the demand for gold out of existence. Actually, they legislate it *into* existence— when their policies send people looking for the safety that gold provides.

The "demonetization" of gold (the ending of the international gold exchange standard in 1971) didn't eliminate the demand for gold. It undoubtedly heightened it. A gold-backed currency is the only substitute for gold itself. When the substitute disappears, people turn to the real thing.

In 1970 I appeared on a television show with a well-known economist who scoffed at my interest in gold. He stated that if the U.S. government "closed the gold window" (as it did later), the price of gold would drop to $2 per ounce. To him, it was governments that imparted value to gold.

It is difficult for many Americans to understand the function that gold performs throughout the world. The troubles of people so far away have never been that real to most of us. But now, with better communications, we're more aware of the turmoil that's the rule in so many areas of the world.

More important perhaps is that the turmoil is now affecting America. Many Americans are no longer so sure that revolution, anarchy, police-state measures, military coups, or currency breakdowns couldn't happen here. Now that they can feel the anxiety personally, and now that they are searching for insurance policies that protect against the worst, they can begin to appreciate the awe with which gold is treated in many parts of the world.

The demand for gold is real, and it's as durable as the metal itself. That doesn't mean gold is never overpriced or that it's always a good buy. But once you see that the demand is something more than fashion, you can begin to weigh the use of gold in your investment program.

INFLATION HEDGE?

Before we look at the role of gold in an investment portfolio, let's first understand what gold isn't.

It isn't an inflation hedge—although many people like to think it is. A true inflation hedge is an investment that responds automatically to the rate of price inflation.

Gold hasn't matched the rate of price inflation in any recent year. It has appreciated by far more than the inflation rate or it's gone down. That isn't an inflation hedge.

It's logical to believe that an increase in U.S. price inflation to 20% per year or more would cause a large increase in the price of gold. It probably would. But if inflation remained at that high level for several years, gold wouldn't necessarily continue to appreciate yearly. More likely, it would rise and fall, as it is doing now.

INVESTMENT USES

Gold currently has two possible functions in an investment portfolio:

1. It can be held as a long-term hedge against economic chaos.

2. Like any other investment, it can be bought in the early stages of an uptrend and sold in the later stages, in order to make a profit.

Chaos Hedge

While gold isn't an inflation hedge, it *is* a chaos hedge. People look to gold as a way out in times of trouble. As a result, gold is sensitive to the level of chaos.

From time to time, an isolated crisis in some part of the world causes the price of gold to rise temporarily. These crisis rallies have three elements. First, individuals in the troubled area are afraid of what may happen, so they convert their assets to gold.

Second, individuals in nearby areas wonder if the problem might spread, and they buy a little insurance in the form of gold. Third, investors elsewhere assume that the crisis will push the price of gold upward, and so they buy in order to profit, but they're usually too late.

The crisis affecting gold can be a military confrontation; actual or potential currency devaluation; a political crisis, as in France or Italy; social upheaval; or terrorism. Anything that threatens lives or property on a large scale qualifies.

There is every reason to believe that an escalation of these isolated disorders into widespread upheavals would be accompanied by large and sustained increases in the price of gold. But investors who buy when the crises occur are usually too late to profit from them.

As the crises begin to affect the U.S. more, the degree of uncertainty will be greater. The United States is the world's largest investment market, and it's also generally respected as the world's most stable country. The more the U.S. is affected by the crises, the more the crises will raise the level of uncertainty throughout the world.

For these reasons gold makes sense as a permanent part of one's portfolio—a permanent hedge against the worst possibilities. When something unexpected happens to damage the other parts of your portfolio, the loss may be largely compensated for by a rise in value for your permanent crisis hedge—gold.

Profit Opportunities

The other investment use for gold is more occasional. Now that gold has overcome the years of price control, I expect it to rise and fall cyclically.

For the long term, gold is in a super-bull trend. And as long as economic and political disorders worsen, the super-bull trend should continue. Thus the price of gold will probably be a good deal higher ten years from now.

But in the course of the super-bull trend, the gold market will experience normal bull and bear trends. And the trends should provide a mirror image of the U.S. stock market—with gold rising when stocks fall, and vice versa.

The stock market drops during periods of tight money and worsening economic prospects—conditions upon which gold thrives. While we have only the price history since 1973 to confirm the relationship between stocks and gold, I believe it's safe to assume that the idea is true until events prove it false.

WHY NOT BARBIE DOLLS?

If gold should be treated now as just one more commodity, why select gold to trade—instead of soybeans, wheat, diamonds, Barbie dolls, or anything that might appear to be in a bull trend at the moment?

There are two reasons that I choose gold.

First, it requires less expertise than most other investments. To enter another investment market, you'll need a good deal of research into recent price trends, supply and demand characteristics, seasonal factors, the choice among various investment media, etc. With gold, you're betting mostly on the trend of current economic conditions.

To do this profitably you must pay attention to economic conditions, but you'll undoubtedly have to do that anyway.

And once you have an opinion regarding near-term economic prospects, no further investigation is needed for gold.

Second, since gold's price movements seem to form a mirror image of the stock market (a reverse image, remember), it provides a logical alternate to stocks and bonds—allowing you to switch back and forth between the two markets as each enters an uptrend.

As long as the inverse relationship between stocks and gold holds up, you can turn to gold when stocks go down—without having to sort through a wide range of possibilities. The great majority of investments tend to move *with* the stock market, because they're dependent upon the general prosperity that a rising stock market seems to forecast. Gold is a fortunate exception.

This doesn't mean you shouldn't consider other investment possibilities. But most investors can't take the time to make a thorough appraisal of an investment, and intelligent investors treat the research of others as suggestions, not commands. With gold, a minimum of research is required.

INVESTMENT MEDIA

There are a number of ways to invest in gold. I'll provide a brief summary of my opinion of each.

Gold Stocks

It's important to limit the number of things upon which you're betting. If you anticipate a gold price increase, you should invest in such a way that the result will depend solely upon the price of gold.

For this reason gold stocks aren't attractive. When you buy a gold stock, you're betting not only on the price of gold, but also on good management, government regulation of the gold mines, labor-management relations, benevolent geological conditions, etc.

In 1970, in my *Devaluation* book, I suggested gold stocks because at that time gold bullion and low-cost gold coins were illegal for Americans to own. Fortunately, the gold stocks did very well between then and 1974.

By January 1974, when my *Monetary Crisis* book was published, U.S. laws had been amended to permit the ownership of certain low-cost gold coins. I suggested that the coins were a much better gold investment than stocks—for the reason I've just stated.

Now, with gold bullion and all gold coins legal, there's no reason to use gold stocks—except for investors who want to follow them closely and take more speculative positions.

Jewelry, Medallions, Rare Coins

The argument against gold stocks applies against most other types of gold investments—such as jewelry, medallions, rare coins, commemorative issues of gold coins, and small bars of gold.

With each of these you're investing in more than just gold. You'll pay an extra price for workmanship or rarity, and you'll have to hope that the extra you've purchased will go up in value with the bullion—or at least won't drop in value.

There are small wafers of gold available—ranging from one-sixth ounce to a full ounce or more. These wafers are expensive to produce in the limited quantities in which they're usually made. When you buy them, you will pay for the cost of manufacture. But when you sell them, you can expect to receive only the current value of the gold they contain, with no premium for the workmanship.

In whatever form you purchase gold, you should find out the exact weight of the item you're buying and the fineness of the gold. The fineness should be at least .995 in all cases. Multiply the weight times the day's bullion price; if the price you're asked to pay is more than 7% above that calculation, you're probably paying more than you need to.

Gold Futures

Gold is traded in several commodity futures markets in the U.S. You can buy a contract to take delivery of a specified amount of gold (usually 100 ounces) in a specified month in the future, at a price determined today. Generally, you deposit 10% of the value when you make the contract.

When the contract falls due, you pay the balance and take delivery of the gold. Or you can sell the contract before the delivery date. An early sale would give you a profit or loss, depending on whether the price had risen or fallen.

Futures markets are especially useful for short-term trading. You can operate with small deposits, commissions are low, and trades are executed quickly. The markets are appropriate for those who hope to gain from short trends that may last only a week or a month.

For investors who hope to buy early in a normal bull market and hold the gold until the end of the uptrend, the futures markets have certain drawbacks.

One drawback is psychological. The deposit required is so small that, although you may have allocated $20,000 for your gold budget, you will need to put up only $2,000 in cash. Once in the market, the temptation to buy more gold than you can afford is strong. It would be easy to use the entire $20,000 as a deposit and commit yourself for $200,000 worth of gold. Then it would take only a 10% drop in the price to wipe out your entire $20,000 capital.

The second drawback is the threat of government interference. If you believe that the government might change the rules in the middle of the game, you'd probably be more comfortable having the gold outside the country.

Forward contracts are available at Swiss banks, but they aren't quite the same as the standardized futures contracts traded in the U.S. Each forward contract is tailored for an individual transaction and can be closed out only by selling it back to the bank from which you purchased it. There are no published price quotations for your contract, and you're dependent upon the price offered to you by the bank.

Gold Bullion

The most logical investment media for most investors are bullion and coins.

Gold bullion can be purchased in the U.S. from gold dealers and from some banks and brokers. It can also be purchased easily through a Swiss bank.

Contrary to popular mythology, the transaction costs aren't high, and unless you buy the gold off the back of someone's truck, you won't need to have it assayed.

If you buy bullion through a Swiss bank, it will be kept with the bank's own inventory, in its vault or in the vault of another bank. It is the bank's responsibility to see that the bullion it receives for you is genuine; you don't need to inspect the gold when you buy it or certify the gold when you sell it.

Handling gold is very inexpensive, compared to its value, so the transaction costs are relatively minor. The spread between the price at which you can buy and the price at which you can sell is usually around ½% (0.5%). At most banks, you also pay a commission of 1% when you buy or sell. Storage and insurance costs are generally around ⅓% of the market value per year. So if you hold the gold for two years and then sell, the costs would total just over 3%.

Most Swiss banks deal in standard gold bars. The smallest standard bar is one kilogram (32.15 ounces). At $200 per ounce, the cost would be $6,430. Each purchase or sale must be in units of kilograms or in units of 100 ounces ($20,000 at $200 per ounce).

However, a few banks allow purchases or sales in any quantity—as long as your overall account at the bank meets the required minimum. The fractional quantities are accommodated by pooling; the bank buys enough bars to cover the purchases of all its customers and then credits each customer with the number of ounces he has paid for.

Because the gold market is much newer in the U.S., the marketing systems are less standardized. Consequently, you shouldn't buy gold in the U.S. without checking with at least three different sellers to determine what you ought to pay in commissions and storage costs. And given the ever-present possibility of gold ownership again being declared illegal, I don't like the idea of leaving gold on deposit with a dealer in the U.S.

Gold Coins

If you are buying gold through a Swiss bank, the choice between bullion and coins is not too important. But for purchases in the U.S., I believe gold coins make more sense.

A gold coin is a self-contained package of gold, with a readily identifiable quality and a standardized weight. Because of the convenient packaging, coins are easy to trade. They don't have to be assayed, although they are easily checked for counterfeits.

Coins don't have to be stored with a dealer, so you can keep them in a safe-deposit box or elsewhere. You don't have to depend upon a dealer's integrity or his ability to stay in business. And you don't have to leave the coins where they would be an obvious target of government confiscation.

Gold coins that are no longer minted have a rarity value, and they sell for much more than the value of the gold they contain. However, some coins are still being minted and have no rarity value. These "bullion coins" include:

South African KrugerRand, 1 ounce fine gold
Mexican 50-peso, 1.2053 ounces fine gold
Austrian 100-crown (krone), .9886 ounces fine gold
Hungarian 100-crown (krone), .9886 ounces fine gold
Soviet Union Chervonitz, .2488 ounces fine gold

For the past few years, each of these coins has generally traded at a price within 5% of the value of its gold content. The premium of 5% or so is the price you pay for the packaging. But when you sell the coin, you probably will receive a similar small premium over the coin's bullion value.

Gold Options

Another gold investment medium is the gold option. Like any other option, a gold option is a right to purchase something (gold) at a specified *striking price* anytime between the day you buy the option and the option's *expiration date*.

Commodity options, of which gold options are only one kind, have acquired a bad reputation in the U.S. Recently, some operators have been discovered selling them, at extremely high prices, to their most gullible customers. The sale of gold and other commodity options is now severely restricted in the U.S.

But it isn't illegal for an American to buy gold options, if he chooses to do so. Nor is there anything inherently shady about commodity options. Like anything else, an option can be a good investment if the price is right and a very bad investment if the price is too high.

For some time, gold and silver options have been sold by members of the various London commodity exchanges. However, these options are newly created each day. They are good for a specified number of days from the date of purchase, and the striking price is the price then prevailing.

This practice means that there are thousands of different options in existence at any time. There is no uniform market in which to sell them, because each one is different. You can check the value of your option only by asking the dealer from whom it was purchased to buy it back.

Fortunately, in 1976, when Valeurs White Weld in Geneva, Switzerland, began making a market in gold options, it decided to use standardized options. At any given time, there are only two or three different expiration dates available—from one to seven months away. And there are usually only five or six striking prices available—in $5 increments around the current market price of gold.

If, for example, the current price of gold is $187 per ounce, there will probably be options with striking prices of $175, $180, $190, and $195. And if the current month is October, there will be a choice of options expiring at the end of November, February, and May—for each of these striking prices. And you could expect that sometime in January, Valeurs White Weld would begin quoting prices for options expiring at the end of August.

Thus there are at most fifteen to twenty different options being traded at any given time. Because the variety of options is restricted, there are always many people dealing in the same option, which gives it liquidity. Buying and selling prices for each option are quoted daily. Although prices aren't published in the U.S., any broker in the U.S. (or elsewhere) who subscribes to the Reuters Monitor price quotation system can obtain current quotes by punching the code VWWW.

Each option covers five kilograms (160.75 ounces) of gold. However, the price is quoted in dollars per ounce of gold. Thus, an offer to sell a given option at $6.00 means that you would pay $6 per ounce for an option to purchase 160.75 ounces, or a total of $964.50.

An option that is about five months from its expiration date and has a striking price close to the current bullion price will cost about 6% of the bullion price. For example, if the current bullion price is $200, an option to purchase at $200, with five months remaining, would cost around $12 per ounce.

If the price of gold drops below the option's striking price, the value of the option will decline. If the price of gold rises above the striking price, the option's value will increase a little less than $1 for every $1 increase in the price of bullion

—and the original 6% premium will gradually evaporate as the expiration date draws closer.

You don't have to exercise an option, by taking delivery of the gold, to profit from it. You can sell the option back to Valeurs White Weld, which makes a continuous market for all the options it issues.

For the past year the spread between the price at which you can buy an option and the price at which you can sell has been $1 per ounce. In addition, the bank you deal through will charge a commission of $\frac{1}{8}\%$ of the striking price.

You can calculate the increase in the price of gold required to make an option purchase profitable. Suppose you buy an option with a striking price of $200 when bullion is at $199, and the option has five months to go until it expires. The option will cost around $12 per ounce, and you'll have to pay a commission of $0.25 per ounce—a total of $12.25 per ounce.

If gold has risen to $213.25 per ounce at expiration date, the option will have a value of $13.25 per ounce—since the option will permit you to purchase an ounce of gold worth $213.25 for only $200. Valeurs will buy the option back from you for $1 less than the closing value, or for $12.25—which in this case was your original cost. So the gold price has risen by $13.25, or 6.6%, and you have broken even. Every dollar increase over that will provide a dollar of profit.

Valeurs White Weld doesn't sell directly to investors. It deals only with banks and other gold dealers. It is through one of them, probably a Swiss bank, that you can purchase options. As the market is only a little over two years old, not all Swiss banks handle gold options. However, in Chapter 32, I'll provide the names of five banks that do.

Gold options are a way by which you can lessen your potential loss. They can be used as a low-cost way of hedging if you expect a bull market in stocks and a bear market in gold. They are also a low-cost way of taking an initial position when you're not sure that a new gold trend has begun.

Gold bullion, coins, and options will all play a part in the strategy I'll suggest in Part IV.

GOLD OPTION PRICES

Striking Price & Expiration Date	Bid Price	Ask Price	% of Bullion Price
$185, August 1978	$ 4.00	$ 5.00	2.7%
$185, November 1978	$10.00	$11.00	5.9%
$190, August 1978	$ 1.50	$ 2.50	1.3%
$190, November 1978	$ 7.50	$ 8.50	4.6%
$195, August 1978	$ .50	$ 1.50	0.8%
$195, November 1978	$ 4.50	$ 5.50	3.0%
$195, February 1979	$ 9.00	$10.00	5.4%
$200, February 1979	$ 6.25	$ 7.25	3.9%

Date: July 10,1978   **Gold bullion price:** $185.875

Striking Price is the price at which the option-holder may purchase gold bullion at any time prior to the expiration date.

Expiration Date is the last day of the month shown.

Bid Price is the price at which you can sell the option.

Ask Price is the price at which you can buy the option.

% of Bullion Price is the percentage of the current bullion price ($185.875 on this date) represented by the ask price.

All prices shown are for each ounce contained in an option comprising 160.75 ounces (5 kilograms). Thus the purchase price of one option is 160.75 times the ask price.

Source of prices: Valeurs White Weld, Geneva.

PROSPECTS FOR GOLD

When gold is in a bull market, as it has been since 1976, it can withstand adverse publicity and absorb increased supplies. The gold auctions by the U.S. government and the International Monetary Fund have been assimilated fairly easily—although at the time of their announcement, the IMF auctions seemed ruinous to many gold investors.

However, the hoard of one billion ounces held by the governments of the western world hangs ominously over the market. I'm not concerned that anti-gold fervor will inspire a campaign to sell this gold to knock the price down. But when the crises heat up, many governments may sell gold simply to raise cash. This is gold's greatest vulnerability.

For the present, gold is in the latter stages of one of its uptrends. When this book went to press, in July 1978, gold was still in the bull trend that began in mid-1976.

I expect the current uptrend to last through the end of 1978, but, of course, I can't be sure of it. In any event, by the time you read this, it could easily be too late to profit from this bull market.

If you're already holding gold, you should be preparing to sell the portion of it that isn't being kept as a long-term hedge against chaos.

If the trend is still in progress when you read this, it may be very much in the news. A constantly rising price can be a powerful attraction, but I hope that won't influence you.

When the gold price is soaring and people are talking about it, the time has come to sell—not buy. The next big opportunity to buy gold will come when the stock market has regained its reputation and is reaching new highs and gold is scorned as a bygone fantasy.

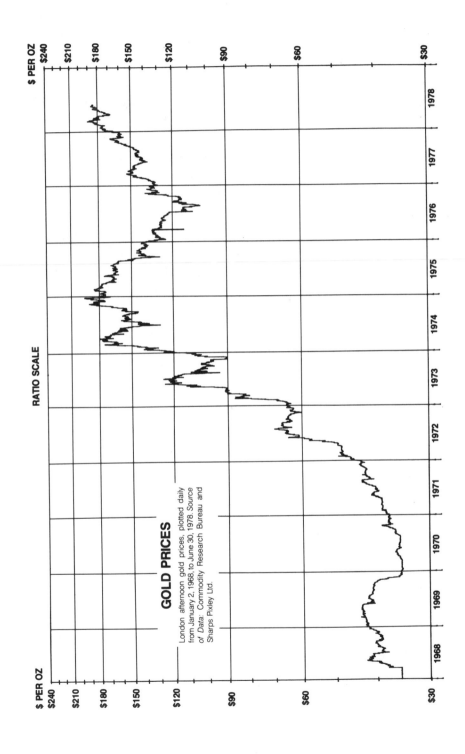

GOLD PRICES

London afternoon gold prices, plotted daily from January 2, 1968, to June 30, 1978. Source of *Data*: Commodity Research Bureau and Sharps Pixley Ltd.

RATIO SCALE

$ PER OZ
$240
$210
$180
$150
$120
$90
$60
$30

1968 1969 1970 1971 1972 1973 1974 1975 1976 1977 1978

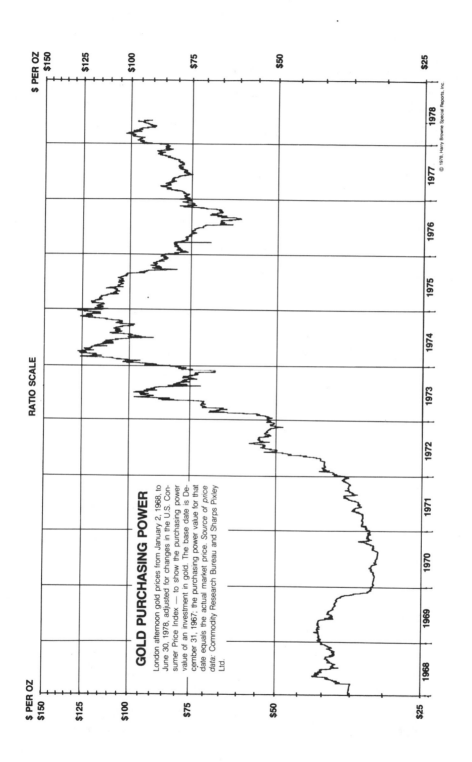

RATIO SCALE

GOLD PURCHASING POWER

London afternoon gold prices from January 2, 1968, to June 30, 1978, adjusted for changes in the U.S. Consumer Price Index — to show the purchasing power value of an investment in gold. The base date is December 31, 1967; the purchasing power value for that date equals the actual market price. *Source of price data*: Commodity Research Bureau and Sharps Pixley Ltd.

16

FOREIGN
CURRENCIES

THE SWISS FRANC HAS BEEN GOOD TO MANY OF US. THE GRAPH on page 205 shows just how good. From June 1970 to June 1978, the franc's price (in dollars) appreciated by 132% and from January 1974 to June 1978, the rise was 80%.

The Swiss franc isn't through as an investment, although I don't expect future rallies to be as intense as those of 1973, 1974, and 1977–1978. The franc has overcome the years of price control that made those rallies so powerful, but it can still serve a valuable purpose in the long-term portion of your portfolio.

In addition, there will be short-term opportunities for profit in the Swiss franc and other currencies. The trading opportunities, however, will be of a different sort from those of the recent past.

A few years back, it was possible to take a long-term position in a strong currency and be confident of earning a sizable profit. No particular analysis was needed, because it was obvious that the strong European currencies (such as the Swiss franc, German mark, Austrian schilling, and Dutch guilder) were being underpriced by the system of fixed exchange rates.

Now these currencies have appreciated and no longer represent investment bargains. If they appreciate further, it will

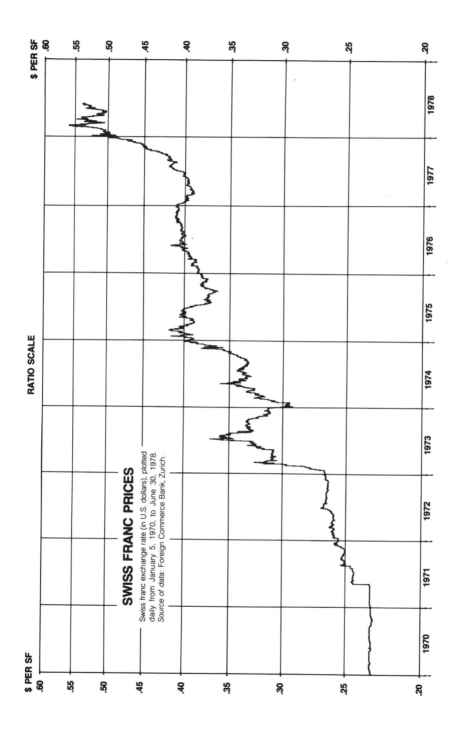

SWISS FRANC PRICES

Swiss franc exchange rate (in U.S. dollars), plotted daily from January 5, 1970, to June 30, 1978.
Source of data: Foreign Commerce Bank, Zurich.

RATIO SCALE

$ PER SF

$ PER SF

.60 .55 .50 .45 .40 .35 .30 .25 .20

1970 1971 1972 1973 1974 1975 1976 1977 1978

be because of conditions existing now and in the future; so I can't give you a list of sure winners.

To trade in currencies you'll have to: (1) use fundamental analysis; (2) use technical analysis; (3) better yet, use both; or (4) rely on someone to do the analysis for you.

In this chapter I'll present a brief summary of the fundamental method I use for analyzing currency prices. One conclusion reached from that analysis is that the Swiss franc is still the best choice for investors who don't want to trade actively, but who do want to hold a foreign currency as a hedge against inflation.

I'll also discuss the various forms a currency investment can take.

Then you can decide whether currency trading is appropriate for you. If it isn't, it's best to leave currencies alone, or limit yourself to a static, long-term holding of Swiss francs. But if trading is appropriate, it can be a source of great profit —because the currency markets include one element that is unique in the investment world.

THE ACCOMMODATING LOSER

I call this unique element the "accommodating loser."

In a free market, investment prices are determined by investors who compete for profits. Competition among them is a race to foresee how prices will change, and to buy or sell before much of the change has taken place.

If you see a price rise coming, you want to buy before everyone else sees what you see—before other investors push the price up. Once the need for the rise becomes generally known and accepted, the rise will probably already have occurred.

Can you imagine an investment market in which the price stood still until nearly all investors could see that it was going to rise? Such a thing seems impossible.

For such a market to exist, there would have to be an investor who was willing to ignore what everyone else knew and to sell at a bargain price to one and all. After this seller had accommodated all interested buyers, the price would rise, and the seller would suffer a considerable loss—hence his title, the "accommodating loser."

Surprisingly, such markets actually exist. Think back to the gold market of 1961–1968. Despite the inevitability of higher gold prices, thousands of investors were allowed to purchase all the gold they could handle at $35 per ounce. When the price finally broke free, they made great profits, and the accommodating loser registered great losses.

Who was the accommodating loser? The U.S. government, assisted by six other governments. The silver market worked the same way, and so did the currency markets.

The accommodating loser has withdrawn from the silver market and today really only dabbles in gold. But there are still accommodating losers in the currency markets.

When a currency's price is destined to rise, the accommodating loser (the currency's government) sells the currency—holding its price down. He *knows* the price will have to go up eventually; he's never yet beaten reality.

Currency intervention is expensive. A government buys an overpriced currency and then lets the price drop; or it sells an underpriced currency and then lets the price rise. In either case, the value of the government's reserves declines. Governments suffer from the big-losses, no-profits disease.

Of course, the government isn't trying to accommodate investors; it's simply carrying on its usual business of fighting with reality. The government's peculiar effect upon the currency markets stems from its peculiar motivation. An investor acts on what he *expects* the price to be; a government acts to *make* the price what it *wants* it to be.

The investor wants to profit by trying to perceive reality. The government wants to defeat reality by controlling prices —even though that means losing in the long run.

The presence of governments as accommodating losers makes the currency markets unusual. This doesn't mean currency forecasting is easy. There's much more to it than just spotting the loser and betting against him. But if you're willing to work at it, you'll find an unusual market—one in which the profits are often enormous and the risks can be kept small.

Floating Currencies?

A government tries to hold its currency's price down so that favored industries can continue to export their products. Or the government holds its currency's price up in order to restrain the prices of imported consumer goods, or because the government imagines that its prestige is at stake.

Before 1973, the rules of the International Monetary Fund required each country to maintain a *par value* for its currency in terms of gold. This par value was automatically translated into a price for the currency in terms of U.S. dollars. By buying or selling its own currency, usually for dollars, each government kept the price within 1¼% of the par value. This was the fixed exchange-rate system.

When the system collapsed in January 1973, governments didn't quit caring about currency prices. They continued to intervene, but they no longer announced the prices they would maintain.[1]

Despite the constant references in the press to "floating" exchange rates, most governments of the world are interfering with currency prices on the same scale as before 1973.

Intervention creates wide disparities between actual prices and fundamental values. Because the disparities eventually must be closed, the investor who can recognize them can profit from the intervention.

CURRENCY FORECASTING

Most forecasters estimate fundamental values with some variation of the *purchasing power parity* (PPP) theory of ex-

[1] An exception is the fixed exchange-rate system of the Common Market (the "Snake"). In addition, almost all small countries maintain announced par values in terms of a major currency such as the U.S. dollar, the French franc, or the British pound. But none of the *major* currencies has kept a fixed rate since 1973.

change rates. I do, too, but I've added a few wrinkles of my own.

The PPP theory is really very simple. But like so many simple things, it becomes quite complicated when you try to explain it—especially if you try to cover all the possible exceptions or objections. To provide you with everything you might need to begin using it would require a separate book.

However, you can understand what is happening in the currency markets much more easily if you at least understand the idea of purchasing power parity. The following pages provide a brief summary.

The Theory

The PPP theory states that exchange rates will tend to move, over a period of time, in a direction dictated by the differences in price inflation between countries. If the rate of price inflation is higher in the U.S. than in Switzerland, for example, the Swiss franc should appreciate against the U.S. dollar.

A lower inflation rate in Switzerland will make Swiss products less expensive than American products. Americans (and buyers all over the world) will prefer to buy Swiss products. To do so, they will exchange dollars (or other currencies) for Swiss francs—creating a greater demand for francs and less demand for dollars.

Suppose, for example, that typewriters were the only product traded internationally. And suppose the prevailing prices were these:

Exchange rate: 1 Swiss franc = $0.50 (50 cents)
U.S. typewriter price: $200 (or SF400 at present exchange rate)
Swiss typewriter price: SF300 (or $150 at present exchange rate)

A Swiss typewriter is cheaper at the present exchange rate. The incentive to buy Swiss typewriters will lead Americans (and others) to convert their money into francs. Eventually, the demand for francs will push the exchange rate up until these conditions prevail:

Exchange rate: 1 Swiss franc = $0.67 (67 cents)
U.S. typewriter price: $200 (or SF300 at new exchange rate)
Swiss typewriter price: SF300 (or $200 at new exchange rate)

Notice that the cost of a typewriter is the same now, no matter where it is bought.

Although typewriter prices haven't changed in either country, the new exchange rate has eliminated the advantage of buying in Switzerland. When translated by the exchange rate, typewriters cost the same in both countries. The incentive for acquiring francs has been eliminated, and the exchange rate will tend to stay near $0.67 until, perhaps, some new price inflation disturbs the balance.

Since more than typewriters are sold internationally, we're interested in the general movement of each country's price level. The consumer price index is one measure, but it includes many services that are purely local. The wholesale price index provides a better measure, because it concentrates more on the prices of goods that can be traded across national boundaries.

The PPP theory says that if wholesale price inflation this year is going to be 0% in Switzerland and 10% in the U.S., the Swiss franc's *value* will rise 10% during the year. The rise in value implies that the *exchange rate* eventually will rise— assuming that the present exchange rate already reflects general price levels faithfully. Unfortunately, this assumption is seldom correct, since we know that governments are always interfering with exchange rates. Later, I'll show how an allowance for previous interference can be made.

When a currency is priced at its PPP, the country will export the products it is best suited to produce and import those things it is ill-suited to produce—in effect, paying for its imports with its exports. But when the exchange rate is at an unrealistic level, there will be an unsustainable imbalance between imports and exports—and there will be pressure on the exchange rate to move to a level that will correct the imbalance (just as the price of anything moves to a level at which supply and demand are in harmony).

The PPP theory doesn't assume that people in general are aware of foreign prices and are alert to changes in exchange rates. It's the job of importers and exporters to watch these things; finding foreign bargains is the way they make their living.

Criticisms

The most common criticism of the PPP theory is that it doesn't consider all the factors that affect a currency's price. What about interest rates, tariffs, exchange controls, and differences in product quality?

Surprisingly, the purchasing-power approach either allows for all these factors indirectly, or it overrules them. Many things can speed up or slow down the movement of a currency's price toward its purchasing power parity, but the PPP always has the last word.

For example, Switzerland is a favorite haven for flight capital. It's easy to imagine that investors seeking a safe currency could push the franc up indefinitely.

However, any upward movement makes Swiss products more expensive internationally. With less of these products being sold, the commercial demand for francs is reduced. The demand for a safe currency displaces the commercial demand for Swiss products.

At first, both sources of demand are felt, and the exchange rate rises. But the higher exchange rate soon dampens demand for Swiss products, and so the exchange rate drifts back down toward its purchasing power parity—at which point Swiss products are again salable.

Similarly, an increase in interest rates (caused, perhaps, by government borrowing) can attract money from foreign investors. But this pressure on the exchange rate works itself out in the same way as the pressure from flight capital. There is a temporary rise, followed by retreat to a level at which local products are again competitive in international markets.

Another criticism of the PPP theory is that it doesn't acknowledge exchange controls, trade restrictions, and quality or technological differences. Presumably, these factors could prevent the exchange rate from ever reaching the level dictated by the PPP.

But factors such as trade restrictions or quality differences are fairly stable. Whatever these factors might be for a particular country, there is some exchange rate that will make the country's products competitive in world markets. If the price level in the country changes, the exchange rate will have to shift also—to keep the country's products competitive.

Thus, considerations apart from inflation rates (trade restrictions, capital movements, quality differences, etc.) don't invalidate the PPP concept. In some cases, they create disparities that a PPP forecaster can exploit.

Balance of Payments (BOP)

Many people see a balance of payments surplus as an indication that a country is more competitive, and thus that its currency will appreciate. Conversely, a BOP deficit is taken to indicate a weak currency. It may be that no currency topic is more misunderstood.

Part of the misunderstanding is the notion that an imbalance in the country's payments will cause the government's international reserves (gold and foreign currencies) to change. A BOP surplus increases the reserves, and a deficit depletes the reserves. It's almost as though the central bank were rewarded or penalized for its country's business practices.

I can understand how this belief arises. In fact, since no one can count all the transactions that make up the balance of payments, the final result is determined by measuring the change in the central bank's reserves. It's assumed that the reserves must have changed because of the balance of payments.

Unfortunately, no one seems to ask *how* changes in official reserves occur. Do foreigners buy airplanes or wheat from the Federal Reserve? Do they buy chocolates or cheese from the Swiss National Bank? Do foreigners seeking a safe haven open accounts at a nation's central bank—adding to the central bank's assets? Obviously, the answer to all these questions is no.

The only contact a central bank has with foreign economies is through *currency trading*—buying and selling in the currency markets. If a central bank didn't intervene in the currency markets, its reserves would never change. And if the reserves didn't change, the statisticians would never discover a balance of payments surplus or deficit.

The figure that is published as a country's balance of payments is an indication only of the extent to which its government has intervened in the currency markets; it is not an indication of the country's ability to produce salable products (as is often believed). A balance of payments surplus persists because a government persistently buys foreign currencies (trying to prevent the price of its own currency from rising).

BOP figures for the United States are calculated indirectly. The Federal Reserve intervenes only slightly in the currency markets, and so its reserves change very little. Instead, other governments intervene by buying and selling dollars, and the statisticians measure the U.S. balance of payments by changes in the foreign governments' dollar reserves.

The chronic U.S. balance of payments deficits are the result of currency intervention by foreign governments. It is they who buy dollars, not the Federal Reserve who buys foreign currencies. I don't believe the U.S. government deserves the criticism it has received for its policy of "benign neglect" of the dollar. It has been more willing than other governments to allow the dollar to find its own natural level.

As a currency forecasting tool, balance of payments figures

can have a limited usefulness. The figures indicate the directions in which a government and the market are pushing against each other. A surplus means the government is trying to hold its currency price down; a deficit means the government is trying to hold it up. In the absence of more detail, the balance of payments figures are better than nothing.[2]

The Starting Point

I said earlier (on page 210) that the PPP forecaster must select a starting point from which to track the accumulated differences in inflation between two countries. This means finding a date on which a currency's price was equal to its PPP.

Unfortunately, there have been no periods that stood out as moments of harmonious equilibrium in the currency markets. Intervention has been nearly continuous since the end of World War II. Although there have been times when currencies were allegedly "floating," a study of any central bank's balance sheet will show that its reserves were changing constantly.

There is no obvious starting point from which to measure the accumulated effect of differing rates of inflation, though a starting point is needed. As a result, most forecasters pick an arbitrary starting date and follow inflation rates from there.

I believe that the record of government intervention is the key to finding a starting point. By noting the amount of intervention at any given time, you at least gain an idea of whether the currency was overpriced or underpriced. And by watching the price and the amount of intervention over a period of time, eventually there's only one PPP that fits all the facts.

The graph on page 215 shows monthly prices for the Swiss

2 Only the overall balance of payments figures are useful for this purpose. The trade figures and the current account figures have no bearing; surpluses and deficits in these accounts can exist without intervention and are not significant.

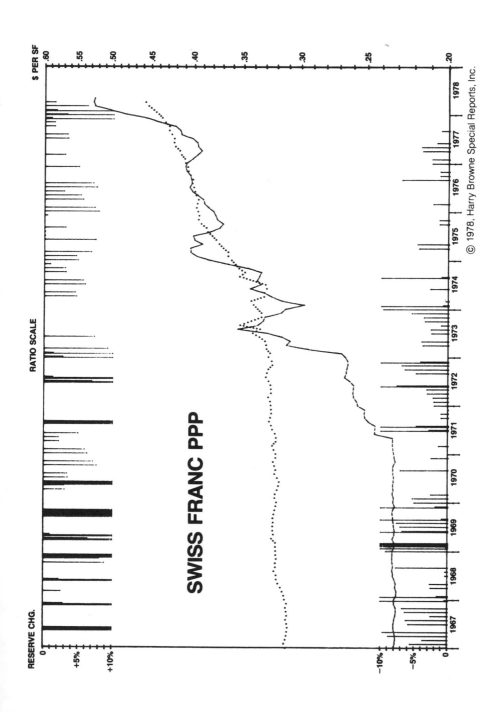

SWISS FRANC PPP

© 1978, Harry Browne Special Reports, Inc.

franc (in U.S. dollars) from 1967 to 1978. The vertical lines at the top and bottom of the graph show the extent of intervention by the Swiss government—as measured by monthly percentage changes in the government's holdings of foreign currencies. Lines at the top indicate government pressure to hold the price down; lines at the bottom indicate pressure to hold the price up.

The dotted trendline shows the accumulated difference between inflation in the U.S. and inflation in Switzerland. If price inflation in the U.S. exceeds inflation in Switzerland in any month, the dotted line moves upward; if Swiss inflation is greater, the dotted line moves downward.

Differences in inflation determine the *shape* of the dotted line, but one must choose a price at which to *begin* the dotted line. (No matter where you begin, the line will still have the same shape.) I have placed the line where it best fits the movement of the actual price after allowing for the influence of Swiss government intervention.

For periods when the Swiss were buying dollars to push the price of the franc down, the price is below the purchasing power parity (the dotted line). When there is relatively little intervention, the actual price moves toward the PPP line.

There has been much less intervention since 1973, and so the price moves more freely. It loops over and under the PPP line—much as price chases value in any free market.

The graph indicates that the actual price rose far above the fundamental value in the spring of 1978. If my analysis is correct, the price should retreat somewhat during 1978. As of June 1978, the fundamental objective was $.4723, while the actual price was $.5382.

We can also see that the fundamental price objective is continually rising. Wholesale prices in the U.S. are rising by about 7½% per year, while wholesale prices in Switzerland are *dropping* by about 3½% per year. So there is pressure on the franc to rise by about 11% per year—the difference between the two inflation rates.

If conditions remain as they were in June 1978, the fundamental value of the franc should be around $.5280 in June

1979. However, I expect U.S. price inflation to begin dropping around the beginning of 1979, perhaps reducing the inflation differential between the two countries to 7% or so.

TECHNICAL ANALYSIS

The PPP system can be used to find a currency's fundamental value. However, government intervention, capital flows, or misguided speculation can cause a currency to move quite a distance from its fundamental value before the PPP exerts its influence. An underpriced currency, like any investment, can become *more* underpriced before fundamental values take over (a process I discussed in Chapter 8).

It would be a mistake to invest in a currency the moment you see that it's underpriced. When I discover a disparity, I watch the price to see if the disparity is growing or shrinking. I wait until the price has started a trend in the right direction—toward its PPP—before investing.

Thus, I use both fundamental and technical analysis to guide currency investments. It's important, I believe, never to go against the prevailing trend. Don't buy a currency that's going down just because you believe it must go upward eventually. "Eventually" can be a long time.

For example, the recent history of the British pound's price and PPP are shown on page 218. The pound's purchasing power parity has been dropping steadily since 1973—because of the high British inflation rate. Until almost the end of 1976, the actual price was dropping, too, whenever the British government refrained from intervening. By late 1976, the pound had sunk to $1.58. Then, buoyed by international loans to the British government and by excitement over the prospect of North Sea oil, the pound began to rise.

The PPP continued to drop, while the actual price was rising. The British government even bought dollars in the marketplace to keep the pound from going higher. The disparity between the actual price and the PPP grew larger and larger until, finally, in February 1978, the price began to fall.

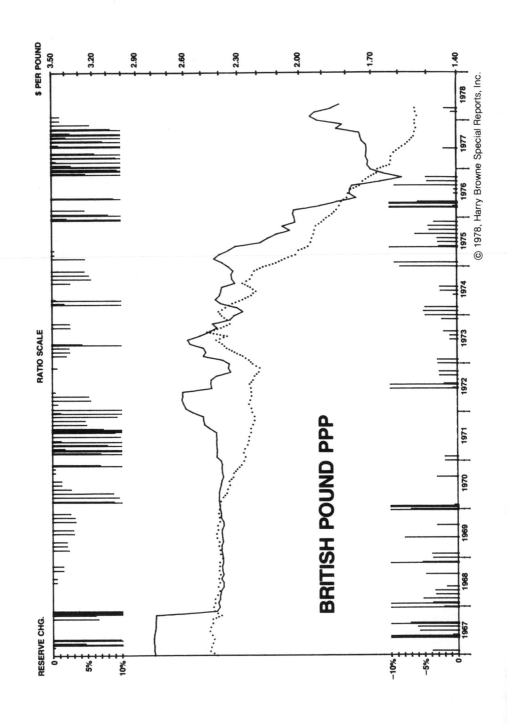

BRITISH POUND PPP

$ PER POUND

3.50
3.20
2.90
2.60
2.30
2.00
1.70
1.40

RATIO SCALE

RESERVE CHG.

0
5%
10%

-10%
-5%
0

1967 1968 1969 1970 1971 1972 1973 1974 1975 1976 1977 1978

The peak was $1.98. When the price had dropped to $1.85, the downtrend was clearly established, and I sold short. At that point, the fundamental objective was $1.55—a drop of 16%. A reasonably leveraged futures sale could turn that into a high profit.

I can't tell you how the story ended, because the book went to press in July 1978. But the price was on its way. It took patience to wait out 1977 without acting, but patience is a necessary part of investing.

Other examples were provided in early 1978 by the Swiss franc, the German mark, and the Japanese yen. All rallied to well above their fundamental objectives. But I waited until the uptrends were clearly over before selling my holdings and switching to dollars.

When the trend changed, I had the PPP theory on my side to let me know there was a *reason* for the change—the currencies had gone too far.

I believe that both fundamental analysis (the PPP theory) and technical analysis (the respect for trends) are necessary to invest profitably in currencies.

The PPP records for the German mark, Japanese yen, and Canadian dollar are shown on pages 220 to 222.

GOLD BACKING

I used a different method of forecasting in my *Monetary Crisis* book of 1974. At that time, there was too little history of moving currency prices to use the PPP theory. And so I computed a "potential price" for each major currency by comparing its gold backing with its money supply.

The main purpose was to discover which governments were the most cautious about inflation. While the method was not nearly so precise as the PPP theory, it served its purpose.

From the twenty-six currencies analyzed, I selected five that I believed were suitable for investment, with the Swiss franc the clear leader. The five selected are shown, in order of suitability, in the left-hand column, while the right-hand column

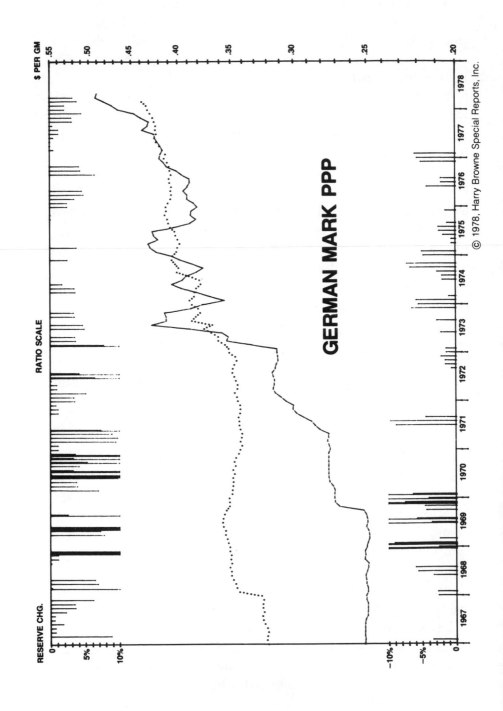

GERMAN MARK PPP

$ PER GM

RATIO SCALE

RESERVE CHG.

© 1978, Harry Browne Special Reports, Inc.

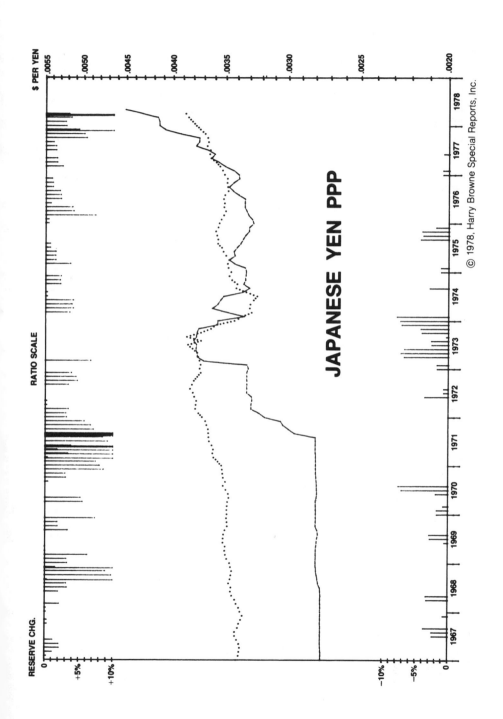

JAPANESE YEN PPP

$ PER YEN

RATIO SCALE

RESERVE CHG.

© 1978, Harry Browne Special Reports, Inc.

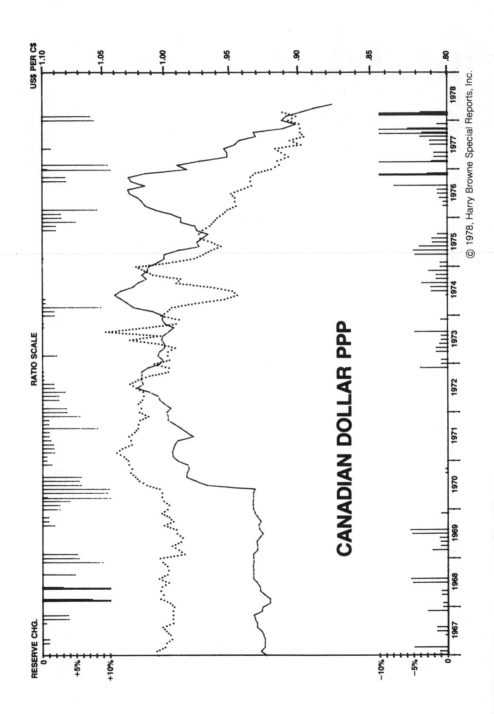

CANADIAN DOLLAR PPP

shows the five that appreciated the most from June 18, 1973 (when the analysis was made) to March 31, 1978:

SUGGESTED	RESULTS
1. Swiss franc	1. Swiss franc
2. Netherlands guilder	2. Austrian schilling
3. Belgian franc	3. German mark
4. Austrian schilling	4. Netherlands guilder
5. German mark	5. Japanese yen

The Belgian franc, which was ranked third, actually finished sixth. I also mentioned the Lebanese pound as a speculative "sleeper." Despite the civil war, it managed to finish twelfth among the twenty-six currencies.

The gold-backing method worked well when nothing else was available. But that was partly because it was easy to see that large changes were coming, and the indications of inflationary attitudes could point to the currencies likely to move the most.

Today, however, the situation is different. Future movements won't be on such a grand scale. The PPP theory is much better suited for spotting transient disparities in currency prices.

INFLATION HEDGE

I've said that an investment qualifies as an inflation hedge only if its appreciation is tied in some way to the rate of price inflation.

According to the PPP theory, the Swiss franc should appreciate yearly by a little more than the U.S. wholesale price inflation rate, because Swiss inflation is currently negative. This makes the Swiss franc an inflation hedge for Americans.

At present inflation rates, the franc should appreciate about 11% per year against the dollar. As of June 1978, the franc was priced about six cents above the value indicated by my PPP analysis. But that gap may have closed partially or completely by the time you read this.

If the franc is not above $.5400 at the end of 1978, I believe it will be safe to buy it as an inflation hedge. The franc will continue to be a hedge until the day price inflation returns to Switzerland.

The franc's status as an inflation hedge has been confirmed by the record of the past five years. This isn't noticeable when you look at a normal price graph. But when the price of the franc is adjusted for changes in the U.S. consumer price index (as in the graph on page 225), the constant relationship between the franc price and U.S. inflation is obvious.

Since 1973, the franc's real purchasing power (in terms of U.S. dollars) has fluctuated mostly within 10% of .275 on the graph. Compare this constancy with similar graphs constructed for gold (on page 203), U.S. stocks (on page 16), and silver (on page 260). On each of those graphs, the real purchasing power of the investment fluctuates widely.

An investment that moves upward during a period of inflation isn't necessarily an inflation hedge; it's just a good investment. An inflation hedge is an investment that moves *because* of inflation. And only the Swiss franc has that link today.

There are other major countries that currently have negative wholesale price inflation rates (Austria, Belgium, Japan, and West Germany). However, I don't believe that the political commitment to maintain this condition is as great in any of those countries as it is in Switzerland. I believe it's safest to stick with the franc—at least until wholesale price inflation is no longer negative.

Such a situation, if it arises, won't be foreseeable; you'll just have to react to it when it happens. Money supply figures are available for the Swiss franc, just as for the dollar, but the Swiss figures are less useful. American demand to hold dollars is quite stable; it changes only gradually. Consequently, any marked increase in the money supply disrupts the monetary equilibrium.

The situation is different in Switzerland, however. Much of the demand for francs comes from foreigners. And the foreign holdings of francs have little effect upon price inflation, since most of the foreign-held francs are reinvested outside of Switz-

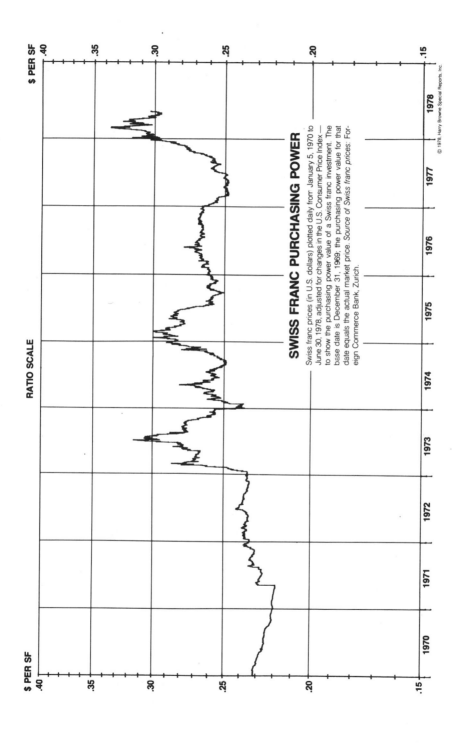

RATIO SCALE

$ PER SF

SWISS FRANC PURCHASING POWER

Swiss franc prices (in U.S. dollars) plotted daily from January 5, 1970 to June 30, 1978, adjusted for changes in the U.S. Consumer Price Index — to show the purchasing power value of a Swiss franc investment. The base date is December 31, 1969; the purchasing power value for that date equals the actual market price. Source of Swiss franc prices: Foreign Commerce Bank, Zurich.

© 1978, Harry Browne Special Reports, Inc.

$ PER SF

.40 .35 .30 .25 .20 .15

1970 1971 1972 1973 1974 1975 1976 1977 1978

erland. This foreign demand for francs is erratic. When it increases, the Swiss National Bank will sometimes accommodate it by allowing the money supply to increase—knowing that the domestic supply of francs won't be changed much by the increase.

In April 1978, for example, the 12-month rate of increase in the basic money supply (M_1) was 16.7%. But the M_2 money supply, which includes domestic savings accounts, had increased by only 9.9%—and the rate was dropping.

INVESTMENT ALTERNATIVES

There are a variety of ways to invest in currencies. I'll use the Swiss franc as an example.

Swiss Bank Account

The simplest method for investing in the franc is through a Swiss franc account in a Swiss bank. If you pick a good bank, the money will be safe from bank failures and be beyond the reach of the U.S. government. I'll discuss this further in Chapter 21.

Most Swiss banks offer accounts in currencies other than the Swiss franc.

In the near future, American banks may offer accounts denominated in foreign currencies. I would resist the temptation to use these accounts, as the government might change the rules once more. And Swiss banks are much better equipped to survive a worldwide deflationary panic.

Swiss Bonds

As of June 1978, the Swiss government prohibited new purchases of Swiss bonds by foreigners, except under circumstances that most foreigners can't take advantage of. However, the government had indicated that it hoped to remove the restrictions by the end of 1978.

Swiss Confederation bonds are the safest interest-earning investment available in Swiss francs. They sell in denominations of SF1,000 (about US$500), and were yielding 3½% in early 1978.

The bonds of any government can be purchased through a Swiss bank.

Swiss Stocks

Many people invest in a country's currency by buying stocks in that country. However, this involves three times as many decisions: (1) you must choose the right currency; (2) you must know when the stock market is going to rise— or at least not fall; and (3) you must select individual stocks that will move with the trend.

The Swiss stock market had a nice uptrend from late 1976 to early 1978. In contrast to the U.S., Swiss monetary inflation isn't cyclical—so you don't see the same broad trends in the Swiss stock market. Instead, Swiss stocks will probably experience a slow, but steady, growth over the next few years. But since you still have the job of selecting individual companies, Swiss stocks aren't appropriate for most investors.

At present, foreigners are prohibited from purchasing Swiss stocks. However, as with bonds, there were strong hopes that the restriction would be removed by the end of 1978.

Swiss stocks can be purchased through a Swiss bank.

Currency Futures

Futures contracts for eight foreign currencies are traded at the International Monetary Market in Chicago. The currencies are the Swiss franc, German mark, Japanese yen, British pound, Canadian dollar, Mexican peso, Netherlands guilder, and French franc. Information about the IMM can be obtained from most U.S. stock and commodity brokers.

Swiss banks will provide forward contracts for major currencies. Normally, contracts are written for any period of time up to one year. The usual margin requirement is 10% to 20%.[3]

Banknotes

A simple method of investing in foreign currencies is by purchasing banknotes (the actual cash) from a foreign currency dealer in the U.S. You can store the banknotes in a safe-deposit box or at home. Dealers are usually listed in the Yellow Pages under "Foreign Exchange Brokers."

The principal drawback of this method is that the spread between buying and selling prices is greater for banknotes than for deposits in a Swiss bank. Generally, the spread for a bank deposit will be around 1½%, whereas the spread for banknotes is about 5% (because the dealer actually inventories the banknotes). This means the price of the banknotes must rise by 5% before you'll break even.

However, banknotes are practical if the amount you want to invest is less than $5,000—a typical minimum for opening a Swiss bank account.

Swiss Life Insurance and Annuities

It is possible to buy annuities and life insurance contracts denominated in Swiss francs. While no Swiss companies are licensed to solicit business in the U.S. (to the best of my knowledge), it isn't illegal for an American to buy insurance wherever he pleases.

The biggest drawback of a long-term insurance or annuity contract is that you can't know what the currency will be worth ten years from now. However, if you need such a con-

---

[3] A forty-one page chapter in my book, *The Complete Guide to Swiss Banks*, explains all the mechanics of forward contracts and margin accounts.

tract, I believe it would be safer to make it in francs than in dollars.

The long-term outlook for the franc is more promising and more reliable. And Swiss companies are probably safer than American companies, because the Swiss economy is less vulnerable to a deflationary crash.

Insurance contracts have, so far, been excluded from all investment restrictions that the Swiss government has applied to foreigners. Also, Swiss insurance contracts aren't bank or securities accounts, so they don't have to be reported to the U.S. Internal Revenue Service.[4]

Other Currencies

I've used the Swiss franc as the example in this section, but the same considerations apply to other currencies. They can be purchased through a Swiss bank or traded at the International Monetary Market, as discussed before. However, I'm not acquainted with the insurance systems in other countries, nor is there any currency other than the Swiss franc in which I would want a long-term insurance contract.

CURRENCY PROSPECTS

Currency forecasting isn't as easy now as it was four to eight years ago, because the major currencies have risen to offset the price distortions created by the fixed exchange-rate system. Instead, you'll have to analyze and monitor currencies, or rely on someone to do it for you. If these alternatives aren't feasible, it is best to stay out of the currency markets.

The one exception is the Swiss franc. Because of Switzerland's low inflation rate, the franc should continue to appreciate by a modest amount almost every year. It can play a small, but important, part in the investment strategy I'll suggest in Part IV.

[4] Both of these matters are discussed further in Chapter 21.

U.S. Dollar

Currency investors will need to get used to the fact that the U.S. dollar is no longer greatly overpriced against the European currencies. It should depreciate mildly against the strong currencies each year, but there are no longer any large, pent-up distortions to be corrected. Any dramatic exchange-rate movements are likely to be reversed soon afterward.

It's easy for an American to recognize the foolish policies of the U.S. government and, thus, to believe that the dollar is sick. But it isn't so easy to be aware of similar policies being pursued by most other governments—policies that are creating a world of sick currencies. And since currency prices can move only in relation to *each other*, the dollar probably won't look so sick by comparison.

Anyone who looks closely at the economies of other countries may be surprised to discover that the "free enterprise" giants are just as socialistic as the U.S. The German "miracle," for example, has long since dissolved into a welfare state along classical European lines. The Japanese "superstate" has been a welfare state almost from the beginning—although somewhat disguised by its unique structure.

The table on page 231 provides some sobering figures. It shows the level of government spending, as a percentage of Gross National Product, in various countries. This provides a partial index of government interference—partial because it doesn't tell *how* the government spends or the extent to which regulations further hamper the economy.[5]

Nor does the table reveal the precarious conditions created by monetary inflation in each country. With the possible exception of Switzerland, there isn't a major country in the world that isn't walking the same tightrope between inflation and deflation that I described for the United States in Chapter 3.[6]

[5] The concept of "Gross National Product" is as imaginary as the balance of payments. I use it here only because we don't have the space to examine alternative measures of economic activity.

[6] More about Switzerland in Chapter 21.

TAXES & GOVERNMENT EXPENDITURES
IN 23 COUNTRIES

Country	(A) Government Expenditures as % of GPD 1976	(A) 1965	(B) Total Taxes as % of GNP 1974	(B) 1965	(C) Total Taxes $ per Person 1974	(C) 1965
Australia	N.A.	N.A.	27.2%	23.8%	$1,473	$ 605
Austria	N.A.	N.A.	38.1%	34.3%	1,668	453
Belgium	45.2%[1]	32.1%	38.1%	30.5%	2,109	552
Canada	39.7%	28.1%	34.8%	27.3%	2,213	709
Denmark	N.A.	N.A.	46.7%	30.2%	2,789	639
England	46.1%[1]	35.3%	35.6%	30.5%	1,215	563
Finland	N.A.	N.A.	36.3%	30.7%	1,686	538
France	41.7%	37.3%	37.5%	36.5%	1,902	739
Germany	45.9%	36.0%	37.6%	32.7%	2,326	642
Greece	N.A.	N.A.	22.4%	19.6%	495	140
Ireland	N.A.	N.A.	32.4%	25.0%	716	243
Italy	46.2%	32.9%	31.9%	29.1%	860	328
Japan	25.0%[1]	19.5%	22.2%	18.2%	945	168
Luxembourg	N.A.	N.A.	40.9%	31.6%	2,433	650
Netherlands	57.4%	34.8%	45.2%	35.1%	2,321	544
New Zealand	N.A.	N.A.	32.7%	26.1%	1,415	525
Norway	N.A.	N.A.	45.3%	33.5%	2,605	633
Portugal	N.A.	N.A.	22.4%	19.1%[2]	342	87[2]
Spain	N.A.	N.A.	18.8%	16.0%	461	107
Sweden	54.8%	34.6%	44.2%	35.6%	3,036	1,013
Switzerland	30.5%	20.9%	26.2%	21.0%	1,998	490
Turkey	N.A.	N.A.	20.4%[3]	16.5%	92[3]	45
United States	34.3%	27.5%	28.9%	24.9%	1,925	892

N.A. = Not available.
[1] 1975
[2] 1966
[3] 1972

EXPLANATION

Section A: Percentage of Gross Domestic Product expended by all levels of government. *Source:* Bank for International Settlements, *Annual Report, 1976-1977*, page 26.

Section B: Total taxes for all levels of government, including Social Security, as a percentage of the Gross National Product. *Source:* Organization for Economic Cooperation & Development, *Revenue Statistics of OECD Member Countries 1965-1974*, page 74.

Section C: Average total taxes per person, translated into U.S. dollars at 1974 exchange rates. *Source:* Same as Section B, page 96.

You can believe that it is America that is leading the way to the world's destruction. But if so, most of the other countries are willing followers. Don't assume that everyone elsewhere is sensible.

If you're going to trade in currencies, you should be as prepared to sell other currencies short as you are to sell the dollar short.

WHERE WE ARE NOW

The following pages will give you an indication of how the major currencies stood in June 1978. The table on page 233 provides a summary of the PPP positions of the five most important currencies, and the current indications of future trends. The table on pages 234 and 235 shows the "Vital Statistics" for the twenty-three major currencies—monetary and price inflation rates, gold backing, and past price changes.

Chapter 32 lists a number of sources for updating this information.

PURCHASING POWER PARITIES
FOR SELECTED CURRENCIES

Currency	As of	PPP	Price 6-30-78	Potential Change	Inflation Rate Difference
British pound	May 1978	$1.5528	$1.8615	− 16.6%	− 1.6%
Canadian dollar	March 1978	.9436	.8897	+ 6.1%	+ 1.8%
German mark	May 1978	.4487	.4825	− 7.0%	+ 9.2%
Japanese yen	April 1978	.003911	.004885	− 19.9%	+ 10.0%
Swiss franc	June 1978	.4723	.5382	− 12.2%	+ 11.7%

As of: Month for which latest wholesale price inflation information was available, and so the month for which the purchasing power calculation was made.

PPP: The Purchasing Power Parity created by the data available at the "as of" date. This is the currency's fundamental price objective, as dictated by the Purchasing Power Parity theory.

Price 6-30-78: Actual price of the currency (in U.S. dollars) on June 30, 1978.

Potential Change: The percentage price change necessary to bring the actual price to the PPP level from its June 30 price.

Inflation Rate Difference: The difference between the currency's most recent 12-month wholesale price inflation rate and the rate in the United States. This provides an estimate of the long-term trend dominating the currency's price movement. A plus (+) symbol means the country's inflation rate is lower than that of the U.S.

Note: As the table indicates, all these currencies (except the Canadian dollar) were overpriced as of June 30, 1978. This suggested that they would be subject to price declines in the near future. However, all the currencies (except the British pound and perhaps the Canadian dollar) had favorable long-term inflation differentials. This suggested that, after the potential short-term declines, they would resume their long-term upward trends.

Sources of data: News releases and publications of the central banks involved; *International Herald Tribune.*

Figures may not agree because of rounding.

VITAL STATISTICS FOR MAJOR CURRENCIES

Currency	Gold Backing @ $180	Money M₁	Money M₂	Price Consumer	Price Wholesale	Price 6-30-78	Change Since 6-30-77	Change Since 6-30-70
Australian dollar	10.6%	4.9%[2]	5.0%[2]	8.2%[2]	7.6%[2]	1.1490	+ 2.6%	+ 3.3%
Austrian schilling	37.5%	5.0%[4]	10.8%[4]	3.9%	− 0.5%[4]	.06692	+ 15.3%	+ 73.5%
Belgian franc	34.4%	9.4%[12]	9.1%[12]	3.7%[6]	− 3.3%	.03030	+ 9.3%	+ 50.5%
British pound	9.0%	37.6%[5]	25.5%[5]	7.4%[6]	9.5%	1.8615	+ 8.2%	− 22.3%
Canadian dollar	14.8%	8.5%[6]	9.3%[6]	9.0%	5.8%[3]	.8897	− 5.7%	− 8.0%
Danish krone	3.4%	3.9%	6.3%	10.8%	4.3%	.1773	+ 6.9%	+ 33.0%
Finnish markka	6.9%	6.4%	13.2%	9.0%[3]	3.3%[4]	.2353	− 4.5%	− 1.2%
French franc	15.9%	11.4%[12]	13.9%[12]	9.0%	0.9%[3]	.2223	+ 9.4%	+ 22.7%
German mark	20.8%	13.5%[5]	9.9%[5]	2.5%[6]	− 1.4%	.4825	+ 12.7%	+ 75.2%
Hong Kong dollar	0.0%	25.1%	23.3%	4.3%[3]	N.A.	.2152	+ 0.5%	+ 30.3%
Italian lira	14.5%	18.7%[11]	20.3%[11]	12.2%[4]	8.2%	.001170	+ 3.6%	− 26.4%
Japanese yen	1.5%	11.2%[4]	12.7%[4]	3.5%	− 2.1%[6]	.004885	+ 30.7%	+ 75.2%
Mexican peso	3.8%[2]	31.1%	37.6%[67]	17.5%[3]	18.2%[3]	.04384	+ 1.4%	− 45.2%
Netherlands guilder	38.0%	10.3%	11.0%	3.5%	3.6%[2]	.4479	+ 10.9%	+ 62.4%
New Zealand dollar	0.2%	3.6%[2]	18.5%[2]	14.6%[2]	14.2%[11]	1.0335	+ 7.0%	− 7.0%
Norwegian krone	2.8%	8.3%	15.2%	7.7%	3.5%[4]	.1849	− 1.5%	+ 32.2%
Portuguese escudo	75.4%[4]	16.6%[26]	17.0%[26]	6.1%[4]	33.1%[1]	.02191	− 15.1%	− 37.0%

		— Inflation —				— Currency Prices —		
	Gold Backing @ $180	Money		Price			Change Since	Change Since
Currency		M₁	M₂	Consumer	Wholesale	Price 6-30-78	6-30-77	6-30-70
Singapore dollar	N.A.	10.1%[2]	8.4%[2]	5.1%[4]	4.6%[1]	.4311	+ 6.4%	+ 31.9%
South African rand	33.9%	5.1%[4]	11.9%[4]	9.5%	9.3%	1.1522	+ 0.3%	- 17.2%
Spanish peseta	7.5%[4]	17.8%[4]	16.8%[4]	21.7%[4]	12.8%[3]	.01270	- 10.3%	- 11.4%
Swedish krona	13.5%	12.8%[5]	14.8%[5]	11.4%	8.5%[4]	.2186	- 3.7%	+ 13.5%
Swiss franc	47.9%	16.7%[4]	9.9%[4]	1.1%[6]	3.6%[6]	.5382	+ 32.7%	+132.3%
U.S. dollar	14.3%	7.9%[6]	8.7%[6]	7.0%	7.7%[6]	—	—	—
Average of all	**17.6%**	**12.9%**	**14.3%**	**8.2%**	**6.6%**	**—**	**+ 5.3%**	**+ 20.9%**

[1] As of January 1978
[2] As of February 1978
[3] As of March 1978
[4] As of April 1978
[5] As of May 1978
[6] As of June 1978
[11] As of November 1977
[12] As of December 1977
[26] As of December 1976
[67] As of June 1977
N.A. = Not available

EXPLANATION

Gold Backing @ $180: The percentage of the nation's money supply (M₁) that is covered by the government's gold supply, when the gold supply is valued at $180 per ounce. Figures are for May 1978 unless footnoted otherwise.

Inflation Rates: Change over previous 12 months.

M₁: Currency outside of banks plus demand deposits at commercial banks. Figures are for March 1978 unless footnoted otherwise.

M₂: Savings accounts at commercial banks plus M₁. Figures are for March 1978 unless footnoted otherwise.

Currency Price Changes: Change in currency's price from the dates shown through June 30, 1978. A plus symbol (+) means the currency appreciated against the U.S. dollar.

Average of all: Unweighted average of all the currencies for which information is shown.

Sources of data: International Monetary Fund *International Financial Statistics,* July 1978; Union Bank of Switzerland *Foreign Exchange News,* various issues; *International Herald Tribune,* July 1, 1978; *The Wall Street Journal,* July 3, 1978.

17

SILVER

SILVER SHOULD BE THE EASIEST OF THE HARD-MONEY INVEST-
ments to analyze. In contrast to gold or currencies, it's possible to find statistics on both the demand for silver and the
production of it. With these statistics, one should be able to
learn just what the market is doing.

Unfortunately, it doesn't work out that way. The published
statistics are slippery and turn out to be only informed
guesses. And there are important segments of the market for
which there are no statistics at all.

As I described in Chapter 5, the U.S. government bought
silver for over a century to hold the price up, and in the
process acquired a hoard of two billion ounces. Later, that
hoard was sold off—in order to keep the price down.

The low price encouraged industrial uses of silver that
wouldn't have been economical on so large a scale if prices
had been higher. Since the production of silver is relatively
static, regardless of the price, silver consumption grew while
production lagged behind.

So long as the government made up the difference, the
industrial use of silver could continue to grow. But now the
government has dropped out as a supplier, and the world
must make do with less. The deficit between production and
consumption is being met (at progressively higher prices) by

using up existing stockpiles—a large part of which is in the hands of investors who bought the silver the U.S. government sold during the 1960s.

As that "above-ground" supply is gradually depleted, the price inches upward. Well, it's not so much inching as a combination of sitting and jumping. The silver price sits quietly for a while, then jumps forward, then sits again. The reason for this frog-like pattern isn't hard to understand, and we'll discuss it shortly.

The big mystery in the silver market is the size of the above-ground supply. Almost everyone who investigates the silver market comes up with a firm idea of the size or availability of the above-ground supply, but these firm estimates are all different. Someday, the answer will be obvious; for now, there is no one who really knows.

There are three possible answers to the mystery of the above-ground supply:

1. The available supply will be exhausted soon (within two or three years), causing silver to shoot upward from its present range of $5 to $6 to a level far higher—perhaps between $10 and $25.

2. The available supply will keep the market well stocked for many years to come, and the price will be quite stable, perhaps rising in line with general price inflation.

3. While the supply is unknown, the stockpiles will be made available to consumers only at progressively higher prices. Silver will continue to rise for many years—not dramatically, but at a rate that's faster than for most other prices.

I lean toward the third opinion. I believe that silver will continue to rise, but the rise may never be as dramatic as many people expect, or as I once expected. Even if it isn't, it should still provide a decent return in an era when very few other investments have that potential. In addition, silver is less vulnerable to government interference than most investments.

Whatever the case, I believe it's possible to take advantage of periodic silver rallies. So you don't have to swear allegiance to one of the three opinions I've outlined.

In this chapter, I'll explain what is known about the silver situation, and I'll describe the investment media for owning silver. In Part V, I'll suggest tactics that can be used to move in and out of silver as conditions dictate.

We'll begin by reviewing briefly the record of production and consumption, and what is known about the available supplies. As we do so, bear in mind that the figures for silver are all very tentative.

Handy & Harman, the New York silver dealer, is the principal clearinghouse for worldwide silver statistics. All figures given in this chapter, unless otherwise noted, are from Handy & Harman's *The Silver Market 1977* and *The Silver Market 1973*. Each year's market review normally contains extensive revisions of previous years' figures, indicating that the numbers should not be regarded as precise.

CONSUMPTION

The consumption of silver can be divided between industrial use and coinage.

Industrial Use

The biggest use of silver is in photographic film. But silver also has properties that make it especially useful in small electrical circuitry and for certain types of soldering and brazing. Silver is also used in mirrors, batteries, and bearings, and as a catalyst—in addition to its better-known uses in jewelry and silverware.

In all but the last two applications, silver represents a small part of the cost of the end product. As a result, the price of silver doesn't exert much influence on the amount that's used—unlike the case with other raw materials. Substitutes for silver would become attractive only at much higher silver prices.

The annual consumption of silver has been little affected

by a price rise from $1.29 in 1971 to $5.40 in 1978. Instead, industrial consumption has risen and fallen with the cycle of general business activity.

The table on page 240 shows this pattern—with industrial use (line 1) rising above the norm during the economic expansion of 1972 and 1973, and then declining in the following years.

Coinage

Surprisingly, the world's governments still devote 20 to 40 million ounces yearly for coinage—even though no country uses silver coins as hand-to-hand money. Instead, governments attempt to raise revenue by selling special issues of coins—such as the Canadian commemorative coins for the 1976 Olympic Games.

The amount used for coinage (line 2 on the table) is no more than 10% of total consumption.

PRODUCTION AND SALVAGE

The primary source of silver is production from mines, but this is augmented by the recovery of silver from the developing of film and from salvage.

New Production

About 75% of the world's newly mined silver is a by-product of copper, lead, and zinc. Because the value of the silver coming from a mine might be as little as 2% or 3% of the mine's overall production, the price of silver has very little effect on the amount of silver produced. It is the price of copper, lead, or zinc that determines how much silver will come from a mine. In addition, silver deposits are concentrated on the surface of the earth; deeper mining for the other metals yields progressively less silver.

THE SILVER MARKET, 1969-1977
(millions of ounces)

	1977	1976	1975	1974	1973	1972	1971	1970	1969
Consumption									
1. Industrial[1]	389.0	399.2	366.0	424.0	477.8	389.9	351.4	338.9	350.6
2. Coinage[2]	22.0	30.0	38.8	27.9	29.2	38.4	27.2	26.9	40.0
3. Total Consumption	**411.0**	**429.2**	**404.8**	**451.9**	**507.0**	**427.3**	**378.6**	**365.8**	**390.6**
Production									
4. Newly Mined[2]	248.0	246.7	238.3	239.4	253.7	245.7	245.1	255.6	241.3
5. Salvage[3]	80.0	76.2	73.4	65.7	60.4	45.3	35.0	18.3	14.6
6. Total Production	**328.0**	**322.9**	**311.7**	**305.1**	**314.1**	**291.0**	**280.1**	**273.9**	**255.9**
7. Production-Consumption									
Deficit	**83.0**	**106.3**	**93.1**	**146.8**	**192.9**	**136.3**	**98.5**	**91.9**	**134.7**
Deficit Covered by:									
8. Government Sales[4]	5.4	8.3	21.1	11.8	52.9	12.3	7.5	77.7	108.4
9. Investor Sales[5]	33.0	35.0	19.0	93.0	101.0	105.0	75.0	(15.0)	(10.0)
10. Sales from India	44.6	63.0	53.0	42.0	39.0	19.0	16.0	16.0	25.0
11. Sales from U.S.S.R.	N.A.	N.A.	N.A.	N.A.	N.A.	N.A.	N.A.	13.2	11.3
12. Average Price	$4.623	4.353	4.419	4.708	2.558	1.685	1.546	1.771	1.791

[1]For non-communist countries only. Includes private mints.

[2]For non-communist countries only.

[3]When salvage by an industrial consumer is reused within the company, neither the salvage nor the second consumption is counted on this table.

[4]Mostly from U.S. government.

[5]Excess of investor sales over investor purchases. For 1970 and 1969, investor purchases exceeded investor sales.

N.A. = Information not available. U.S.S.R. sales are included in investor sales, but specific amounts are unknown.

In some cases, figures may not agree because of rounding.

Source: Handy & Harman's annual review of the silver market.

As the table on page 240 indicates, there has been very little change in the amounts of new silver flowing to the market (line 4). Since 1969, annual production has ranged from 238 to 256 million ounces—a variation of only 7% during nine years.

It is unlikely that the production of new silver will increase enough to ease the world shortage.

Salvage

The recovery of silver is a different story. Higher prices have made salvage more profitable. From 15 million ounces in 1969, the yearly salvage yield (line 5 on the table) has increased to 80 million ounces in 1977—with every intervening year showing an increase.

In future years, at higher silver prices, we can expect the amount of silver recovered to increase.

EXISTING SUPPLIES

The yearly deficit between production and consumption, of around 100 million ounces (line 7), is offset by sales from existing stockpiles. The yearly amounts entering the market from each source are shown on lines 8 through 11 of the table on page 240.

The table on page 242 shows the depletion of these stocks since 1968. It is estimated that the overall above-ground supply has declined from two billion ounces in 1968 to one billion ounces at the end of 1977.

U.S. Government

At the end of 1977 the U.S. government owned 185 million ounces of silver.

Of the total, 39 million ounces were held by the U.S.

ABOVE-GROUND SUPPLIES OF SILVER
(End of Each Year — Millions of Ounces)

	1977	1976	1975	1974	1973	1972	1971	1970	1969	1968
U.S. Government[1]	185.2	185.6	186.9	189.6	190.6	191.5	193.8	196.3	264.0	372.4
Other Governments	77.0	82.0	89.0	107.4	118.2	170.2	180.2	185.2	195.2	195.2
Users' Inventories	33.4[2]	30.6	34.6	35.0[3]	35.0[3]	35.0[3]	35.0[3]	35.0[3]	35.0[3]	35.0[3]
Investor Holdings[4]	418.9	454.7	485.7	504.3	597.3	698.3	803.3	878.3	863.3	853.3
Indian Silver Available[5]	300.0	344.6	407.6	460.6	502.6	541.6	560.6	576.6	592.6	617.6
Total	**1,014.5**	**1,097.5**	**1,203.8**	**1,296.9**	**1,443.7**	**1,636.6**	**1,772.9**	**1,871.4**	**1,950.1**	**2,073.5**

[1] Includes strategic stockpile.
[2] As of September, 1977.
[3] Estimated by author.
[4] Includes holdings of U.S. silver coins.
[5] Calculated by using Charles Stahl's estimate for 1977, and adding Handy & Harman's estimates of amounts sold in previous years.

In some cases, figures may not agree because of rounding.

Source of data: Handy & Harman's annual reviews of the silver market, except where noted otherwise.

Treasury for future minting of collectors' coins. The government uses in the neighborhood of one million ounces yearly for this purpose.

Another 6 million ounces were held by the Defense Department for use in the development of weapons.

The biggest part of the government's holdings were the 139.5 million ounces in the strategic stockpile. The stockpile is meant to hold commodities that might be needed during wartime.

The strategic stockpile is, not surprisingly, a political football. A proposal to unload silver is a feature of every session of Congress, along with similar proposals aimed at other commodities. Industrial users want the silver to be sold, because that would lower the price of their raw material. Miners who produce silver want the government stockpile kept off the market. So far, the producers have had their way, but this could change.

Foreign Governments

The holdings of foreign governments are estimated by Handy & Harman each year, but the figures are not precise. The latest estimate is that foreign governments own about 77 million ounces.

User Inventories

The inventories of U.S. industrial users are relatively static, in the range of 30 to 35 million ounces. Foreign industrial users undoubtedly hold inventories, too, but I've seen no estimates.

In a severe depression, or at some very high price, users might allow their inventories to drop by 10 or 20 million ounces. Otherwise, inventories contribute nothing to the supply of consumable silver.

Investor Holdings

Handy & Harman estimates that investors held around 419 million ounces of silver at the end of 1977. The distribution was as follows (in millions of ounces):

N.Y. Commodity Exchange warehouses	68.5
Chicago Board of Trade warehouses	62.2
London Metal Exchange warehouses	19.2
Unreported bullion holdings	22.0
U.S. silver coins	220.0
Foreign silver coins	27.0
Total	*418.9*

As the table on page 242 shows, investor holdings have decreased every year since 1970. These sales have helped to offset the production-consumption deficit.

Indian Silver

The biggest question mark about silver is the amount available from India.

India's currency was backed by silver until 1927, and so large amounts of silver were imported (very little is produced in India). Charles Stahl of the Economic News Agency estimates that 2.9 billion ounces were imported between 1874 and 1932.[1]

Handy & Harman estimates that Indian industry currently consumes about 17 million ounces per year. The rest of the silver has been consumed, is being held in the form of bullion, has been smuggled out or lost, or has been made into simple jewelry as a store of value. Most observers believe that bullion holdings are minor. A good part of the jewelry would probably be available to the world if the price were right or if the need to sell were great enough.

[1] *Green's Commodity Market Comments,* Nov. 30, 1977.

Charles Stahl estimates the net Indian silver holdings available to the world at 300 million ounces. In the table on page 242, I have used this figure for 1977, and then computed the earlier years by adding the amounts Handy & Harman has estimated were sold from Indian stocks.

Supply Summary

As the table on page 240 indicates, silver consumption has outrun production by about 100 million ounces in all but the boom years of 1972–1974, when the deficit was larger. The deficit is offset by sales of silver from governments and investors, and from India.

We've reviewed the available figures covering these sources of supply. The meaning of the figures is a matter of controversy.

RECENT HISTORY

The daily price chart on page 246 begins in 1967, when the U.S. government gave up trying to hold the price at $1.29. The government continued to sell limited amounts of silver until 1970.

The market was so glutted with government silver that a genuine rally couldn't get off the ground until 1971. Then the price began the super-bull trend that's still in progress.

As the price moved upward, it stalled at various levels along the way. At each stalling point, sales from investors were large enough to offset the deficit.

1974 Rally

At the beginning of 1974, silver was ready to move upward again—this time from the $3.00 range. At the same time, the falling dollar, the sick stock market, and poor economic con-

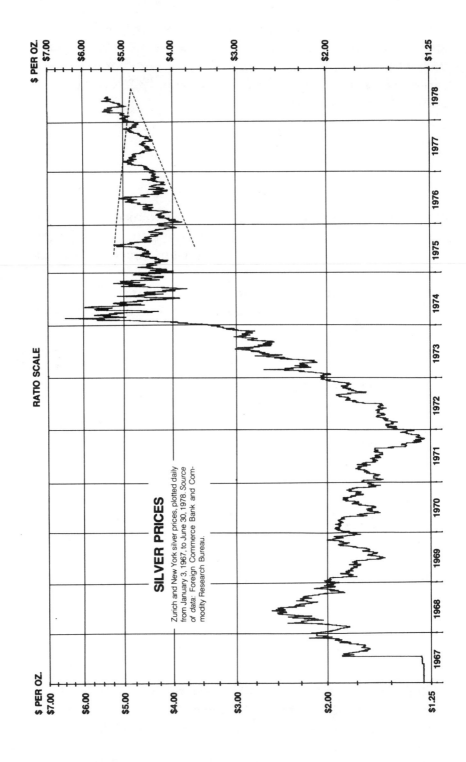

RATIO SCALE

SILVER PRICES

Zurich and New York silver prices, plotted daily from January 3, 1967, to June 30, 1978. Source of data: Foreign Commerce Bank and Commodity Research Bureau.

ditions had most investors looking for an alternative. Many found it in silver. Their purchases caused the price to leap to $6.50 in four months.

The $6.50 price was unsustainable at that time, and the price dropped back to the $4 to $5 range. This left thousands of investors holding silver purchased at prices between $4.75 and $5.50 (where most of the trading had taken place).

When the price retreated to under $5.00, many of these investors abandoned their dreams and hoped only for a price rise that would allow them to break even. Consequently, the market was well stocked with sellers whenever the price approached $5.00. The result of the 1974 excitement was that the price remained dormant for four years—mostly fluctuating between $4.00 and $5.00.

The period from 1975 to 1978 is characterized by the dotted triangle that's been added to the graph on page 246. During that period, the price moved up and down within a restricted range that grew progressively narrower. The price continued to fluctuate, but the declines tended to halt at gradually higher prices. The rising low-points define the lower line of the triangle.

Similarly, the rises ended at gradually lower prices. The falling tops define the upper line of the triangle. Whereas the first swing carried the price through a range $1.50 wide (from $5.25 to $3.75), the last swing was only $.45 wide (from $4.40 to $4.85).

I interpret this pattern to mean that many investors were losing patience and lowering their objectives for getting out (the declining tops), while, at the same time, the number of these desperate investors was shrinking (the rising low-points).

Finally, in early 1978, the market ran out of $5.00 sellers, and the price was able to work higher. However, there was still a lot of silver available between $5.00 and $5.50, no doubt from 1974 buyers who had waited out the entire period.

Although I can't tell you what happened next (because the book had gone to press), it was my guess that the price would break through the $5.50 level sometime during the summer of 1978. Once through that level, there would be much less selling resistance. And so, if my forecast was correct, silver may be over $6.00 by the fall of 1978.

Future Moves

Where this rally will end, I can't say. But it isn't difficult to foresee how future rallies will be needed to cause industrial consumption to fall to the level of production.

From time to time the market will run out of sellers at the current price. The price will begin to move up. This will attract the attention of new investors who will jump aboard the bandwagon. Their purchases will send the price up to an unsupportable level.

The price will retreat from its high and then stabilize. The new price will be above that which preceded the rally, but considerably lower than the rally's high point. The retreat will leave a number of investors in a loss position.

Many will wait with their silver until the price returns to the level at which they purchased. At that price, they'll welcome the opportunity to get out without a loss, and their sales will help to hold the price back. When they have finally run out of silver, the price will move to a new peak—and the entire process will be repeated.

Only one feature will change. The periods during which the price stalls should be shorter from one sequence to the next. This is because the amount of silver in the investment markets is constantly shrinking. Thus, fewer investors will have an emotional interest in any given price.

SILVER'S FUTURE

Most observers of the silver market are agreed that consumption outruns production, that the deficit must be made up from above-ground stocks, that these stocks will be exhausted someday, and that the price will eventually be higher. The disagreements come from estimates of the above-ground supply available to the market—which means the controversy is over the length of time required to use up these stocks. If it will take twenty years, the matter appears to be of no importance to an investor today.

However, I believe the argument misses one important point. The market isn't going to run out of silver suddenly on a specific day in the future—two or twenty years from now. It is gradually running out of silver every day.

The cost of luring silver from the remaining holders will get progressively higher, which is what eventually will force industrial users to cut their consumption. The price will move up step by step until the world's consumption is reduced to the level of new production. Then the price will level off— and future price movements will result from future conditions, just as with any other commodity.

So the argument isn't whether silver will rise in price. Rather, it's whether the increase will be rapid enough to make an investment worthwhile.

I believe the long-term pattern will show a gradual increase. But, just as in the past, the price will move upward in occasional spurts, with relative tranquillity in between.

The big rallies could be relatively brief (as with the four-month rally in 1974), and there may be fairly lengthy periods between the rallies (four years from 1974 to 1978). If you think you will be able to spot the rallies at the start, you may not want to hold silver straight through. In Chapter 29, I'll offer some suggestions for moving in and out.

How Long?

How long could this pattern continue in the silver market? That depends upon how long the above-ground stocks hold out. And that, of course, is what the argument is all about.

The answer will hinge on three variables:

1. How much silver really exists in India, and how much of it will be available to the market, and at what price?

2. Will the U.S. government sell any or all of its silver stockpile?

3. What is the minimum permanent amount that investors will want to hold?

No one can answer these questions with certainty. But I don't consider the answers to be critical because I believe the price will move in a long-term upward pattern while the stocks are being depleted. In addition, it's possible to stay out of the silver market during the pauses, so that one's capital doesn't have to be tied up continuously.

But you may have a different view; you may feel that it's important to know how long the silver stockpiles will last. For this reason, I've constructed the table on page 251. It shows the length of time required to use up the available supplies—assuming different combinations of the variables.

There are two ways of looking at the Indian situation. One is to accept the estimate that 300 million ounces (or some other amount) are potentially available. The other is to disregard the amount available, and to assume instead that approximately 50 million ounces will be exported by India each year—enough to cover about half the yearly deficit. The table lets you choose between these two approaches.

Another variable concerns the U.S. government's stockpile. The table shows projections with and without the government's 185 million ounces available.

And lastly, the table lets you choose between the possibility that all investor stocks and user inventories (currently about 450 million ounces) will eventually be sold, and the possibility that investors and users will always hold at least 150 million ounces (which I consider more probable).

But, as I've said, I'm not sure that any of these figures is important. The market is running out of silver. We don't know how long it will take, but as long as the price moves upward while it's happening, the duration isn't critical.

YEARS OF SILVER
AVAILABLE TO THE MARKET
(Dependent upon Various Conditions)

Condition	Available[1] Supply	Yearly[1] Deficit	Year Stockpiles Run Out
If there are 300 million ounces available from India			
& the U.S. government sells its stockpile			
& all user inventories & investor holdings are sold	900	100	1986
& inventories & investor holdings are reduced to 150	750	100	1985
& the U.S. government doesn't sell any silver			
& all user inventories & investor holdings are sold	715	100	1984
& inventories & investor holdings are reduced to 150	565	100	1983
If Indian stockpile is disregarded but India continues to supply 50 million ounces per year forever			
& the U.S. government sells its stockpile			
& all user inventories & investor holdings are sold	600	50	1989
& inventories & investor holdings are reduced to 150	450	50	1986
& the U.S. government doesn't sell any silver			
& all user inventories & investor holdings are sold	415	50	1985
& inventories & investor holdings are reduced to 150	265	50	1982

[1] Millions of ounces

POTENTIAL PROBLEMS

Everything I've said up to now assumes a continuation of present economic conditions—that is, the boom-and-bust monetary cycles that we've had since World War II.

There are three possibilities we should examine: (1) a continuation of the boom-and-bust cycles, with further recessions on the scale of the 1974–1975 recession; (2) a runaway inflation, and (3) a deflationary depression.

Recession

Industrial consumption increases during the boom years of a monetary cycle and then falls off during the recession years. This can be seen in the table on page 240.

However, the desire of investors to hold silver apparently increases during the recession years. As a result, the price jumps to an unsupportable level and then declines to a quiet trading range.

The long-term price uptrend isn't stopped by the recession. But the pattern of the uptrend changes—from a slow, steady increase to a pattern of occasional spurts.

Runaway Inflation

In a runaway inflation, all prices rise drastically—but some rise more than others.

Productivity in all areas is impaired, and so business profits and stock prices fail to rise by as much as prices of food and other consumption goods. Demand centers more and more upon absolute necessities.

Silver isn't a necessity; hungry people won't buy sterling silver, jewelry, and electrical circuits. I wouldn't expect silver to be among the price leaders during a runaway inflation.

If there's an increased demand for silver as a store of value, it will be registered by silver coins, not silver bullion. Coins would sell for more than their silver content, but the price of silver bullion probably wouldn't be affected by the demand for silver as money.

I don't believe that silver bullion will be a bad investment during a runaway inflation; there will be others that will probably do much worse. But I don't see it as first class. Gold and stable foreign currencies should do better.

Since it would take many years for industrial activity to return to normal after a runaway inflation, silver's super-bull trend would be brought to an end with the conclusion of the runaway inflation.

Deflationary Depression

As I stated in Chapter 3, I believe a deflation within the next three years is a greater possibility than a runaway inflation.

It's of no value to examine past deflationary periods for indications of how silver would behave, because silver wasn't in a free market prior to 1970. In the depression of the 1930s, silver prices were chosen by the government for political reasons.

In addition, silver's industrial use was limited mostly to jewelry and silverware until World War II; coinage was by far the larger function. Since the war, silver has become a full-fledged industrial metal.

We can only assume that the industrial demand for silver would drop rapidly during a deflation. And so it makes sense to avoid holding silver through such a depression. There will be buying opportunities for silver (and for many other things) at the bottom of the depression.

EVENTUAL PRICE

The statistics on production, consumption, and stockpiles are neither complete enough nor accurate enough to confirm any estimate of silver's eventual price.

But if no deflation occurs before the price reaches equilibrium, it would seem that silver would have to rise to at least

$15.00 per ounce. On the way to reaching a stable level, the price would probably go as much as $10.00 higher and then come back to equilibrium.

Many silver bulls have pointed to the historical ratio of 16 to 1; the price of gold traditionally has been 16 times the price of silver. They expect this ratio to reappear in the future. In early 1978, the ratio was 34 to 1, so a recurrence of the 16-to-1 ratio would require that silver appreciate much faster than gold.

I see no reason to be concerned with this. The 16-to-1 ratio was arbitrarily chosen by the U.S. government in 1792. It's true that prices had often been close to that ratio, but there's no reason for the ratio to be valid today. Silver's function is quite different from what it was in 1792, although gold's has remained substantially the same.

Eventually the ratio may be 30 to 1, 10 to 1, or anything else. Gold and silver must each be evaluated on its own merits —with no concern for the relationship between their two prices.

INVESTMENT MEDIA

The comments I made in Chapter 15 concerning gold stocks, gold rarities, and gold futures apply as well to their silver counterparts, so they don't need to be repeated here.

Silver Coins

American circulating coins minted before 1965 had a silver content of 90%. The Kennedy half-dollars minted from 1965 to 1970 were 40% silver. All other circulating coins minted after 1964 contain no silver.[2]

2 Since 1971, the U.S. government has minted a 40%-silver dollar in limited quantities. Although technically legal tender, it is sold to collectors at premium prices and is more like a medallion than money. Any "silver" dollar you find in circulation contains no silver, unless it is dated before 1936—in which case, don't spend it.

U.S. silver coins, both 90% and 40%, are traded in the investment markets. The trading unit is a *bag*—with each bag containing coins that amount to $1,000 in face value. Thus a bag will contain 2,000 half-dollars, 4,000 quarters, or 10,000 dimes.

A bag of 90%-silver coins will contain 720 ounces of silver—within an ounce or two either way. And a bag of 40%-silver half-dollars will contain about 295 ounces of silver.

The prices of the coins fluctuate in close step with the price of silver bullion. However, because the coins are still legal tender (like paper money), no bag can be worth less than $1,000—no matter how low the price of silver might drop.

The legal-tender status of the coins puts a floor under the price. But as the price rises, the floor falls further behind and becomes less important. The floor for the 90% coins corresponds to a silver price of $1.38 per ounce—since at that price a bag of 90% coins will contain exactly $1,000 worth of silver. For 40% coins, the floor is reached at a silver price of $3.38.

The $1.38 floor was worth something to owners of the 90% coins until early 1974. The coins usually sold at a premium of about 2% to 5% over the value of the silver they contained. But when the price of silver passed $4.00, the floor became meaningless; from then on, the coins were valuable only as a source of silver bullion. Since the coins have to be melted and refined before they can be used as bullion, the coins moved to a discount of about 2% under the value of their silver content.

The $3.38 floor was still important enough for the 40% coins to have a premium of 5% in early 1978, when silver was still below $5.00. But the 1978 rally has already caused the coins' premium to drop to about 3%. And if silver is above $6.00 when you read this, the premium on the 40% coins will probably have disappeared; the coins could be selling at a discount of about 2% or so.

After silver reaches its equilibrium price, the coins should continue rising, so that they once again trade at a premium—

because of their rarity. But the rarity won't be of the same degree as for numismatic coins, nor will it appear suddenly. The silver coins will appreciate, but at a slow rate.

They'll sell at a premium because some investors will want to keep them as a hedge against runaway inflation. The coins would be useful as money if the paper currency system were to break down, because the coins offer silver in a recognizable form and weight.

I believe that anyone who takes the threat of runaway inflation seriously should keep a small supply of these coins on hand, even after silver reaches its equilibrium price. A "small supply" might be anywhere from one-half bag to five or ten bags—depending upon the size of your family, your ability to provide safe storage for the coins, and the seriousness with which you view the threat.

The coins should be kept in a safe-deposit box, or at home if you believe you have a safe place for them. They can be purchased from coin dealers in the United States, but they shouldn't be left in storage with a dealer. Coin dealers have been the object of many government crusades, and some have gone out of business as a result of the harassment. Others have gone under completely on their own.

U.S. silver coins are generally available only in the United States.

Silver Bullion

To speculate on a rise in silver, it is best to purchase silver bullion. The two principal retail sources (outside of the futures markets) are U.S. coin dealers and Swiss banks.

It's impractical for most people to store silver bullion themselves, so silver purchased in the U.S. would have to be stored with a dealer. For the reasons just stated, I prefer not to do that.

It is better, I believe, to buy and store silver at a Swiss bank. Costs are nominal. There's usually a 1% commission for a purchase or a sale, and the spread between the buying

SILVER COIN PREMIUMS

Date	Bullion/Oz.	90% Coins		40% Coins	
		Price/Bag	Premium	Price/Bag	Premium
December 26, 1975	$4.258	$2,978	− 2.9%	$1,358	+ 8.1%
December 31, 1976	4.355	3,035	− 3.2%	1,355	+ 5.5%
December 30, 1977	4.765	3,343	− 2.6%	1,440	+ 2.4%
June 30, 1978	5.23	3,703	− 1.7%	1,585	+ 2.7%

The *premium* is the percentage by which the price of a coin exceeds the value of the silver in the coin. A minus symbol (−) indicates that the coin is selling at a discount from its silver value.

Source: Monex International Ltd.

and selling prices is never more than 1%. Annual storage costs run about ⅓% of the silver's value.

Swiss banks will be discussed in more detail in Chapter 21, and the names of banks that handle silver will be given in Chapter 32.

Silver Options

In 1977, Mocatta Metals Corp. of New York began making a market in silver options—similar to the Valeurs White Weld gold options described in Chapter 15. However, the marketing of these options has been sidetracked by the regulatory problems described in Chapter 15.

If the options are available when you read this, they can be a useful way of taking a position in silver at times when you believe a new rally is underway or imminent. You can inquire at a Swiss bank or a securities or commodities broker in the U.S.

SILVER AS AN INVESTMENT

I hope I've made it clear that I have no definite answers to the many questions concerning silver's future.

However, the existing stockpile hasn't held the price down so far. Silver is in a long-term bull market, caused by an imbalance between consumption and production. How long it will take for this imbalance to be eliminated is a matter of conjecture, but it's clear that the trend is up.

The uptrend has been irregular so far, and it should continue to be so. There will be hectic rallies occasionally, followed by declines that erase part of the gain, and then periods of stability.

If you hold silver through thick and thin, the odds are in favor of your earning a good average annual profit. But you'll do better yet if you can buy near the beginning of each rally and sell near the end.

In addition, such a trading strategy would remove you from the silver market after the final rally—even if you don't know that it *is* the last rally. And the strategy would have you out of the silver market during a deflation, in which the price might drop by 50% or more.

In Chapter 29, I'll suggest tactics for moving in and out of the market.

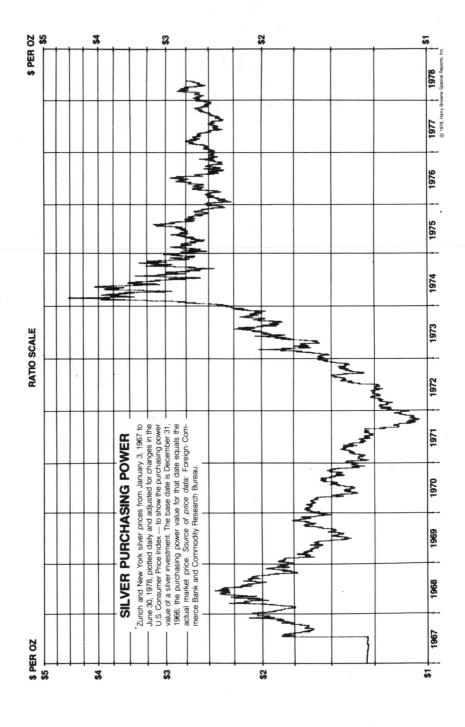

RATIO SCALE

$ PER OZ

SILVER PURCHASING POWER

Zurich and New York silver prices from January 3, 1967 to June 30, 1978, plotted daily and adjusted for changes in the U.S. Consumer Price Index — to show the purchasing power value of a silver investment. The base date is December 31, 1966; the purchasing power value for that date equals the actual market price. Source of price data: Foreign: Commerce Bank and Commodity Research Bureau.

18

COMMODITIES

In Chapter 15 I explained why I believe gold is different from soybeans, pork bellies, tin, and other commodities. Because the demand for gold is a demand to hold it, rather than to use it up, the price is little affected by considerations of production and consumption. The price responds to the world's general level of confidence or uncertainty.

Silver, too, is unique—because of the production-consumption imbalance described in Chapters 5 and 17.

What, then, of other commodities? Are they an appropriate field for part-time investors? It depends.

Commodities in general are appropriate only for an investor who's going to watch them constantly. The big attraction of the commodities market, namely the extreme volatility of prices, is also its biggest danger. You can't expect to keep up with the market unless you're always ready to act.

The profit winners in commodities are mostly full-time commodity investors. Occasionally, a part-time investor strikes it rich. But such a strike can be as dangerous to the winner as a lucky first win at the gambling tables. It can serve merely to intensify the winner's confidence and thereby intensify his later losses.

LEVERAGE

Commodity futures markets in the U.S. allow you to make a large investment with only a tiny deposit. For example, you can acquire a stake in $100,000 worth of a commodity by making a deposit of only $5,000.

It isn't hard to imagine that a favorable price change of only 5% would produce a $5,000 profit, doubling the investment. But, of course, an *un*favorable price change of 5% would wipe out the investment—a possibility many people tell themselves they're prepared to accept when, in reality, they don't believe it can happen.

With such thin margin you can expect things to happen quickly. The price movements of the next few hours or days will be critical. There's nothing wrong with that in itself; the question is one of appropriateness. Is it appropriate for *you* to be in the game? If not, you've found a sure way to lose money.

Leverage doesn't have to be used if you don't want it, however. If you believe the price of a commodity will increase over the next year, you can make what amounts to a cash (nonleveraged) investment by depositing 100% of the contract's value with your broker. For this purpose you can deposit Treasury bills or other interest-earning securities. Or you could put the equivalent of the contract in a bank account or money market fund.

So long as you have cash earmarked for the full value of the contract, a commodity investment is quite similar to any other nonleveraged investment. You can afford to sit out small setbacks that would wipe out an investment made on only 5% margin.

NEW BLOOD

For those who like to gamble, to follow markets closely, and to trade actively, commodities can be an exciting avocation.

But it's foolish to assume that you can enter this market with no background, compete against professionals, and come out ahead. The market is something of a race to analyze trends and take positions first. If you're not at the head of the pack, you won't win.

As you sit in your armchair in the evening, your price graph in one hand and your handbook of charting techniques in the other, trying to come to a decision, more experienced traders (who react intuitively to price movements) have already eliminated the possibilities for profit that you're discovering.

That doesn't mean there's no room for new blood in the market. It's just that you must be prepared for what you're doing, or your new blood will be quickly shed.

You should begin by studying the literature on technical analysis. Then trade on paper (without actually investing money) to develop your skill. Keep track of your trades as though you had put your money on the line, and see how you do.

If your paper investments are successful enough, then start making real investments. But use very little leverage; keep the potential profit or loss small. If your success continues, begin taking larger risks. If you never get to that point, your education will have been time-consuming but not terribly expensive in money.

GOVERNMENT INTERVENTION

One seldom recognized risk in the commodity markets is the threat of government intervention. As the crises get worse, changes in the rules will be more frequent and more startling. I'm sure there are plenty of people in the government who can imagine how handily inflation could be eliminated by ridding the commodity markets of speculators. And I'm sure that there are many other "giant steps for mankind" being planned—and commodity traders may be among those who get stepped on.

I was given a firsthand demonstration of this. In 1971 the

West Coast Commodity Exchange decided to trade futures contracts for gold coins. At the time, it was illegal for Americans to own gold bullion, but it was not illegal to own certain gold coins, including the British sovereign.

Since prices were to be quoted in dollars per ounce, it occurred to me that some traders might fail to allow for the premium that the sovereign commanded over gold bullion. At the current gold price of $40 per ounce, a sovereign was selling, in effect, for $54 per ounce. I thought that the coins might for a while be quoted at something less than $54 per ounce, enabling me to buy a futures contract for less than the coins would cost from a dealer.

On the morning that trading was to begin, I went to the exchange with a floor trader. He was to go to the "pit" when trading began and to report immediately the opening price. Just after the opening bell sounded, he ran over to me and shouted, "They're bidding $59 per ounce."

It took me only a moment to realize that I could *sell* at that price while buying from a dealer at $54 per ounce. I couldn't lose. "Sell short!" I screamed.

During the day the price rose even higher, closing at $62. The rise didn't bother me, because I knew I could simply purchase the coins at a lower price from a dealer and deliver them to fulfill the contract.

The next day the price began to move downward, closing the day at $61.50. I was still $2.50 per ounce behind, but reality was beginning to assert itself.

The following morning I rose early, full of anticipation that the price would plunge sharply as dealers entered the market to sell their coins at prices higher than they could get from retail customers. But the market never opened. Overnight, the government had ruled that trading in British sovereigns was a form of speculation in gold and was not a legitimate "numismatic" investment.

The governors of the exchange met and decided that all contracts would be settled at the previous day's closing price. That meant I would lose $2.50 per ounce. No deliveries would be accepted, so I didn't have the option of covering with coins from a dealer, where I could get them for $54 per ounce. So, instead of making a "certain" $5 per ounce profit, I suffered a $2.50 per ounce loss.

It was an expensive education, but probably a very useful one. Now I'm prepared for anything the government might spring.

PLATINUM

I've been asked often if platinum, as a precious metal, has a special status as an investment—the way gold and silver do.

Gold's special attraction comes from being a store of value for investors all over the world. Silver, to a smaller extent, is also a store of value, but silver's principal attraction is the long-term production-consumption imbalance caused by years of government intervention.

Platinum has no special qualities of this kind. It has never, to the best of my knowledge, been used as getaway money or insurance—although platinum coins and medallions have occasionally been minted. Governments have never played more than an incidental role in the platinum markets.

Platinum is in the same position as any other commodity. At any time, it might be a buy, a sell, or an object of indifference—just like coffee or pork bellies. There are no long-term considerations based upon platinum's status as a precious metal.

COMMODITY FUNDS

There are mutual funds that deal solely in commodities and currencies, just as most mutual funds deal in stocks. As with any other industry, some of these funds do well and others not so well.

If you should believe that the stock market is ready for a general rise, you might take advantage of the rise by investing in a mutual fund that holds stocks. But it would be a mistake to apply the same reasoning to a commodity fund.

Commodity funds are organized to trade, not to hold; and in the commodity markets, it's as easy to go short as it is to buy. Even though you might expect a general increase in commodity prices, the fund in which you invest might expect a drop and so go short. Thus your investment wouldn't be in keeping with your expectation.

You can select a commodity fund by evaluating its record and its philosophy toward the markets, but you can't pick one because you agree with its forecast. An agile commodity trader is prepared to change his mind instantly and bet the other way, so any opinion he gives you early in the morning might not last past lunch.

When you invest in a commodity fund, you aren't investing in commodities, you're investing in the skill of the fund's manager. If your judgment about the manager's skill is correct, you will profit, just as you would from a correct judgment about a commodity. And, of course, if your judgment is incorrect, you will lose. The availability of commodity funds doesn't rescue you from the need to make a correct decision; it merely changes the kind of decision you have to make.

COMMODITIES

Again, my answer to the question of trading in commodity markets is, "It depends."

You shouldn't approach commodities as just one more element in a diversified portfolio. You have to place your capital in the hands of a commodity trader or mutual fund that will make decisions for you, if you can find one that inspires your confidence. Or else you have to think of commodities as a business, requiring skill and attention.

If that's more than you had in mind, just ignore all the excitement and stick to what you know.

19

COLLECTIBLES

You may have read that spectacular prices are being paid for various collectibles—works of art, diamonds, antiques, postage stamps, rare coins, rare guns, or rare anythings. And you may have wondered why you're not exerting yourself to participate in these booming markets.

One very good reason may be that you don't know anything about them. It's a good reason, because these are specialist markets—in which amateur investors trade at a definite disadvantage.

TWO TYPES OF PARTICIPANTS

I can make this clearer by dividing participants in the investment markets into two categories—the professionals and the amateurs.

A professional is an individual who makes his living executing trades, either for his own account or for his customers. The professionals include dealers, brokers, and the floor traders at the stock and commodity exchanges.

The amateur is the outsider for whom trades are often made. He is the investor who goes to the professional in order to make his investment.

The investor who trades full-time is still an amateur—in

that he isn't a part of the profession. He must execute his trades through a professional.

There's no gospel saying that the professionals have to make lots of money and the amateurs have to lose it. For many professionals, their business is simply a business—making an ordinary rate of profit on their capital. As with any business, the more skilled will make big profits—and the less skilled may go bankrupt.

TWO TYPES OF MARKETS

We can carry the analysis further by recognizing that there are two kinds of investment markets, each with amateur and professional participants. I'll refer to them as "public markets" and "specialist markets."

A *public market* is one in which a great deal of pertinent information is available to everyone, including the amateur investor. He can easily obtain current and past prices, trading volume, and fundamental data on the investment. Examples of public markets are stocks, bonds, currencies, and commodities (including gold and silver).

In such a market the investor is on a nearly equal footing with the professional. The amount of information to which only the professional has easy access is relatively insignificant compared with the body of important knowledge available to everyone.

A *specialist market* is one in which the major part of the relevant knowledge is easily available only to the full-time professional. He knows the general climate of supply and demand; he knows the recent prices; he knows which of the many similar investments are doing well and which aren't.

The outside investor knows none of these things—except as he is told by the professional. In other words, a specialist market is one in which the important information is available to the investor only through the professional. Collectibles of all kinds, as well as real estate, trade in specialist markets.

A public market is characterized by the existence of *multiple-copy* investments—what are generally called *fungible* investments. The best example is a share of XYZ company's common stock; one share of XYZ stock is exactly the same as every other share. If you know the value of any one share, you know the value of them all.

On the other hand, there is only one copy of Gainsborough's *Blue Boy*. Knowing its current market value will tell you only a little about the value of other paintings—even of other paintings by Gainsborough.

Thus the price lists that are published for specialist markets will be of no use to you—unless you're a professional. Why, for example, does one painting by Chagall sell for ten times the price of another Chagall of the same size?

Of course there are exceptions, even with the examples I've used. A stock that isn't traded publicly doesn't fulfill the qualifications I've given for a public market. And a collectible of which there are a thousand or more copies (such as a famous postage stamp or rare coin) doesn't fit the description of a specialist market as precisely as an original painting.

Generally, however, collectibles trade in specialist markets and stocks trade in public markets.

SPREADS

Each type of market sets prices in its own way.

In the public markets, a dealer offers both to buy and to sell, and he quotes two prices—the *bid* and *ask* prices—for any item. The bid is the price he'll pay right now for the item. The ask is the price at which he'll sell you one right now. The range between bid and ask is the *spread*.

Bid-ask spreads tend to be small, and the prices themselves tend to be standard from dealer to dealer. The spread is small because every trade in the investment provides an evaluation, or market appraisal, of every other copy of the investment. The prices are standard because every dealer in the investment is trading exactly the same thing.

In the specialist markets, there are no standardized prices because there are no standardized inventories. A dealer can't quote both a price to buy and a price to sell a given item, because he can do only one or the other—buy if he doesn't have the item or sell it if he does have it.

A dealer in a specialist market will buy an item, hoping to sell it eventually for a great deal more than he paid. Unlike a dealer in a public market, who might operate on a spread of 1% to 5%, the dealer in a specialist market may be hoping for a markup of 100% or more on a particular transaction—meaning that he would buy the item back from you for only about half the price you paid.

Thus a dealer in a specialist market resembles an investor. He buys for price appreciation only, with no intention of making a two-way (continuous buying and selling) market.

RELATIVE VALUE OF RELATIVES

It happens that my uncle has been an art dealer for over thirty years. He handles paintings and sculptures for a limited clientele.

If I should be tempted to invest in works of art, I need only think of him. What he knows about art markets, appraisals, historical trends, etc. is completely inaccessible to me—except as he chooses to share what he knows. How could I expect to do as well as he does—without first acquiring the same education?

If he were a gold dealer or an over-the-counter securities dealer, his thirty years' experience wouldn't intimidate me. Most of his knowledge would be available to me or to anyone else.

LIQUIDITY

If you have an interest in a public market, you can look in *The Wall Street Journal* or other newspaper to find recent prices. You can't do this in a collectibles market, because virtually every investment that traded yesterday was a one-of-a-kind item. The list of trades would be endless, and it still wouldn't tell you what your holdings were worth.

The constant availability of price quotations is one of the two basic ingredients of liquidity. An investment is liquid if you can base a change of plan on a realistic price quotation whenever you need to.

And if the quotes are genuine, you have the other ingredient of liquidity, which is the ability to sell the investment promptly at any time—and to do so without paying for your haste. That requirement is only partially met with collectibles. In a time of rapidly falling prices, an investor can sell a stock, a commodity, or a bond at a price not too far from the last price at which the investment traded.

If prices are falling rapidly in a collectibles market, a dealer may prefer not to buy at all. Of course, there's always some price at which he won't refuse to buy—but that price may be only 10% to 50% of what you would expect to receive by your most cautious estimate.

So collectibles markets aren't liquid markets.

BOOMING PRICES

Still it's hard not to be impressed when you hear of the fantastic profits.

Frequently, you can read in the newspaper of a high price paid for a work of art. Possibly the price will be 100% to 500% more than the seller paid only a few years before. Why didn't *you* invest in something like that?

First of all, you may not have the $500,000 or more to invest in the class of items whose sales show up in the newspaper. Any investment you make might be in a different world from the one you're reading about. Do the paintings of Sam Nobody appreciate at the same rate as those of Goya?

Secondly, you're reading of the sale of a one-of-a-kind item. You would have obtained the same investment result only if you had purchased the same item at the same time—in other words, only if you are reading about yourself. A similar, but different, item might have earned a very different profit or no profit at all.

It isn't possible to follow even the general trend of collectibles prices because there's no way to track all the sales and average them out. The published reports of trends are almost always misleading.

For example, one investment newsletter presents a review of investment trends every January and covers a wide variety of markets.

For 1976, the newsletter showed that U.S. common stocks were up by 18%—using the Dow Jones Industrial Average. Gold bullion was down by 4%—using the London daily price fixings.

Turning to the world of collectibles, the newsletter said that surrealist paintings were up by 490%. How was that determined? It seems that the highest price recorded in 1975 had been the $340,000 paid for Dubuffet's *Echange des Vues,* while in 1976 someone paid $2,000,000 for Pollock's *Lavender Mist.* Since $2,000,000 is 490% higher than $340,000, surrealist paintings were said to have appreciated by 490%. Thus the comparison was based upon the prices of two different paintings—neither of which indicates the value of any other work. The 490% figure is as surrealist as the paintings.[1]

The same logic was applied to other types of paintings, and to classic automobiles, carpets, numismatics, war medals, books and manuscripts, vintage wines, and firearms.

I can understand the writer wanting to do this—since there's no other way to make price comparisons in a professional market. But no investor can logically make his investment decisions by comparing imaginary results in the specialist markets with actual results in the public markets.

---

[1] Please don't write me to point out that Dubuffet and Pollock were abstractionists, not surrealists. I'm only quoting the survey of investment prices.

DEFLATIONARY CONDITIONS

An inflationary period is the most plausible time for a boom in collectibles. Many people become afraid to hold too much in cash or fixed value investments when the purchasing power of money is depreciating at a noticeable speed. And so they turn to "things"—because they've heard that "things" hold their value.

During deflationary periods, when cash is appreciating in purchasing power, we would expect collectibles to fall in price faster than other assets. There are no price histories to verify this, so only a dealer who had been in his market for the past fifty years would know for sure. And we aren't dealers.

But I think it's fairly safe to assume that collectibles aren't a hedge against deflation. Unlike tin or copper or the products of many companies, collectibles are luxury items. We can't expect luxury items to appreciate in value during deflationary periods.

DIAMONDS

Diamonds are in a gray area between a collectibles or specialist market and a public market.

Although each diamond is different in some way from every other diamond, there are grading characteristics—size, cut, color, clarity, lack of flaws, etc.—that make it easier to compare one diamond with another.

In the U.S., the Gemological Institute of America grades individual diamonds and issues descriptive certificates. The information in the certificate is sufficient for appraising the diamond. Thus, you can read a certificate over the telephone to a diamond dealer and obtain a reliable price quotation. With a painting or sculpture, you could do this only if the work were schoolbook famous, or if it were, at least, by a famous artist.

Price quotations for diamonds are possible because the millions of diamonds in the world can be described by a relatively small number of characteristics. The small number of characteristics makes each diamond more or less comparable with every other diamond.

The diamond market is still a specialist market, however. Pertinent information is accessible by you only through a professional. And price spreads remain typical of such an exclusive market. There are bid-ask prices, but the spreads are wide, so you need a substantial price rise just to break even.

There appears to be a movement afoot to create auction markets or, perhaps, a formal network of over-the-counter dealers. If this should succeed, you might find the prices of the most popular categories of diamonds being published in *The Wall Street Journal* and in other daily newspapers.

The new market would make diamonds more liquid, and buy-sell spreads would narrow. At the same time, diamond prices might rise—merely because the improved liquidity would make the diamond market more attractive.

But until that day arrives, the diamond market remains the province of professionals. No amateur investor should expect to do well in it unless he's willing to devote a great deal of time to his education before he invests.

SHOULD YOU?

The collectibles markets differ from normal investment markets in several ways:

1. Collectibles are less liquid. There is no market-maker standing ready to buy your holdings, and it is difficult to learn their real value.

2. The information needed to invest properly is available to you only through dealers and other professionals.

3. The dealer from whom you buy your investment is your

competitor. Both of you are trying to buy low and sell high. But a dealer in a public market usually thinks of you as his customer; he hopes to make money from the *volume* of your transactions, not from the prices he can induce you to pay. His competitors are the other dealers.

4. To succeed, you'll have to negotiate (bargain) with the dealer, unless you buy only at auctions.

My purpose isn't to dissuade you from entering the collectibles markets. It's only to point out that they're different from the investment markets you're used to. Consequently, an amateur—attracted by the stories he hears—may be separated from his capital very quickly.

If you buy a bad stock, you'll see the price dropping before your eyes—and you'll know what to do. When you buy a bad painting, you won't know it until you try to realize the profit you thought you'd made.

If you buy an antique, it should be because you want to have it in your home—not because the salesman tells you, "Antiques are a good investment; the prices continually rise." They may be a good investment for him—because he knows what will sell and because he has a steady market from people like us. But his situation is considerably different from ours.

If you show an occasional profit from things you buy for pleasure, consider it pure gravy—not an invitation to speculate.

SUGGESTIONS

However, there's a lot to be said for investing in markets that are particularly interesting to you. It should be true generally that you can do better investing when the work is more like recreation. (And if you lose, at least you've received some enjoyment for your money.)

I have little to suggest if you find that a collectibles market attracts you. But this might help avoid some losses:

1. Find a dealer who will act as your *broker*—buying and

selling for you on a commission basis. He may even be willing to work for you for a percentage of the net profit, using your capital and his knowledge.

2. Start with low-cost items, so that your risk is low until you're sure you know what you're doing. Through your broker, make a few small purchases.

3. Check these purchases by asking for offers for the items from other brokers or dealers. Don't expect to be offered an instant profit. But if what you're offered is way below what you've paid, you'll know you're doing business with the wrong broker—or that you can't beat the market's price spreads. (For low-cost items, expect a bigger buy-sell spread than for higher-cost items.)

4. When you've decided that you can rely on your broker, increase the level of investment—but slowly.

5. Always spread your capital over a number of items—rather than concentrating on one or two very expensive items. Don't expect to stumble upon the "find" of the twentieth century.

6. Continue regularly to get independent opinions of your purchases, and be prepared to change brokers or systems at any time. Always be sure that the price quotes are offers to buy—not abstract appraisals.

7. Sell something from your inventory at least every three months. That way, you'll keep in touch with the real market (not the published market). Actual sales will also help you get serious quotes from dealers.

8. Anytime your sales begin to tell you that the market may be turning weak, unload as much of your inventory as you can—as quickly as you can without creating a distress sale.

9. Watch the general economic indicators for deflationary signs. A bear stock market isn't necessarily a deflationary sign, but a series of bank failures should certainly cause you concern. Anytime you think the economy may be heading for a deflationary period, sell all your holdings except for those you enjoy having in your home.

These suggestions aren't the distilled wisdom of thirty

years in the collectibles markets; they're only common sense for someone who doesn't know what he'll find when he enters a new world.

Realize that to make money in any kind of collectible, you'll have to enter the market as a professional, or at least be in business with one. You can't dabble in it and hope to do well.

It's probably true that a great deal of money is being made today by professionals in these markets. It would be hard for them *not* to, since so many people like us are ready to plunge.

But a lot of money is being made today in computers, videotape products, and pornography. And I don't think I'll try to profit from buying and selling any of them.

20

SELLING SHORT

WHEN STOCKS APPEAR TO BE HEADED DOWNWARD, MANY IN-vestors ask, "Why not sell short?" And if gold is going to have periodic bear markets, why not sell it short?

Selling short is a reversal of the normal pattern of buying an investment first and selling later. With a short sale, you sell something you don't own, and buy it later—at a price you hope will be lower.

The word "short" is used because you have committed yourself to deliver something you don't yet have; you are "short" the required asset, and you'll have to buy it eventually in order to fulfill your commitment.

In general, selling short is neither more speculative nor riskier than buying. When you sell short, you're acting on your belief that the investment's price is going to fall, just as buying reflects your anticipation of a rise.

However, my major concern in this book has been with stocks, bonds, and gold—because of their cyclical behavior. With these particular investments, selling short has some clear disadvantages.

Selling short isn't appropriate for everyone. For one thing, some people simply don't understand it. For another, there often are alternative ways to profit from a declining price—and sometimes these alternatives are safer and simpler.

This chapter will be of interest mainly to the investor who has already decided to include short-selling in his kit of investment tools. The chapter will discuss some of the supposed risks, as well as some considerations that aren't usually noticed. If the material seems overly technical, that may be a sign not to involve yourself in selling short.

We'll begin by looking at the way a short sale works.

TYPES OF SHORT SALES

There are two types of short sales: (1) selling for future delivery something you don't own now, and (2) selling borrowed assets for current delivery.

Future Delivery

Selling for future delivery is common with commodities and currencies, and the practice has recently been extended to Treasury bills and other U.S. government securities.

In the futures market, you can sell an investment for delivery on a specified future date—at a price determined today. Later, you close your position (end the short sale) by buying the same investment—for delivery on the same future date.

If the price is lower when you close the position, you'll have a profit.

Borrowed Assets

In the U.S. stock markets, there are no sales for future delivery; all transactions are settled within a few days. To sell short, you have to borrow another investor's shares and sell them for immediate delivery. Later, you buy the shares and return them to the lender.

Again, if you purchase the shares at a lower price than at which you originally sold them, you'll have a profit.

UNLIKELY DISADVANTAGES

A number of clichés are invoked to warn against selling short. I'll deal with two of them here.

"Infinite Loss" Theory

The classic argument against selling short is the "Infinite Loss" theory. It goes like this: If you buy a stock (for example), it can drop no further than to zero, so you can never lose more than your original investment. But if you sell short, there is no limit to what you might lose, because there is no limit to how far the stock might rise.

This idea might be renamed the "World Cruise" theory. It can apply only to the man who sells a stock short and then takes off for a six-month cruise around the world, leaving no instructions with his broker.

If it's your practice to place a stop-loss order when you buy an investment (instructing your broker to sell automatically if the price drops too much), you can and should do the same thing when you sell short. Your short position will be closed out if the price *rises* to the point you have chosen as the maximum loss you can tolerate.

So while the investment might indeed rise infinitely, you won't be short when it does.

Limits

A second, similar argument concerns what are called *trading limits*—day-to-day price controls imposed by the rules of the commodity and currency futures markets. On any day, an investment is allowed to rise or fall no more than a specified distance from the previous day's closing price. Whenever the limit prevents the price from moving enough to bring buyers and sellers together, trading comes to a halt.

If you've sold an investment short, a government announcement or other surprise could cause the price to rise the limit several days in a row. You would be locked in, and your stop-loss order would have no effect.

It would be a painful situation, but it would be just as painful to have *bought* an investment that is having a series of limit-*down* days. Since limit days rarely run a price up by 100%, the risk from limits is just as great when buying as when selling. It isn't a risk that applies only to selling short.

Protection

If you exercise no discipline when investing, selling short can involve greater risks. If you refuse to place stop-loss orders and do nothing else to close out losing investments, your ultimate loss could be greater with a short sale than with a purchase. But if you use stop-loss orders, the risk is the same whether you sell short or buy.

SHORT-SALE DIFFERENCES

Although there needn't be any special risks with a short sale, there are mechanical differences between selling short and buying. Not all these differences are widely known, but some of them can work to your disadvantage.

Borrowing Shares

Before you can sell a stock short, your broker has to locate and borrow the shares for you. Generally, this isn't a problem. But for thinly traded securities, such as many warrants or over-the-counter stocks, it may take a few days to find a lender.

After the short sale has been made, the investor from whom

the stock was borrowed can demand the return of his shares at any time. He may want to sell them, for example. If that happens, your broker will have to replace the shares by borrowing from someone else.

Again, this usually doesn't create a problem. But if the stock is thinly traded, your broker might be unable to find replacement shares for you. In that case, you would have no choice but to obtain the needed shares by purchasing them in the open market. You would be forced to close out your short position—perhaps at an inopportune time.

Uptick Rule

In addition to difficulties with borrowing, a short sale in the stock market sometimes can be obstructed by the "uptick" rule. You can sell short only if the last change in the stock's price was an increase (an uptick).

Normally the uptick rule won't bother you. Unless the stock you have in mind is thinly traded, there will probably be upticks and downticks every day. But if you're trying to jump onto a bandwagon that's speeding downhill, you may not be able to. You'll have to take your short position either before the trend gets underway, or later—during a reversal that you'll hope is temporary.

Neither the uptick rule nor the need to borrow the investment applies when you sell short in a futures market.

Dividend Payments

After shares have been lent to a short-seller and sold in the market, the lender is no longer the registered owner, and so he misses out on any dividends the company pays. The short-seller must compensate the lender by reimbursing him for any dividends that are declared.

This is irrelevant in a short sale of a warrant or of a stock that isn't paying dividends, and it has no application in the futures markets. But if you short a stock that is paying dividends, the dividends represent an additional cost that must be overcome before you can make a profit.

Cash Requirements

If you buy an investment and the price changes, you need only decide whether to hang on or sell out. No one asks you for more cash if the price comes down. And if the price goes up, that only means the investment has become more valuable; you don't realize any cash from it until you sell or borrow against it.

When you sell short, the situation is different. Your cash requirement is adjusted daily, dollar for dollar, for any change in the investment's price. If the price goes up, you must put up more cash. If the price goes down (a gain for you), funds are automatically released to you—which you can use elsewhere or use to sell more of the same investment short.

Finite Profit

Although the "Infinite Loss" problem of a short sale is easily eliminated, the drawback of a "Finite Profit" is real.

When you purchase an investment, you can hope it will rise by 200%, 300%, or more—whatever your analysis or dreams tell you. But when you sell short, you can hope only that the investment will drop to zero.

The potential profit of an unleveraged short sale is limited to 100% of your original investment, but even 100% is unlikely—since investment prices rarely drop to zero. At least once in your life, you should be able to buy an investment for $5 and sell it for $20—a 300% profit. But you'll never sell an investment short at $5 and see it drop to minus $15.

As mentioned before, money is released to the short-seller automatically, as the investment's price falls. These funds can

be reinvested in additional short sales on the way down—
thereby increasing the potential profit. However, the reinvestment of profit isn't automatic; each reinvestment would
be a new transaction, requiring a new decision.

Math Problems

The limitation on short sale profits is affected by the
simple arithmetic of buying and selling. Suppose, for example:
1. You buy a stock at $30 and then sell it at $50.
2. Later, you sell the stock short at $50 and it drops back
to $30, at which price you close out the short position.
On both trades you made a profit of $20 per share, but the
percentage returns were different. On the first transaction
your profit was 67% (a $20 profit on a $30 investment); on the
second transaction your profit was only 40% (a $20 profit on a
$50 investment).
There is a profit bias on the purchase side which isn't often
recognized. Obviously, the stock could have fallen to $17,
which would have provided a 67% profit. But because
many investments are affected by the monetary cycles, they
tend to trade within a defined range—rising to a certain price,
then falling back to the original price.
By the arithmetic of buying and selling, the money you
invest can produce more when the investment is rising than
when it is falling.

Government Intervention

In a major deflation the politicians may decide it's unpatri-
otic or inhumane for speculators to profit from the falling
prices that are hurting other investors. They may even believe that short sales are the cause of falling prices.
An excess-profits tax could be levied on short sales. The tax

might be 50%, 75%, even 100% of the profits. And, of course, it would be retroactive, to cover profits made before the tax was announced.

Even if the politicians ignore your profits, they may want to halt the losses other investors are suffering. The investment markets could be closed by the government, allegedly to allow matters to "cool off" before trading resumes. You'd have some anxious moments waiting for the cooling-off period to end.[1]

Every risk of government interference with short sales can be turned around to apply to purchases as well. Special taxes could be imposed on speculators who profit from soaring food prices, or markets could be closed when prices are rising rapidly.

But there's a definite, though indefinable, emotional bias against selling short. Sanctions against short-sellers would be easier to invoke and more widely praised, and the damage to the economic system would be harder for most people to recognize. In a time of renewed chaos, desperate political leaders will be throwing wild punches—just to be doing something.

Stocks, Bonds, and Gold

Short sales would seem to have the best potential and the least risk with the cyclical investments—stocks, bonds, and gold. When it appears that monetary policy has turned against one of these investments, the time would be ripe for a short sale.

However, these three investments hold special problems for short-sellers.

With stocks, I've already covered the problems. Your obligation to compensate the lender for missed dividends in-

[1] During the past few years, governments in several major countries have closed currency markets for a day or more following hectic trading periods.

creases the price drop you'll need in order to make a profit. The possibility that borrowed shares may not be available when needed imposes another special risk.

With bonds, the problem is that only U.S. government and government-agency issues are traded on an organized futures exchange. While these are the safest bonds to *buy* when you expect interest rates to drop, they aren't the safest to sell short.

You would sell bonds short during a period of tight money because you believe interest rates are going to rise. If any one of these periods escalated into a general deflation, interest rates temporarily would go even higher than you expected.

That would seem to be an added bonus for anyone who sold bonds short. And it *would* be for *corporate* bonds. But the opposite might be true for government bonds. The flight of cautious money (such as trust funds or pension accounts) out of corporate bonds and into government bonds could cause the latter to *rise* in price—resulting in a loss on your short sale.

If a futures market for corporate bonds should develop, that would be the place to sell bonds short.

As we've seen, gold prices should continue to be cyclical— moving opposite to stock prices. The bear trends in gold should last for a year or two at a time, and they might appear to be ideal periods for selling gold short.

But it's always risky to short gold. Gold is too sensitive to political and military troubles. Even during periods of apparent tranquillity, a sudden event unrelated to the monetary cycle could have a spectacular effect upon the price of gold. An entire bull market could occur in one day.

Would you like to be short gold on the day that Russia invades China, or the day the first terrorist group sets off an atomic bomb somewhere? I don't know if these things will ever happen; they're only hypothetical examples. But *any* kind of nonfinancial disaster that causes worldwide fear can also cause gold to jump by 25%, 50%, or more almost in an instant. The jump would be too fast for a stop-loss order to be executed.

ALTERNATIVES

There are ways to bet on a price decline without selling short. In some cases, you might find one of these alternatives more attractive.

Puts

A *put* option is the reverse of the *call* option. A call gives you the right to purchase an investment at a fixed price anytime prior to the call's expiration date. A put entitles you to *sell* the investment at a fixed price anytime prior to the put's expiration date.

A put option, like a call, enables you to limit your loss to the cost of the option—no matter how far the price moves against you. As long as you're prepared to lose the entire cost of the option, you don't have to worry about catastrophic events or whether your losses should be cut.

Puts on stocks work more smoothly than short sales. There is no need to borrow shares (and, therefore, no need to compensate the lender for missed dividends), and no uptick rule.

There are 25 blue-chip stocks for which listed put options are available (on the Chicago Board Options Exchange and elsewhere). More listed puts may be available in the future. In addition, puts on other stocks can be purchased from over-the-counter dealers.

The Commodity Futures Trading Commission, the U.S. government's regulator of commodity trading, is currently wondering whether to permit trading in commodity options. Presumably, put (and call) options for commodities will be available in the U.S. eventually, but right now the situation is uncertain. And, to my knowledge, Swiss banks don't offer put options on investments.

However, it's possible to create your own put option on gold at a Swiss bank. You can purchase a call option (described in Chapter 15) and sell a forward contract short for the same expiration date. The net result is the same as having a put.

If the price rises, the loss on the forward contract will be offset by the profit on the call. Your net loss will work out to be the cost of the call option. If the price drops, you'll gain on the forward contract while losing only the cost of the call option. In both cases, your total risk is the price of the option—just as if you had purchased a put.

Contrary Investments

Another alternative to selling short is to purchase an investment that should move in the opposite direction. Today, that means stocks and bonds on the one hand and gold on the other. They move in cyclical opposition to each other, as I've been discussing throughout the book.

You can bet on a falling stock market much more safely by buying gold options than by selling stocks and bonds short. And there's less risk in purchasing warrants than there is in selling gold short.

In other words, for most investors, the purchases suggested by this book make more sense than short sales.

INVESTMENT MEDIA

Any stock or commodity can be sold short on the exchange where it's traded. Major currencies, as well as U.S. government bonds and Treasury bills, can be sold short on the Board of Trade and the International Monetary Market, both in Chicago. These investments and listed puts can be handled through a U.S. securities broker. Or a Swiss bank will handle them for you by placing the order, in its own name, with its U.S. broker.

Forward sales in gold, silver, and currencies can also be made in Switzerland through a Swiss bank.

The International Monetary Market is especially attractive if you intend to trade frequently, because commission costs are very low. The disadvantage is its vulnerability to U.S. government intervention.

Selling gold or currencies short at a Swiss bank puts your dealings beyond the reach of the U.S. government. But trading costs are higher, and you can close out a short sale before the delivery date only at a price set by the bank. These disadvantages are small if you don't trade frequently; but if you plan to buy and sell every week, they can be important.

SELL SHORT?

I've attempted to call attention to some details of short-selling that aren't frequently recognized. The importance of any of the details will depend upon your own plans.

If you don't understand the process and mechanics of selling short, stay out of it—no matter how sure you may be that a price is going to fall or how strongly others may be advising that you sell short. As always, stick to what you understand and what you believe you can handle.

21

A SWISS
BANK ACCOUNT

IF YOU'RE CONCERNED ABOUT POTENTIAL GOVERNMENT INTER-ference, you might feel safer if some of your assets were outside the country.

Under U.S. law you're required to file a form along with your income tax return, listing all foreign bank, securities, and commodity accounts—if you have any. Nevertheless, there's an advantage to having a foreign bank account. It's easy for the government to confiscate assets within its reach; it can do so at a time of *its* choosing, a time that might be especially harmful for you.

But for assets outside the U.S., you could delay your compliance without getting into legal hot water. You would have time to dispose of the newly illegal assets profitably.

FUTURE DECISIONS

A foreign bank account is also a way to postpone critical decisions. If all your assets are held with banks and brokers in the U.S., compliance with almost any new investment law will be automatic, since U.S. banks and brokers will have no choice but to cooperate in enforcing the law. By keeping assets in the U.S., you are deciding in advance to comply with future laws.

If assets are outside the U.S., however, you can decide whether to comply with a new law—when it's decreed—because its enforcement won't be automatic.

At this moment, you might believe that you will always comply with *any* law—no matter how foolish or distasteful it might be. I think that such a view is unrealistic, however; and there are people in many countries who would agree with me.

You have only to look at their legal systems to realize why. In some places, mere survival depends upon breaking the law. The legal system of any of those places could be the U.S. system someday.

The unthinkable has already become the rule. Even if you've adjusted to all the unthinkable edicts of the past, the day could come when your government will go too far—even for you. Then it will be too late to send money out of the country.

This isn't a suggestion to break the law. It's a suggestion to deal with today now, while reserving judgment on the future. A foreign bank account is one way of doing so.

WHY SWITZERLAND?

There are nearly two hundred countries in which you can have a bank account. I choose Switzerland because its traditions and its legal system provide the best protection for an investor. Of the major countries, it is furthest from having an omnipotent government.

There is a drift toward the welfare state in Switzerland, just as in other countries. But the drift is much slower, probably for two reasons.

Referendum

The principal reason is the system of referendum. It is a permanent obstacle in the way of "progress."

If the Swiss parliament passes a law, anyone who can obtain fifty thousand signatures on a petition can force the law to be put to a referendum. It is typical of voting patterns everywhere that anyone in favor of a proposed law, or indifferent to it, can be kept from voting by any small obstacle, such as bad weather. But those who are opposed to the law will almost certainly show up to vote against it. Consequently, only a small minority of laws survive the referendum process.

Most new legislation isn't very revolutionary and doesn't provoke a referendum. But whenever something radical is passed, a referendum is sure to undo it. In fact, radical legislation is seldom passed by parliament, simply because it's known in advance that the measure won't survive.

Comparative Benefits

The second reason for Swiss stability is that its benefits are easy for any citizen to see. The referendum has prevented Switzerland from keeping up with its more "advanced" neighbors, and the difference is obvious to all but the most dedicated socialists.

In all the countries around Switzerland, you find unemployment, inflation, terrorism, bankruptcies, and oppressive taxes. But not in Switzerland.

Price inflation is between 1% and 2% per year. The unemployment rate is ⅕%. The Swiss currency is the strongest in the world, providing bargains for Swiss consumers. A kidnapping in Geneva in October 1977 was big news because it was the first reported kidnapping in Switzerland since 1952.

In 1978 a law was passed that lowered the legal workweek from forty-four hours to forty—requiring overtime rates for all hours over forty. Of course, a referendum was demanded, and the new law was repealed. Can you imagine such a disapproval in the United States?

A constitutional amendment that would have established uniform tax rates for all cantons (Swiss states) was submitted to voters in 1977. In any other country, citizens of high-tax areas would demand that others "pay their fair share." But not in Switzerland; voters in every canton turned it down. They probably understood that uniform tax rates eventually mean tax rates that are uniformly high.

A labor-union strike of small proportions occurs once every few years at most. Unions aren't privileged to invade property or to chase off workers who would gladly take the jobs that strikers complain about. And there are no minimum wage laws to prevent wages and prices from dropping when economic conditions require it.

The Swiss economy was badly hurt by the fixed exchange-rate system. But because the Swiss economy is less regulated, it was able to make a "soft landing" from a 24% monetary inflation rate in 1971 to a zero monetary inflation rate in 1973.

Such a thing would be impossible in the U.S.; reducing the rate of monetary inflation sharply would provoke a massive deflationary washout. With rigid wages and prices, there would be millions of unemployed workers and mountains of unsold goods. Switzerland could make the adjustment because there were no obstacles to smooth changes in prices and wages.

I'm not saying there's no government interference in Switzerland. There are farm subsidies, welfare, and some crazy laws. But it's all on a tiny scale compared to what an American takes for granted.

The Future

After spending the last seventeen months living in Switzerland, I could write page after page about how exceptional the country is. You have only to spend a few days here to notice it. You can search throughout Zurich for a slum area, but you won't find one. The city's cleanliness and prosperity are unequaled by any American city. You can walk through any part of Zurich in the middle of the night, trying to get mugged, but you won't succeed.

Swiss banking laws and practices are only the outgrowth

of a culture with very deep roots. Superficial changes in the banking laws are made from time to time as a result of some scandal. And Swiss politicians occasionally impose new regulations in order to placate foreign politicians and tax collectors. But nothing really changes.

The Swiss way of life is founded on a respect for privacy, for individualism, and for self-sufficiency. This isn't going to change next month or next year—no matter how frustrating it may be to foreign politicians. Swiss citizens aren't going to trade the benefits of freedom for the alleged benefits of the welfare state.

BANK SECRECY

Bank secrecy is typical of the Swiss concern for privacy. Because the secrecy laws are seldom understood by foreigners, events sometimes make it seem that bank secrecy has been breached or repealed.

For example, a great flap was made about the "breach" of Swiss bank secrecy when the Clifford Irving case was publicized in 1972. Irving claimed to be ghostwriting the autobiography of Howard Hughes, and asked that royalty checks be made out to "H. Hughes." The book was a fraud (Howard Hughes disowned it); the checks were being deposited into a Swiss bank account that Irving's wife had opened in the name of "Helga Hughes."

Once it was suspected that a Swiss bank account had been used in a fraud, no one who understood Swiss banking was surprised that information on the Helga Hughes account was turned over to the authorities. Bank secrecy hadn't been "breached"; no such case ever receives the protection of Swiss bank secrecy.

The system is very simple. In Switzerland, it is against the law for a bank employee to divulge information about a customer or his account to anyone. It is difficult for an American to understand that "anyone" includes the Swiss government.

Exceptions are made only if a court order directs the release of information. To obtain a court order, the government must demonstrate that a crime has been committed under Swiss law and that banking information is needed in the prosecution of the case.

If a foreign government is seeking information, the matter still hinges on the Swiss definition of what is criminal. A foreign government may obtain banking information only by demonstrating that the bank customer is being prosecuted for something that is a crime by *Swiss* law.

The ordinary crimes of assault, theft, and fraud are prohibited by the Swiss legal code. But two activities that are considered crimes elsewhere are not illegal in Switzerland.

One is maintaining a private foreign bank account. No Swiss bank can be made to reveal information about an account on the grounds that the account violates the exchange controls or other laws in some country.

The second activity concerns taxes. Tax evasion isn't a crime in Switzerland. If the government believes a citizen hasn't paid enough tax, the case is taken to civil court. If the government wins the case, the citizen must pay what the court says he owes, but no criminal charges are involved. The evasion is treated as an unpaid bill, not as a crime. Consequently, the Swiss government does not cooperate with foreign governments in ordinary tax cases.

However, there *is* a Swiss law concerning tax *fraud*. Tax fraud is defined as the falsifying of documents (other than the tax return itself) in order to evade taxes. If a taxpayer creates dummy invoices for fictitious payments, for example, he can be accused of tax fraud (a criminal offense) just as if he had defrauded another citizen. But as long as he merely understates his income or overstates his expenses, he isn't committing a crime.

Except in exchange-control and nonfraudulent tax matters, Swiss bank secrecy doesn't shield criminal activities. If you rob liquor stores, embezzle from your employer, or kidnap people for ransom, don't expect a Swiss banker to hide your money or keep your secrets.

But if you have no plans to defraud anyone, the Swiss banks

are as secret as you would like them to be. The Swiss government isn't interested in your relationship to your government or your relatives.

FACILITIES

There are large gold, silver, and currency markets in Switzerland; a Swiss bank can deal in these investments for you easily, with low transaction costs.

In addition, a Swiss bank can make investments for you in any other market in the world—such as U.S. stock and commodity exchanges. The investment is made in the bank's name, and you remain anonymous. The charges will be the same as if you had made the investment directly, plus a nominal commission for the bank's services.

It's tempting for me to try to detail the many services and types of accounts available at a Swiss bank. But I had that idea in 1976, and I wound up writing a 515-page book on the subject. It includes listings of banks, types of accounts, commission rates, account minimums, tax considerations, sample letters, suggestions for privacy, and much more.[1]

However, there are a few matters that I believe should be touched upon now.

U.S. DOLLAR ACCOUNTS

Most investment portfolios will include some funds in U.S. dollars. It is possible to keep the dollars in a Swiss bank account.

However, it isn't commonly recognized that a dollar account at a Swiss bank isn't as secure as a Swiss franc account. A franc account is like any bank account anywhere; it is a liability of the bank, owed to you no matter what. But a U.S. dollar account is treated as an investment that the bank makes

[1] *The Complete Guide to Swiss Banks,* listed in the *Suggested Reading* on page 449.

for you—such as purchasing gold or stocks. The bank doesn't owe you the money. The bank places the money for you in an American bank; if the American bank fails or if the U.S. government imposes exchange controls, it is *your* loss—not the Swiss bank's.

Every currency account is ultimately kept in the country of that currency. U.S. dollar accounts are placed in an American bank; German mark accounts are placed in a German bank, etc. This is the case regardless of where the bank you deal with is located.[2]

You won't even know the name of the bank where the currency is kept (unless you ask) until the day your Swiss bank informs you that the money has been lost in a bank failure.

Consequently, keeping a U.S. dollar deposit at a Swiss bank is no safer than keeping it in an American bank. Either way, you are exposed to the weakness of the U.S. system.

At the same time, there's no reason not to purchase Treasury bills or money-market fund shares through a Swiss bank. You won't be vulnerable to the U.S. banking system, and your name wouldn't be registered as the owner.

EUROCURRENCY ACCOUNTS

Any Swiss bank will place funds for you in the Eurocurrency market, in any currency but the Swiss franc.

The risks here are the same and, again, many people don't recognize them. The deposits aren't an obligation of the Swiss bank. The funds are placed with another bank (unknown to you). If that bank fails, you lose money.

A safer way to invest in a foreign currency is to have your Swiss bank purchase the bonds of the country's national government.

---

[2] There are exceptions, but they are rare. However, you can keep U.S. dollars with no vulnerability to the U.S. banking system by asking any Swiss bank to purchase dollar banknotes and hold them for you in the bank's vault.

STOCKS AND BONDS

As mentioned in Chapter 16, the Swiss government has restricted the purchase of Swiss stocks and bonds by non-residents. The restrictions may have been removed by the time you read this; any Swiss bank can tell you whether this is the case. If the restrictions have been removed, Swiss confederation bonds (the bonds of the national government) are my choice as the safest and easiest way to invest in Swiss francs. The bonds come in denominations of SF1,000 (about $500).

A Swiss bank can also be used to purchase U.S. stocks and warrants. The bank places the order through its broker in the U.S. The commission schedule is rather complicated, but in most cases the commission will be a little more than dealing directly with a U.S. broker.

In addition, eighty-four major U.S. stocks are traded on the Zurich Stock Exchange (the list is shown on page 299). The prices are quoted in Swiss francs, but the dollar equivalents are comparable to New York prices. Thus, if the franc is worth $.50, and the stock is trading in New York at $40, it will trade in Zurich at SF80. Since you'll be holding a stock, not a currency, changes in the exchange rate won't affect your investment. Commissions for these stocks range between ⅝% and 1%.

By purchasing through a Swiss bank, you can invest in U.S. stocks with privacy. In addition, since the shares are in the hands of the bank, you can switch to or from gold without having to transfer money from and to the U.S.

Buying U.S. stocks on the Zurich Stock Exchange makes sense if you intend to hold the stocks through an entire bull market. The costs are nominal and the inconvenience involved in transmitting instructions may arise only once every other year. But if you intend to trade in and out of the market, you will probably find it is more convenient to use a U.S. broker.

U.S. STOCKS TRADED
ON THE ZURICH STOCK EXCHANGE

Aetna Life
Amax
American Cyanamid
American Tel. & Tel.
Amexco

Baxter Labs
Beatrice Foods
Black & Decker
Borden
Burlington Industries
Burroughs Corporation

Caterpillar Corporation
Chessie System
Chrysler Corp.
Citicorp
City Investing Co.
Coca-Cola
Colgate-Palmolive
Consolidated Natural Gas
Continental Can
Continental Oil
Control Data
Corning Glass Works
CPC International
Crown Zellerbach

Dow Chemical
du Pont de Nemours, E.I.

Eastman Kodak
Exxon

Firestone Tire & Rubber
Fluor Corp.
Ford Motor Co.

General Electric
General Foods
General Motors
General Tel. & Electronics
Genstar
Gillette
Goodyear Tire & Rubber
Grace & Co., W.R.
Gulf Oil
Gulf & Western

Haliburton
Honeywell

INCO (International Nickel)*
IBM
International Paper
International Tel. & Tel.

Kennecott Copper
Kraftco

Lilly, Eli
Litton Industries

Minnesota Mining & Mfg.
Mobil Oil
Monsanto

National Cash Register
National Distillèrs & Chemical
Norton Simon

Occidental Petroleum
Otis Elevator
Owens Illinois

Pacific Gas & Electric
Penn Central
PepsiCo.
Philip Morris
Phillips Petroleum
Proctor & Gamble

Rockwell International

SmithKline
Sperry Rand
Squibb
Standard Oil

Tenneco Inc.
Texaco
Transamerica

Union Carbide
Uniroyal
United States Gypsum
United States Steel
United Technologies

Warner-Lambert
Woolworth

Xerox

Zenith Radio

*Canadian company.

SWISS RESTRICTIONS

Since November 1974 the Swiss government has limited the number of Swiss francs that can be held in a bank account by a nonresident of Switzerland.

The present maximum is SF100,000 (about $50,000) in any one account, of which no more than SF20,000 (about $10,000) can draw interest. You may have only one account at any bank, but you can have an account at each of many different banks, and each account may have up to SF100,000. The limits apply to households (individuals living under one roof).

If you had a Swiss bank account prior to October 31, 1974, the limit for that account is SF100,000, plus whatever was in it on that date. Even if some of the funds have been withdrawn since then, the limit remains the same—so long as the account remains open. The absolute account maximum, regardless of the October 1974 balance, is SF5,000,000.

These limits apply only to Swiss franc accounts. There are no limits for accounts in other currencies, or in gold, silver, stocks, bonds, etc.

CHOOSING A SWISS BANK

The Swiss system of reporting bank assets and liabilities is particularly useful to investors. Unlike the balance sheets of banks in other countries, you can get a good idea of a Swiss bank's liquidity by reading its financial statement.

A bank's liquidity is its ability to honor every demand for a withdrawal. Liquidity is measured by comparing the (1) assets that can be turned into cash immediately with (2) the deposits that are presumed to be withdrawable on demand. If a bank is 100% liquid, it can satisfy every possible demand. If it is 75% liquid, it can satisfy 75% of the demands.

Normally it isn't necessary for a bank to be 100% liquid, because it isn't imagined that every depositor will ask for his money at once. However, during a worldwide banking crisis, you might feel a little safer knowing that your bank *could* meet every claim.

I have created a formula by which I measure a Swiss bank's liquidity. About once a year, I publish the liquidity status of some two hundred Swiss banks in my newsletter. The 1978 liquidity ratings for a few of the prominent banks are shown in the table on page 302.

I have visited most of these banks and selected five that are highly liquid and seem particularly suited for Americans— because the officers speak fluent English, and because American ways are understood. These banks are listed on page 410.

In addition, you can make inquiries at other banks. Every Swiss bank is listed, with many details, in the *Swiss Financial Yearbook*—mentioned on page 414. Also, many public libraries have at least one international banking directory— which will contain the names and addresses of numerous Swiss banks.

SO FAR AWAY

I can understand that you might feel uneasy about sending your money five thousand miles or more away from home. It's a big step to take. It would help a great deal if you were to visit Switzerland, meet your banker, and see that the banks are made up of buildings and people, just as they are at home. But, for most investors, such a trip won't be practical.

Most of your investments actually are quite far away from you, even if you think of them as being close by. You may know your local stock broker, for example, but he isn't the real custodian of your capital. Your capital is being used by the managers of the company whose shares you own, and you may not even know their names—much less what kind of people they are.

If you have qualms about sending money overseas, I have a suggestion. Open a Swiss bank account with a small sum, perhaps 5% of your capital. You'll receive letters and bank

SWISS BANK LIQUIDITY
(Selected Banks)

	Assets[1]	Liquidity
Liquid Banks		
Algemene Bank Nederland in der Schweiz, Zürich	73	113.0%
Anlagebank Zürich[2]	39	187.3%
Banca del Ceresio, Lugano[2]	25	107.5%
Banca Privata in Lugano, Lugano	33	110.8%
Bank Heusser & Cie, Basel[3]	87	109.0%
Bank Julius Bär & Co., Zürich[4]	690	79.7%
Bankinstitut Zürich	31	109.1%
Banque de Rive, Geneva	24	119.5%
Banque Indiana (Suisse), Lausanne	24	77.8%
Banque Ormond Burrus & Cie, Geneva	27	110.8%
Banque Pasche, Geneva	37	91.4%
The British Bank of the Middle East, Geneva	57	108.6%
Cambio + Valorenbank, Zürich	76	130.2%
Foreign Commerce Bank, Zürich	245	127.7%
Habib Bank, Zürich	203	109.8%
Handelskredit-Bank, Zürich	36	117.3%
Nederlandsche Middenstandsbank (Schweiz), Zürich[5]	52	129.6%
Big Banks		
Bank Leu, Zürich[4]	3,646	38.5%
Swiss Bank Corporation, Basel[4]	56,621	36.2%
Swiss Credit Bank, Zürich[4]	44,398	41.5%
Swiss Volksbank, Bern[3]	11,606	62.4%
Union Bank of Switzerland, Zürich[4]	56,360	37.9%
Averages		
All 443 Swiss banks, December 1976		45.0%
71 large banks, April 1978		52.0%
All 28 private banks, December 1976		70.7%

[1] Millions of Swiss francs.   [5] Formerly Transitbank Zürich.
[2] As of September 30, 1977.
[3] As of June 30, 1977.
[4] As of March 31, 1978.

All other data is as of December 31, 1977.
Sources: Averages are from data published in *Das Schweizerische Bankwesen im Jahre 1976* and *Monatsbericht,* June 1978, of the Swiss National Bank. Individual bank data is from banks' balance sheets published in *Schweizerisches Handelsamtblatt,* Bern.

statements, and begin to get used to the idea. Gradually, your Swiss bank will become as familiar and comfortable as your local bank.

With a little money in Switzerland, you may notice that you can read the daily newspaper with a little less uneasiness—simply because a small portion of your capital is out of reach of the problems the newspaper describes.

As you add to your Swiss account, you may find that your feeling of security continues to grow, that you no longer feel so vulnerable to federal budgets, monetary policy, and the "save the world" plans of social reformers.

Then you'll start wondering why everyone doesn't have a Swiss bank account.

PART IV

INVESTMENT STRATEGY

22

BACKGROUND

WE'VE COVERED A LOT OF GROUND IN THE FIRST THREE PARTS
of this book. And while I've reached some conclusions along
the way, most of the effort has been working toward the investment strategy to be presented here.

We'll begin this part with a brief summary of the points
I've made that form the basis for the investment strategy.

THE THIRD ERA

The days of a long-term, buy-and-hold strategy for stocks
ended in 1965. The hard-money era that followed ended in
1974.

Any unhedged, buy-and-hold program initiated today
would have to wait out long periods of decline (lasting from
one to three years) that would try the patience of most investors.

Nevertheless, buy-and-hold is the only strategy some investors are prepared to use. For them, I'll suggest a portfolio
that is hedged enough that its worst periods of loss will be
relatively mild.

Most investors, however, will do better by reviewing their
situation every month or so, and by making major changes
in the portfolio every couple of years.

CHAOS

The era of chaos that began in 1970 is likely to remain with us for at least another decade. And although the pattern will be familiar, there will be surprises along the way. A sound investment strategy must be hedged against the unforeseeable.

Government Interference

Government involvement in the economy will continue to grow. Each new crisis will be an excuse for a new government program to offset the consequences of previous programs.

This process will affect us in two ways. There will be government cure-alls that only worsen economic conditions. And there will be interference directed at investments in particular—changes in the tax rules and increased regulation of the markets.

SUPER-TRENDS

A super-trend is a long-term movement in an investment's price. During the period of the super-trend, an investment goes through normal bull and bear markets, but there is an upward or downward bias—taking the bull or bear markets to progressively higher or lower ranges. Not all investments move in super-trends, but most of those we have discussed do.

The stock market has been in a super-bear trend since 1966. Most likely, the trend will last for several years more, as it becomes harder for companies to earn profits for their stockholders.

The bond market is in a similar super-bear trend, because price inflation has created a long-term upward bias in interest rates. Interest rates won't return to "normal" until after a deflationary washout has brought the inflationary cycle to an end.

Gold is in a super-bull trend because it is the world's number one chaos hedge—and we are in an era of escalating chaos.

Silver is probably in a super-bull trend that will be completed when the worldwide consumption of silver is reduced (as the result of a higher price) to the level of new production and salvage.

The Swiss franc is in a super-bull trend because the low inflation rate in Switzerland creates continual pressure for the franc to move higher. The super-trend will end if the gap between inflation rates in Switzerland and the U.S. ever closes.

Each of these investments will also experience normal bull and bear trends, lasting for a year or two. But the trends will occur in progressively higher or lower ranges—depending upon whether an investment's super-trend is bullish or bearish.

With the exception of the Swiss franc, the major foreign currencies are not in super-trends. The differences in inflation between the U.S. and most other major countries are not large enough, or else are not persistent enough, to support long-term trends.

MONETARY CYCLES

The Federal Reserve generates cycles in the rate of monetary inflation—as shown in the graph on page 45. The pattern of monetary cycles isn't likely to change in the next few years, since both inflation and unemployment will remain major concerns. The Fed slows the growth in the money supply when the price inflation rate is rising, and it accelerates monetary growth when unemployment is rising. By fighting one problem, the other problem worsens. As a result, it appears to have no choice but to alternate between expansion and restriction, bringing on one bad consequence and then the other.

Stocks and Bonds

The bond and stock markets are the first areas affected by changes in monetary policy, and these two markets move up and down cyclically—up when monetary policy is expansive, down when it is restrictive.

Up to now it has been possible to take advantage of the cycles by buying and selling when key economic indicators change direction (to be discussed in Chapter 28). It's possible to buy fairly early in a bull trend in stocks and bonds, and get out of the market shortly after the bull trend turns to bear.

There's no guarantee that monetary policy will continue to be cyclical. But I see only two ways in which the cyclical pattern can be brought to an end: (1) with a political discipline that isn't in evidence today; or (2) by an unintentional runaway inflation or deflation that breaks the pattern and provides a fresh start.

Gold

Monetary policy also begins to affect general economic conditions in the U.S. within a few months after it affects the stock market. And the expansion or contraction in the U.S. economy usually influences the rest of the world. Thus, a new trend in the U.S. stock market is frequently a forerunner of general economic conditions throughout the world.

Because the demand for a store of value increases during crisis periods, and because gold is the most popular store of value, gold can be expected to rise in price during periods of severe economic conditions. Consequently, gold should continue to react inversely to the U.S. stock market, rising when the stock market falls and vice versa.

Currencies

In general, foreign currency trends can't be related to U.S. monetary cycles.

Currency prices change because price inflation rates differ from country to country. Since price inflation results from monetary inflation, it would seem that U.S. monetary policy is a key to currency forecasting, but it's not.

Each foreign country will also have its own monetary policy, with zigs and zags that may not be the same as those of the U.S. In addition, the time lag between monetary inflation and the resulting price inflation is so great (in the area of two years) that many other factors can intervene to upset a forecast. The time lag isn't merely long; the length itself varies. Therefore, we shouldn't look for cyclical movements in currency prices.

Silver

Silver prices also lack a clear tie to the monetary cycles. Although we might expect silver, as an industrial metal, to do poorly during periods of recession, so far that hasn't been the case. The reason is probably that investors increase their purchases during a recessionary period.

CONSIDERATIONS

We can summarize these points in three considerations that should control your investment strategy:

1. There will be monetary cycles that first favor stocks and bonds and then favor gold.

2. There will be surprises as the crises unfold in unexpected ways, and surprises as the government changes the

rules. This means that some investments won't live up to your expectations. It also means that some investments will live up to your expectations but then be damaged by special taxes or by other government interference with the profits you have earned.

3. It is unrealistic to expect that your timing will be perfect, allowing you to catch trend changes precisely, or that you will always succeed in dodging government interference.

Therefore, an appropriate strategy should:

1. Be in keeping with the long-term super-trends, but try to take advantage of the normal bull and bear markets within those super-trends.

2. Be hedged against surprises and mistakes.

3. Have as little exposure as possible to the U.S. government, so that losses from rule changes are minimized.

UNIQUE INVESTORS

Every investor works with a unique set of circumstances, objectives, resources, and attitudes. It isn't possible to suggest a single investment portfolio that would suit everyone. Nor is it even possible to suggest a portfolio for a specific individual without knowing a great deal about him.

So I'm offering a basic *strategy*—a way of approaching the investment markets—not a portfolio. I can't tell you how much of your capital should be invested in each possibility, nor which investments you should choose for your portfolio, nor even which form of any investment is right for you. Instead, I've tried to tell you everything I think is relevant concerning these investments, so that you can make your own decisions.

I'll provide portfolio examples so that you can visualize what I mean. But these examples are only starting points from which to develop a program of your own. Even the basic strategy is flexible, so that it can fit individual capabilities and resources.

23

————

TWO PORTFOLIOS

A KEY ELEMENT IN THE BASIC STRATEGY IS THE SEPARATION OF your capital into *two* parts—which I call the *permanent* portfolio and the *variable* portfolio.

A portfolio is a collection of investments. When planning a portfolio, it is common to look for balance, diversification, and hedging.

I have found that it is easier for an investor to plan his strategy by establishing two separate portfolios. One of them, the permanent portfolio, stresses the traditional goals of balance and diversification. The other portfolio stresses the investor's judgment about current trends. Making this division enables him to decide just how aggressive and active he will be, without taking the risk that he will invest himself into the poor house.

PERMANENT PORTFOLIO

The permanent portfolio is a fixed, unchanging collection of investments. It is diversified and hedged, but, on balance, it is aligned with the super-trends now in force. It provides a permanent foundation for long-term profits.

With this foundation in place, you can afford to take greater

risks with the other portfolio, because the permanent portfolio will be immune to short-term trading errors.

The permanent portfolio contains gold and Swiss francs,
because they are the investments with the greatest assurance
of long-term appreciation. A third investment is stock warrants, which serve as a low-cost hedge.

So long as the present era of inflationary disorder continues, the permanent portfolio, once established, will not be
altered. It isn't intended to exploit temporary bull or bear
markets; it is built to ride the long-term super-trends.

VARIABLE PORTFOLIO

The variable portfolio will be more adaptable; you will
change it, as necessary, to capitalize on trend changes in gold
and stocks and, perhaps, in other investments.

In Part V, I'll suggest tools that can be used to spot trend
changes. For now, we'll assume that those tools are at your
disposal.

In managing the variable portfolio, you would buy gold
when it appears to be in a bull market. When the trend
changes, you would sell the gold and use the proceeds to
purchase stocks and bonds, which would be held for as long
as their uptrend lasts. When you expect a rally in some other
investment, such as currencies or silver, your purchase would
be made with funds from the variable portfolio.

Thus, the variable portfolio moves with the times. It is
used to take advantage of current trends.

DIVISION

The first decision to make is how your capital will be split
between the two portfolios. It is also the most important
decision. It will be easier to make after you've finished reading the book, but the main consideration will be the extent

to which you're confident you can run the variable portfolio profitably.

Few people will want to have less than 15% of their capital in the permanent portfolio; many will want to have far more. Each will make a choice according to his ability and willingness to deal with portfolio changes.

SAMPLE

Before we look at portfolios in more detail, it may help to see an example of the division between permanent and variable. For this example, I'll put 35% of the capital into the permanent portfolio and 65% into the variable portfolio.

Throughout this chapter and the next three, I'm going to use $100 in capital for the portfolio examples. This will lessen confusion when the main divisions are broken down into subdivisions.

PERMANENT PORTFOLIO		VARIABLE PORTFOLIO	
Gold	$20.00	Gold vs. Stocks	$35.00
Swiss francs	10.00	Dollars and	
Warrants	5.00	other investments	30.00
Total:	*$35.00*	*Total:*	*$65.00*

As we continue, I'll provide additions and elaborations for the two portfolios, but this example will help you visualize the concept.

In the variable portfolio, the "vs." between gold and stocks indicates that funds would be switched back and forth between the two investments according to current trends. However, the gold (and everything else) in the permanent portfolio just sits—regardless of the current trend.

The "dollars and other investments" in the variable portfolio represents a fund from which other investments will be made as opportunities arise.

We can now look more closely at each of the two portfolios.

24

THE PERMANENT
PORTFOLIO

ONCE DESIGNED, THE PERMANENT PORTFOLIO SHOULD BE LEFT untouched. Its purpose is to keep you aligned with long-term considerations, and they don't change yearly.

One day you'll review your investments and notice that something in your permanent portfolio is currently suffering through a bear market—gold, perhaps. You'll ask yourself, "Why should I have *any* money in gold when it will be at least a year before monetary policy becomes restrictive and gold moves up? I could sell the gold now and buy it back next year at a lower price."

Six months later, the stock market may fall apart and gold will rally. But when this happens, all you will recognize will be minor deviations from what you think are the current trends. When it finally becomes obvious that the trends aren't operating as you had imagined, you'll buy your gold back at a higher, not lower, price.

This could have happened easily in 1976. Monetary expansion wasn't reduced until the middle of the following year, but gold started its latest bull market from a low of $103 in August 1976. No one who waited until 1977 to convert his variable portfolio from stocks to gold was hurt very badly, but the purpose of the permanent portfolio would have been thwarted if the portfolio had been tinkered with in 1975 or 1976.

In the same way, the super-trends will probably end two years or more before the change can be confirmed. To abandon your permanent portfolio's warrants in anticipation of a short-term trading opportunity might prove very costly.

The permanent portfolio should be altered only for one of two reasons:

1. You believe that the current super-trends have finally ended. For this, you would need strong evidence that the economic chaos is over.

2. Personal considerations have changed. You may decide to pay more, or less, attention to your investments, calling for more, or less, of your capital to be in the variable portfolio. In this case, the percentage distribution *within* the permanent portfolio would not change, but the portfolio itself would command a different share of your overall capital.

The variable portfolio should reflect your view of the near-term future. The permanent portfolio should never be disturbed because of an opinion about temporary trends. If you make any changes in the permanent portfolio, they should be changes you expect to stay with for many years to come.

100% Permanent

If trading decisions impress you as an opportunity more for loss than for gain, a buy-and-hold strategy will make your life simpler. You'll probably keep 100% of your capital in the permanent portfolio and 0% in the variable portfolio.

Doing so, you must be prepared for periods when the value of your portfolio will decline. There is no permanent portfolio that will rise continually over the next ten years.

The situation for hard-money investments isn't the same as during the early 1970s. Price declines during the hard-money era were relatively brief, averaging about six months apiece. Now you may have to wait out declines of two years or more.

The 100%-permanent approach isn't necessarily unwise; it's just that you should understand what the choice implies.

PERMANENT INVESTMENTS

Since gold and the Swiss franc are in super-bull trends, they would be the dominant holdings in your permanent portfolio; but they would not be the only holdings.

Hedges

Hedges are required because you won't know immediately when a super-trend ends. Also, by offsetting declines in the portfolio's main investments, a hedge helps you to relax during periods that run counter to the super-trends. And a hedge protects against the possibility that the entire portfolio is misconceived.

A proper hedge has two characteristics. First, it is aimed in the opposite direction from your main investments; it rises when they fall. Second, it must be able to appreciate dramatically when it's needed; otherwise, you'd have to put 50% of your capital into the hedge to obtain full protection.

Stocks are aimed against gold, and dollars are aimed against the Swiss franc. Ideally, to protect against declines in its investments, the permanent portfolio should include a leveraged form of stocks and a leveraged form of dollars.

Stock warrants serve well as a hedge because a small investment, with limited risk, can buy a large interest in the stock market. Unfortunately, there's no comparable way to hedge against a rise in the dollar's value. It would be very handy to be able to purchase call options on long-term government bonds, but no such options exist. Leverage is available in other forms, but without the limited risk that makes warrants so attractive.

The alternative has to be a long-term position in dollars themselves. And although it won't be leveraged, it should be small. Its main purpose will be to provide buying power if you see that the long-term trends have gone against you. The dollars should be in a money-market fund or in Treasury bills.

Cash and Coins

In addition, you might want to hold insurance against a deflationary banking crisis and against a runaway inflation.

Cash (U.S. dollar banknotes) would be valuable in the event of a bank holiday, during which cash would be in great demand. And, most likely, silver coins could be used as spending money if a runaway inflation made the dollar worthless.

A Retreat

Another possibility is a retreat. The economy's troubles will end eventually, but it's unlikely that they'll end quietly. A runaway inflation or a deflationary collapse would have social consequences beyond the obvious financial effects that investment planning normally prepares for. A breakdown in the ability of banks to clear checks or of companies to make payments would undercut all the institutions that make city life as comfortable and safe as it is.

We can imagine how lifelong welfare clients might react when the government is no longer able to support them— either because runaway inflation has made the government's money worthless or because the government must cut back in order to avoid the runaway inflation. And we can only wonder how tranquil the big-city neighborhoods will be if they are blacked out night after night because the power company can neither collect its bills nor pay its employees.

As a form of protection against these and other possibilities, many people have established what is called a retreat. It is a safe haven created away from the cities, to which you would go if economic problems made the cities unfit to live in. Like the small holdings of cash and silver coins, it is a kind of insurance. If it turns out never to be needed, the retreat may still contribute to your peace of mind in the interim.

I devoted a half-dozen pages to the idea in each of two previous books, but I haven't discussed it in this one. One reason I've left it out is that I know very little about storing food, arranging for an energy supply, or any of the limitless details such an undertaking involves. The area involved is vast and requires a separate book—written by someone who knows the subject. My own experience with retreats has been personal and of very little value to anyone else. And since I have lived in Switzerland, the subject has lost its urgency for me.

Another reason I don't discuss retreats is that others choose to put so much emphasis on this one subject, about which I know so little. Six pages on retreats in my *You Can Profit* book earned me a full-page review in the New York *Times Book Review*, discussing my plans for the forthcoming end of civilization. The *Times*' best-seller list summarized my book as "Buy gold, silver, Swiss francs, and a gun"—even though I've never discussed guns in any of my books.

So I'm ignoring a subject about which I know very little. But if a retreat fits your plans, it should be considered part of the permanent portfolio.

Other Investments

Lastly, there may be other investments you'll want to include in the permanent portfolio. These might be a business, your home, life insurance, and other personal property. Beyond these, you might have permanent investments in real estate, collectibles, or whatever. If you don't intend to monitor or alter these investments as trends appear to change, they should be part of the permanent portfolio.[1]

I've indicated that silver rallies should be relatively infre-

---

1 A business that you control should be in the variable portfolio, since you can decide from month to month what direction the business will take. A business in which you have a long-term, illiquid investment that you don't control should be in the permanent portfolio.

quent in the future, making a buy-and-hold policy less attractive. But you may decide to keep silver bullion in the permanent portfolio, either because you want to take advantage of its long-term rise, or because you want an added element of diversification.

BREAKDOWN

There's no way I can tell you how much should be in each investment, as I don't even know which investments you'll select. But we can broaden the permanent portfolio example I gave earlier to include other possibilites. Again, I'll use 35% of the $100 capital as the permanent portfolio's share:

**PERMANENT
PORTFOLIO**

Gold	$12.00
Swiss francs	6.50
Warrants	3.00
Dollar Investments	2.00
Silver Bullion	5.00
Silver Coins	.50
Cash (banknotes)	.50
Life Insurance [2]	.50
Home (equity)	5.00
Total	*$35.00*

Although the investment distribution will depend upon which assets you hold, the emphasis I've given in this example is in keeping with my views. I believe the first three items are the most important.

If you have trouble deciding on percentages, treat this example as a starting point. Scratch out items that aren't applicable and alter the percentages that don't suit you. Once your pencil gets in motion, you probably won't have any trouble finding the right balance.

[2] Cash value of the policy.

ADJUSTMENTS

I've stated that you shouldn't tinker with the permanent portfolio once it's established. It should stand unchanged until you're ready to create a new long-term portfolio that itself will last for many years.

However, the portfolio requires annual maintenance. The percentages you establish should remain constant for many years. Since changes in investment prices will alter the percentages, you will need to make small adjustments each year to restore the proper balance.

For example, let's suppose that you have the simple portfolio used in the last chapter. It has only three items, representing 35% of your total capital of $100.

PERMANENT PORTFOLIO

Gold	$ 20.00
Swiss francs	10.00
Warrants	5.00
Total Permanent:	*$ 35.00*
Variable Portfolio:	*$ 65.00*
Total Capital	**$100.00**

A year later, when you review your investments, you find that your total capital has increased by 20%. Of course, each investment appreciated differently, and the differences have altered each investment's share of your capital:

	CURRENT VALUE	CURRENT SHARE OF CAPITAL	ORIGINAL SHARE OF CAPITAL
Permanent Portfolio			
Gold	$ 15.50	12.9%	20.0%
Swiss francs	10.50	8.8%	10.0%
Warrants	13.00	10.8%	5.0%
Total Permanent:	*39.00*	*32.5%*	*35.0%*
Variable Portfolio:	*81.00*	*67.5%*	*65.0%*
Total Capital	**$120.00**	**100.0%**	**100.0%**

To restore the original percentages, you must buy more gold and Swiss francs and sell some of the warrants. And because the variable portfolio has increased in value beyond its original 65% share of your total capital, something must be sold from the variable portfolio to replenish the permanent portfolio.

When the adjustment is made, the result will be:

	BEFORE ADJUST-MENT	AFTER ADJUST-MENT	NEW SHARE OF CAPITAL
Permanent Portfolio			
Gold	$ 15.50	$ 24.00	20.0%
Swiss francs	10.50	12.00	10.0%
Warrants	13.00	6.00	5.0%
Total Permanent:	*39.00*	*42.00*	*35.0%*
Total Variable:	*81.00*	*78.00*	*65.0%*
Total Capital	**$120.00**	**$120.00**	*100.0%*

Notice that the percentages under "New Share of Capital" are the same as those under "Original Share of Capital" in the preceding table.

The adjustments guarantee that the permanent portfolio will continue to do its job—no matter what the current bull and bear trends may be. By restoring the balance, you restore the safety originally built into the portfolio. Adjustments should be made yearly, more often if there are dramatic changes in investment prices.

Usually, you'll sell from holdings that have appreciated and add to holdings that have depreciated. Thus, maintaining your portfolio's balance is a simple way of honoring the investment truism "Buy low, sell high."

The adjustment of the permanent portfolio should be purely mechanical. If you believe certain investments will do especially well during the coming year, the *variable* portfolio is the place to act upon that belief. For the permanent portfolio, just restore the original percentages.

Home Equity

If you have a home in the permanent portfolio, you won't be able to sell small bits of it to restore the original percentages. If the portfolio's distribution slips 1% or 2% from the original, don't worry about it.

But if your home equity appears to have increased sizably, consider increasing the mortgage on the house. This would reduce your equity and provide funds to balance your portfolio. Or you can increase the size of the permanent portfolio (at the expense of the variable portfolio) so that the main permanent investments get the proper percentages of your overall capital. Or, if you firmly intend to keep the house for many years whatever its value, leave the house out of your portfolio plans. Your unwillingness to sell means that you don't want to treat the house as an ordinary investment.

INVESTMENT MEDIA

Because transactions in the permanent portfolio generally won't occur more than once a year, you can afford to disregard transaction costs and personal inconvenience. You are free to use the safest investment media; for me, that means handling the permanent portfolio through a Swiss bank.

The bank can buy, sell, and hold warrants, Treasury bills, money market fund shares, silver bullion, and gold. Swiss francs can be held in a Swiss franc current (checking) or deposit (savings) account.

If the bank's minimum size for gold bullion transactions is large enough to make yearly changes difficult, use a low-premium coin like the KrugerRand. There usually is no minimum for a purchase or sale of coins after an account has been opened.

Silver coins and cash should be kept in a safe-deposit box near where you live.[3]

A few more considerations for the permanent portfolio will be covered after we look at the variable portfolio.

---

[3] During the bank holidays of the 1930s, most bank offices were open for business; it was the accounts that were closed. You couldn't withdraw funds beyond a specified limit.

25

———

THE VARIABLE
PORTFOLIO

THE VARIABLE PORTFOLIO WILL HOLD INVESTMENTS SELECTED according to your judgment of current trends, and it will be subject to review at least every month.

A large percentage of the variable portfolio, perhaps all of it, would be used to alternate between gold on the one hand and stocks and bonds on the other. To handle the trading decisions, you will need to keep up with the monetary cycles (a task to be discussed in Chapter 28), but little more.

If your interests are broader, part of the variable portfolio would be reserved for other investments. These might include silver, currencies, or anything else. You would have a budget within the variable portfolio from which to draw whenever an investment looks promising. Money not being used can be kept in a money market fund.

If you have 65% of your capital in the variable portfolio, the breakdown could be:

VARIABLE
PORTFOLIO

———

Gold vs. Stock market	$35.00
$ & other investments	30.00
Total:	*$65.00*

STOCK MARKET INVESTMENTS

As I've indicated, I believe the best stock market investments are warrants, rather than stocks themselves. With warrants, you can obtain the same profit with less risk. Bad timing and poor selection are far less costly.

When the time comes to get into the stock market, you would sell the gold held in the variable portfolio and buy warrants. In the example above, you would have $35 to invest.

One dollar invested in warrants can do the work of about four dollars invested in stocks. Investing the whole $35 in warrants wouldn't reduce your risk; it would increase it. Instead, you would invest only about $9—which should have an effect equal to $35 invested in stocks.

The remaining $26 shouldn't be used for another investment. It should remain as neutral as possible, which means cash. The leverage in warrants is being used to limit your risk, not to expand it.[1]

The most neutral form for the other $26 would be to keep it in dollars (T-bills or a money market fund) or in Swiss francs. In fact, if you don't have an opinion on the immediate future of the franc, it might be more neutral yet to split the $26 between dollars and francs.

Thus, during a stock market uptrend, the variable portfolio would look something like this:

Stock market investments		$35.00
of which: Warrants	$ 9.00	
Dollars	26.00	
Other investments		30.00
Total Variable Portfolio:		*$65.00*

---

[1] I have no argument against using margin or other methods to leverage an investment, as long as you understand the risks involved. But that's a separate issue from the principle involved here.

Bonds

As I indicated in Chapter 14, long-term bonds usually appreciate during a bull market in stocks. You may want to divert some of the stock market budget to long-term (ten years or more) U.S. government bonds.

Unfortunately, there's no bond investment with the risk-limitation feature of a warrant. However, government bonds are less risky than individual stocks, and a little diversification between warrants and bonds might be wise.

If you invest in bonds, the money will come from the stock market budget (since the objectives are the same). Let's suppose you take $15 from the $35 in the stock market budget:

Stock market investments			$35.00
of which:	Warrants	$ 5.00	
	Dollars	15.00	
	Bonds	15.00	
Other investments			30.00
Total Variable Portfolio:			*$65.00*

If you choose, the bonds can be purchased on margin, in which case the $15 would represent your equity.

GOLD INVESTMENTS

The normal media for a gold investment are bullion and coins. However, there will be times when a new gold uptrend appears imminent but not certain. At this, or other times, you may decide to invest in gold options, instead of bullion or coins, until you're sure the trend is real.

The principle used for warrants applies here. You should purchase the number of options that cover as many ounces of bullion as your gold budget would have purchased. Since this will use only about 6% of the gold budget, the remaining funds should be kept in dollars (or partly in Swiss francs).

The option series purchased should be for the furthest expiration date and have a striking price close to the current bullion price.[2]

Your variable portfolio would look something like this:

Gold			$35.00
of which:	Options	$ 2.50	
	Dollars	32.50	
Other investments			30.00
Total Variable Portfolio:			*$65.00*

If you later decide that the uptrend in gold has materialized, tell the Swiss bank to take delivery of the gold just before the options expire. If, on the other hand, you decide that the uptrend was an illusion, sell the options and recoup what you can. If you're not sure one way or the other, hold on to the options.

If you choose, you can stay in options throughout a gold uptrend, selling expiring options at a profit and buying new ones. Doing so will cost you around 10% to 15% of your gold budget per year, but you may prefer to pay this in order to limit your risk throughout the trend. If you want to use options in this way, tell your Swiss bank to sell each option two weeks before it expires and purchase new ones. The striking price and expiration date of the new options should be chosen in the same way as they were for the old options.

OTHER INVESTMENTS

If you are not going to restrict your variable portfolio to gold and the stock market, you'll want a fund from which to make other investments as they become attractive. This fund would be kept in dollars (T-bills or a money market fund).

How much you should invest in each opportunity will depend upon your own evaluation of it. But if two investments are attractive, I suggest that you split your funds between

[2] The mechanics of gold options are explained on page 197.

them for diversification—rather than using all the "other investment" funds for the one you like better.

VARIABLE INVESTMENT MEDIA

The investment media for the variable portfolio are similar to those for the permanent portfolio.

Because gold, stocks, and bonds will normally be invested for the duration of an uptrend lasting in the neighborhood of two years, it won't be inconvenient to handle them through a Swiss bank. If you hold Swiss francs as a cash reserve, they should be kept there, too.

Silver, currencies, and other investments that you won't hold for a complete phase of a monetary cycle can be purchased either through a Swiss bank or on the U.S. futures markets. Any rapid in-and-out trading should be done in the U.S. markets for convenience and lower costs.

26

PORTFOLIO DETAILS

IN THIS BRIEF CHAPTER I'LL COVER A FEW SUPPLEMENTARY considerations, and then we'll take one last look at a total investment program.

SEPARATION OF FUNDS

For many investors it will be simpler to keep the permanent portfolio and the variable portfolio in separate bank or brokerage accounts. If all investments are handled through Switzerland, it might be wise to have each portfolio at its own bank. This way, you'll always be able to keep the holdings and the value of each portfolio straight.

If you don't think this is necessary, at least keep separate records. Keep track of the physical quantity of each investment (shares of stock, number of warrants, ounces of gold, number of dollars, etc.) in each portfolio. For example:

Permanent Portfolio
    6 KrugerRands (at Swiss Friendly Bank)
    2,000 Swiss francs (at Swiss Friendly Bank)
    100 ABC Warrants (at Swiss Friendly Bank)
    100 XYZ Warrants (at Swiss Friendly Bank)
Variable Portfolio
    Stock market investments
        100 DEF Warrants (at Joe's Neighborhood Securities)

100 GHJ Warrants (at Joe's Neighborhood Securities)
100 KLP Warrants (at Joe's Neighborhood Securities)
1,500 shares of Infidelity Money Market Fund
2,000 Swiss francs (at Swiss Security Bank)
Other Investment Budget
1,600 ounces of silver bullion (at Swiss Security Bank)
2,000 Swiss francs (at Swiss Security Bank)
1,500 shares of Infidelity Money Market Fund

It's helpful to note where each of these items is kept, so that you know which items belong to which portfolio.

TAX ACCOUNTING

There's a further reason for keeping the portfolios in separate accounts—taxes.

Suppose, for example, that you've made several purchases of gold, totaling 85 ounces—20 ounces for the permanent portfolio and 65 ounces for the variable portfolio—and that all 85 ounces are in the same account. If you sell the variable portfolio's 65 ounces, U.S. tax laws will figure the capital gain by assuming that the 65 ounces sold were the first 65 purchased. This is the FIFO ("first in, first out") rule of cost accounting.

Even though the first 20 ounces you purchased were for the permanent portfolio, the tax man will insist that they are among the ounces you sold. He will tax you accordingly.

If the portfolios are kept in separate accounts, you can sell the gold from the variable portfolio, and the purchase price for tax purposes will be what you paid for *that* gold.

Timing of Transactions

Also for tax reasons, you may want to handle the adjustments in your permanent portfolio around the middle of December. At that time, you can decide whether any sales should be made before the end of the year or be put off until

January. A loss on an investment sold in December could be deducted from the tax paid the following April, while the profit on sales made in January wouldn't be taxed until twelve months later.

INCOME AND OUTGO

In all probability, your capital won't remain static. You may add to it occasionally from outside sources. Or you may use the procedure discussed in Chapter 10 to draw living expenses.

Deposits

When you add a small amount to your capital, it is simplest to add it to the variable portfolio. Within the variable portfolio, place it wherever you believe it will do the most good. That may mean making a new purchase, or it may mean simply increasing your cash. At the time of the annual adjustment, you'll restore the proper division between the two portfolios.

If you receive a large sum, divide it immediately between the two portfolios—subdividing the permanent portfolio's share into the required investments.

Living Expenses

If you intend to draw your income from your portfolio, there are several ways to arrange for it.

The easiest method is to create a special account (call it the *income account*) each year when you adjust the permanent portfolio. The income account should contain enough funds (in dollars and/or Swiss francs) to pay your expenses for the coming year. If you keep the funds at a Swiss bank, you can instruct the bank to send you monthly (or quarterly) checks in dollars during the year.

When you make the annual adjustment, first restore the permanent portfolio to its required percentage of your current total capital. Then establish the income account with the funds needed for the coming year. All remaining funds go into the variable portfolio.

Another method is to sell a little from each investment during the year, using the proceeds as income. However, this is more troublesome, and it can require the sale of such small quantities that the transaction costs would become a hindrance.

TOTAL PROGRAM

The table on page 335 assembles the many elements discussed in this part. It includes items you might not want, so you'll need to rearrange it to suit your circumstances and opinions.

For purposes of example, the table assumes that the stock market is in an uptrend, so the variable portfolio contains warrants and bonds, but no gold. In the alternate part of the monetary cycle, that budget would be in gold alone.

The variable portfolio contains a $25.00 budget for miscellaneous investments. At the time of the hypothetical example, $10.00 is invested in silver bullion, $5.00 in a foreign currency, and $5.00 in another investment you have chosen; an additional $5.00 is held in cash.

The table also allows $5.00 for income through the following year.

The location of each of these investments is shown in the last column. Two Swiss banks are used, to keep the permanent and variable portfolios separate.

CHOICES

The figures I've given aren't meant to tell you what to do. My figures can't be taken literally because I've included

SAMPLE PROGRAM

Item	Amount	Location
Permanent Portfolio		
Gold bullion or coins	$12.00	Swiss bank #1
Swiss francs	6.50	Swiss bank #1
Warrants	3.00	Swiss bank #1
T-bills or money market fund	2.00	Swiss bank #1
Silver bullion	5.00	Swiss bank #1
Silver coins	.50	Safe deposit box
Cash (U.S. banknotes)	.50	Safe deposit box
Life insurance (cash value)	.50	Home
Home (equity)	5.00	Home
Total Permanent Portfolio:	**$ 35.00**	

Item	Amount	Location
Income Account		
Cash for coming year:	$ 5.00	Swiss bank #1
Swiss francs $ 2.50		
U.S. dollars* 2.50		
Total Income Account:	**5.00**	

Item	Amount	Location
Variable Portfolio		
Stock market investments	$35.00	Swiss bank #2
of which:		
Warrants $ 8.75		
U.S. dollars* 13.13		
Swiss francs 13.12		
Miscellaneous investments	25.00	
of which:		
Silver bullion $10.00		Swiss bank #2 or commodity broker
Foreign currencies 5.00		Swiss bank #2 or IMM
Other investment 5.00		?
U.S. dollars* 5.00		Swiss bank #2 and/or U.S. broker
Total Variable Portfolio:	**60.00**	
Total Capital:	**$100.00**	

*In Treasury bills or money market fund.

items that obviously not everyone owns or wants. However, I've attempted to place the emphasis where I believe it belongs.

It won't be difficult for you to decide how to distribute your capital. Start by writing various possible divisions down on paper. You'll soon find the breakdown that makes the most sense—the one that suits your requirements.

Make sure the plan is one that's practical for you to carry out. Don't let anyone pressure you into undertaking an investment approach that doesn't fit your capabilities and objectives. *Your* savings are at stake, not his.

Treat my suggestions in the same way. Often in this book I've used the word "should" because I know you'd get tired of reading "it seems to me" or "you may want to consider," etc. The word "should" is meant to apply to the goal being discussed; that is, if you're trying to accomplish the objective being discussed, "then you should . . ."

PART V

INVESTMENT TACTICS

27

TIMING

WE HAVE NOW SURVEYED ECONOMIC CONDITIONS, DISCUSSED investment philosophy, analyzed major investments, and devised a strategy. But we haven't covered what is the most critical topic of all—when to buy and when to sell.

Several times I've casually mentioned that you can buy near the beginning of an uptrend and sell shortly after it ends, but I haven't said how. It may be obvious that trends exist; it may be obvious that U.S. monetary policy causes cyclical patterns in gold, stocks, and bonds; and it may be obvious when past trends actually began and ended. But how you will recognize the next turning point is another matter.

So I can't blame you if you've become a little impatient with me and have decided I'm taking too much for granted in treating trend changes as obvious. If that's the case, I hope to get back in your good graces with this part of the book.

AUTOMATED TRADING

The goal of the tactics section is good timing. The right tactics should automatically answer such questions as: When do I buy? When do I take a profit? When do I admit defeat and take a loss?

With the right tactics the answers to these questions come automatically. The word *automatic* is important. If your tactical rules are well conceived, no subjective judgment should be required at the time of decision. The answer should be unmistakable. Once you have decided that an investment is promising, the time to buy and the time to sell should be determined by fairly explicit rules.

Many writers stress that you shouldn't be bound by rules. They believe you should base your judgments upon the conditions that prevail at the time of each transaction. I don't agree—at least not for investors who aren't professional traders.

The purpose of a trading system is to let you avoid losses you can't handle, while letting you exploit successful investments to the full. Even the best system won't always be right, but a good system stacks the odds in your favor.

Because trading rules are expected to improve your average results, they can't be effective if used one time and not the next. A system that is followed sporadically is no system at all.

It's true that professional traders don't need strict rules and, in fact, find them a handicap. But we aren't professional traders. Too many suggestions made in investment books disregard the capabilities of the reader. Very few investors are stupid, but many of them are not interested in becoming, or are not suited to become, artful traders. To expect them to exercise proper judgment in a situation for which they have no training is like sending a Sunday driver into the Indianapolis 500.

Stop-Loss Orders

One controversy about automatic decisions involves stop-loss orders. It is possible for the trader who holds your stop-loss order to buy your investment at the stop-loss price, even though the market price was still a little above the stop-loss point. This transaction, of itself, will cause the price history for the day to appear to justify the stop-loss sale; it won't be apparent that your sale was the only transaction at that price.

Some advisors believe you should never enter a stop-loss order, because it invites a market-maker to buy your investment from you on a downturn. They say you should pick your stop-loss price and then keep the decision to yourself. The day the price closes at or below the stop-loss point, tell your broker to sell at the market's opening the next morning.

This appears sensible. But I've seen too many investors waver when the time comes to sell. If the stop-loss order isn't on the broker's books, it doesn't really exist. When the price dips below the stop-loss point, the investor will reopen the question: "Should I sell or should I wait another day to see if the price will rebound?"

Of course, he'll decide to wait another day—and then another and another. Eventually, the price may be 20% below the stop-loss point. At that point, he'll feel he *can't* sell; he must wait for the price to come back so that he can avoid a loss.

Talking about tactics isn't the same as acting when a price is moving and emotions are running high. If the price of your investment is dropping, you won't have the same detachment about the question of selling as you had earlier about the question of buying. You will need rules.

The stop-loss price is chosen at a time when there is no emotional interference. Your choice then is more likely to be correct than the feelings you have when the price has dropped. If the stop-loss is executed automatically, the system will work. If the decision to sell is left up in the air, you have no system.

You must consider your own capabilities when you decide how your investments will be handled. Knowing yourself is as important as knowing the investment. If you recognize the limits of your skills, you can make the most of what you have—and do better than the person who's in over his head. Once you learn how to handle your limitations, you can work to expand those limits, if you choose.

Sometimes a stop-loss will sell your investment just before it rallies. And perhaps once in your investment career a market-maker may use your stop-loss order to take advantage of you (costing you very little). But most of the time, a stop-loss order will get you out just before the price falls further. Certainly, your tactical system doesn't know if the price will rise tomorrow, but no one else knows either.

TECHNICAL ANALYSIS

In Chapter 8, I discussed some of the drawbacks of technical analysis. I mentioned that academic studies have claimed to discredit the system.

However, I also pointed out that the tests were conducted by measuring the performance of every investment that gave a technical buy signal. This approach ignored the idea that the value of technical analysis is not in telling you *what* to buy, but *when* to buy. Fundamental analysis is necessary to pick an investment before technical analysis has any application. And such an approach doesn't lend itself to a computerized test.

I said that buying investments solely for their fundamental values is a risky policy. An underpriced investment often becomes more underpriced before it rises. The buy-and-hold eras are over, and we can no longer rely solely on an investment's fundamentals to take care of us. Timing must be added to the fundamentals, and only technical analysis provides clues for timing.

It isn't my purpose to provide a course in technical analysis; there are many good books available already. But I believe a few simple technical tools can provide most of the tactics you need. Then, if you want to pursue the subject further, a good textbook is listed on page 449.

TOOLS

The next chapter will explain how to spot trend changes within the monetary cycles. The following chapter will offer technical tools that can be used to verify investment trend changes, and Chapter 30 will provide guidelines for placing stop-loss orders. The remaining chapters in the section will discuss how to select stock market investments and where to obtain useful data.

There may be more here than you need. You will have to decide which tools you can use best and which tools you can't use at all.

Go through the range of ideas and weed out the things you don't agree with; from what's left, choose the tools that appear to match your interests and capabilities. My objective is to give you everything that might help and that will fit within the covers of one book. But you don't have to use everything I offer—not even everything that appears to be correct.

So if you come across something you don't think you can handle, don't worry about it. Read through it and then mentally set it aside. Perhaps sometime later you'll read it again, and it will seem perfectly clear.

In the meantime use only what you're sure you can profit from.

28

CYCLICAL
INDICATORS

THE CYCLICAL NATURE OF U.S. MONETARY POLICY HAS BEEN
a key theme of this book. Chapter 7 discussed the way monetary policy generates cycles in stock and bond prices. These markets are the first area of the U.S. economy to be affected by newly created money; if understanding the cycles can be profitable anywhere, it is here.

The dependability of monetary inflation's effect on the stock market can be seen in the graph on page 345. Like the graph on page 45, it shows the money supply's twelve-month growth rate. I've added to the monetary picture by inserting arrows that indicate the start of a major uptrend or downtrend in the Dow Jones Industrial Average.

IMPOTENCY

There is an omen in that graph. The down arrow marking the start of the most recent bear market appears long before the completion of the uptrend in monetary inflation.

This could be a sign that monetary inflation is losing its power to stimulate, that it is getting harder for newly created money to propel the stock market upward. In the 1975–1976 bull market, the Dow Jones Industrial Average would go

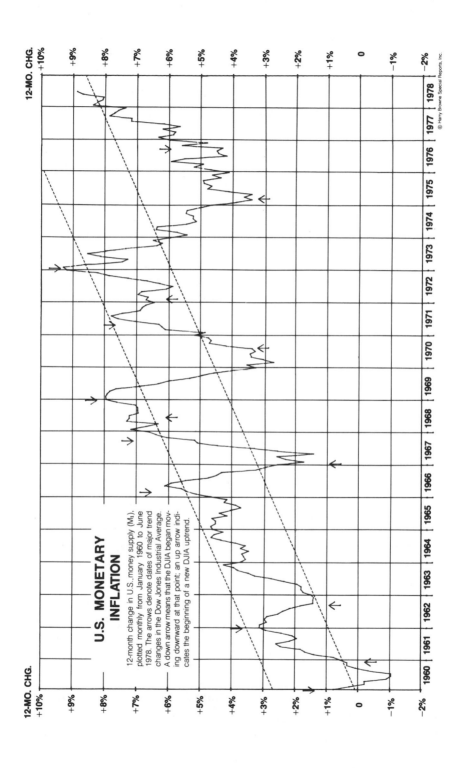

U.S. MONETARY INFLATION

12-month change in U.S. money supply (M₁), plotted monthly from January 1960 to June 1978. The arrows denote dates of major trend changes in the Dow Jones Industrial Average. A down arrow means that the DJIA began moving downward at that point; an up arrow indicates the beginning of a new DJIA uptrend.

12-MO. CHG.

+10%
+9%
+8%
+7%
+6%
+5%
+4%
+3%
+2%
+1%
0
-1%
-2%

12-MO. CHG.

+10%
+9%
+8%
+7%
+6%
+5%
+4%
+3%
+2%
+1%
0
-1%
-2%

1960 | 1961 | 1962 | 1963 | 1964 | 1965 | 1966 | 1967 | 1968 | 1969 | 1970 | 1971 | 1972 | 1973 | 1974 | 1975 | 1976 | 1977 | 1978

© Harry Browne Special Reports, Inc.

just so high and no higher, even though monetary inflation continued to rise.

It is possible that the next bull market in stocks will also wilt prematurely. New money may move the market up to some extent, but with little of the potency it showed in previous cycles. This, I believe, is a further confirmation of the super-bear trend in stocks.

It is also a sign that the long-term inflationary cycle may be nearing its end. If monetary inflation is losing its power to stimulate the stock market, it is also losing its power to stimulate the economy in general. Monetary expansion will become less noticeably a solution to unemployment and more noticeably a source of price inflation. Consequently, monetary inflation may lose its charm for politicians. Less monetary inflation could easily bring on a general deflation of the economy.

Even if future stock market uptrends are less vigorous than before, stocks will still provide a profitable alternative to gold during periods of monetary expansion. With the tactics to be suggested in the coming chapters, you should be able to get out safely even if an apparent stock rally suddenly turns into a crash.

MONEY SUPPLY

Since changes in the growth rate of the money supply are the stock market's prime mover, it might seem that watching the money supply is the key to spotting trend changes in stocks.

A glance at the graph on page 347 will probably serve to discourage that idea. The graph shows the actual level of the money supply week by week over the past eight years. From watching this chart weekly, how would you have known when a significant change had occurred?

The pattern becomes more intelligible when the growth rate, rather than the money supply itself, is plotted—as in the graph on page 345. But here, again, you wouldn't know

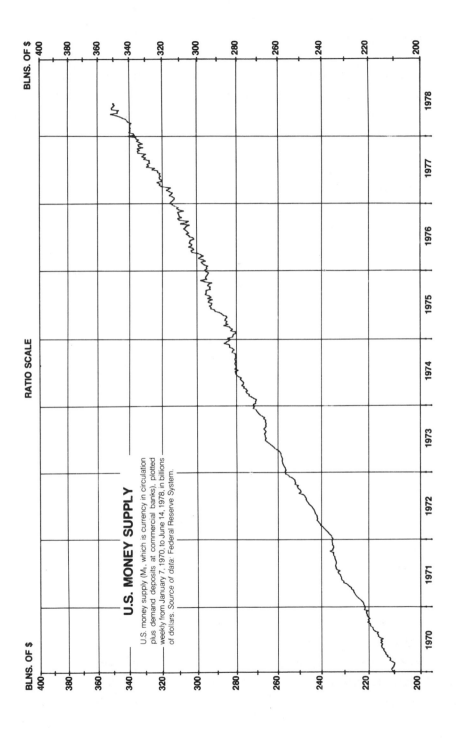

RATIO SCALE

BLNS. OF $

U.S. MONEY SUPPLY

U.S. money supply (M, which is currency in circulation plus demand deposits at commercial banks), plotted weekly from January 7, 1970, to June 14, 1978, in billions of dollars. Source of data: Federal Reserve System.

BLNS. OF $

400 380 360 340 320 300 280 260 240 220 200

1970 1971 1972 1973 1974 1975 1976 1977 1978

for sure that a trend change had occurred until many months after the fact.

Note in the graph on page 345 the apparent change to a monetary uptrend in early 1974, just before the worst of the stock market drop. Notice also the apparent change to a monetary downtrend in 1975, just before the stock market entered the second half of its bull market.

In each case it was many months until you would have realized that the basic trend had not changed. Realizing that such false alarms are possible, you would always have to wait several months after an actual trend change before you would be confident enough to act on it.

The principles of technical analysis can't be used to "chart" the money supply, because it isn't an investment market. The price graph of an investment reveals the decisions made by profit-seeking investors. The trends appearing on a money-supply graph are also the result of deliberate actions, but the motivations behind the actions are different. The theories of investment charting don't apply to economic indicators.

INTEREST RATES

Interest rates are affected directly by the Federal Reserve's monetary policy. As the Fed buys bonds in the marketplace, bond prices are pushed upward, and yields (interest rates) are pushed downward.

However, once again, short-term fluctuations can muddy the water for anyone who is looking for trends in interest rates. Trends are easy enough to spot in retrospect, as the graph on page 349 demonstrates. But at any given time, you have no way of knowing whether a current fluctuation is really the start of a new trend or just a brief disturbance.

We need an indicator that doesn't fluctuate in response to day-to-day pressures. Such an interest rate would be stubborn; it would move only after substantial pressure had developed. Because of its inertia, it wouldn't alert you the

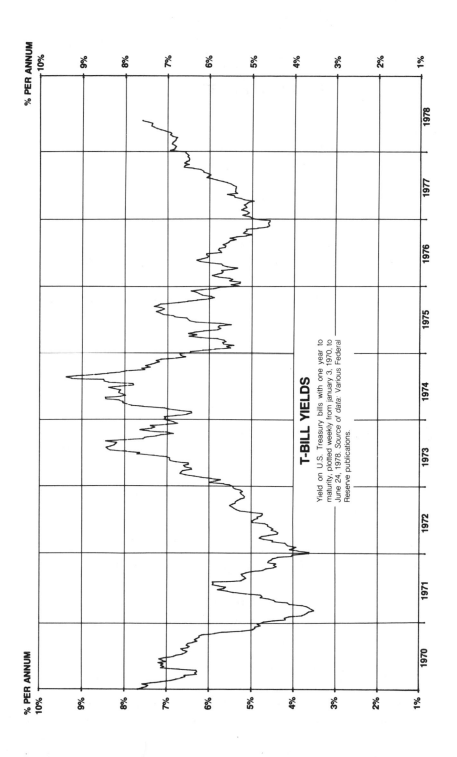

T-BILL YIELDS

Yield on U.S. Treasury bills with one year to maturity, plotted weekly from january 3, 1970, to June 24, 1978. *Source of data:* Various Federal Reserve publications.

% PER ANNUM

10%
9%
8%
7%
6%
5%
4%
3%
2%
1%

1970 1971 1972 1973 1974 1975 1976 1977 1978

% PER ANNUM

10%
9%
8%
7%
6%
5%
4%
3%
2%
1%

moment monetary policy had changed. But any signal it gave would be clear; you would know the trend had changed.

KEY INTEREST RATES

There are two such interest rates—the prime rate and the discount rate. Recent trends for both these indicators are shown in the graph on page 351.

The prime rate is the interest rate charged by commercial banks for loans to their best and largest customers. The discount rate is the interest charged by Federal Reserve banks for loans to commercial banks.

Normally, each of these rates will move only one to six times in a year, although they move as often as monthly during hectic periods like 1973–1974. Both rates tend to follow the yield on short-term securities, such as Treasury bills. The discount rate responds a little more slowly than the prime rate.

We aren't so interested in the movements of the rates themselves as we are in changes in their *direction*—a switch from rising to falling, or vice versa. Because these interest rates move only occasionally, any change in direction provides a strong indication that the monetary tide has turned.

As you can see from the graph on page 351, changes in the direction of interest rates occur only every year or two. And these trend changes occur less often in the discount rate than in the prime rate.

Because the discount rate is more stable, I believe its power as an investment signal is greater. A change in its trend is strong evidence that monetary policy has changed direction. And the monetary change indicates that the stock market will reverse direction—or that it already has.

Recent Record

A trend change is defined as either a rise in the discount rate after one or more falls, or a fall after one or more rises.

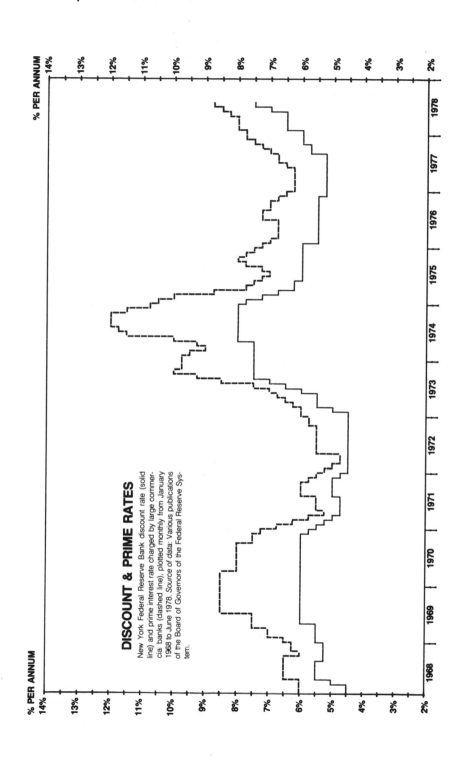

% PER ANNUM

DISCOUNT & PRIME RATES

New York Federal Reserve Bank discount rate (solid line) and prime interest rate charged by large commercia banks (dashed line), plotted monthly from January 1968 to June 1978. *Source of data:* Various publications of the Board of Governors of the Federal Reserve System.

Thus if the rate were rising in steps and then dropped, the drop would constitute a trend change.

Rising interest rates mean that monetary policy is tightening, drawing funds from the investment markets and causing a downtrend in stocks and bonds. Falling interest rates mean that monetary policy is loosening, making new funds available to the investment markets.

So if a new interest-rate trend is downward, the time has come to buy stocks and sell gold. If the new trend is upward, it is time to buy gold and sell stocks. *Gold moves in the direction of interest rates; stocks move in the opposite direction from interest rates.*

Since 1968 there have been eight trend changes in the discount rate. The record these trend changes have earned as forecasters of correct investment policy is shown in the table on page 354.

Each line covers one trend. Column two shows the date the new trend was signaled by the discount rate. Column one shows the investment called for by the trend change. Column three shows the price of the investment two business days after the discount rate signal (to allow an investor time to act).

Column four shows the date a new signal called for the trend to end. The price in column five is the price at which the investor would have sold out two business days later. The gain or loss for the investment is given in column six.

Column seven shows the accumulated investment gain from the beginning of each trend to June 16, 1978. For example, if you had begun using this system on November 19, 1971, you would have purchased stocks, held them until the next signal, and made a profit of 30.2% in that fourteen-month trend alone (as shown in column six). If you had continued to use the system through to June 16, 1978, you would have shown a gain of 550.0% (as shown in column seven). The accumulated gain from any other starting date can be determined by checking the date's results in column seven.

Finally, column eight converts the accumulated gain to an

average annual return. If you had started using the system when the December 1974 signal was given, your average yearly return through 1978 would have been 19.2%. If you had started with any other signal, your average yearly return would have been even better.

For comparison, the table on page 355 shows the record of the prime rate. Here the results are not as good. More investment changes were called for, and they were not so fruitful.

Reliability

Using the discount rate to signal changes isn't a new idea; it's been around for many years. But, although it's widely known, it isn't very widely used. It is probably one of those ideas that is neglected in practice because investors don't quite believe it or are swayed by other considerations when the signals occur.

There is no reason not to use it—so long as it continues to work. It is the ideal signal for the investor who is looking for a solid annual return without having to follow the investment markets closely.

One reason some investors don't use it may be that they are asking for too much. If you note the discount-rate signals on a chart of the Dow Jones Industrial Averages, for example, you'll see that the signal has been early on some occasions and late on others. The verdict is that the signal is not good enough. Perfect timing is demanded, so the discount rate is disregarded.

But the intelligent investor doesn't expect to get in at the very bottom and out at the top of every bull market. His goal, less ambitious but more realistic, is to participate in a large part of each major move.

The standard should not be what is missed, but what is gained. And what has been gained is shown in the table on page 354. Compare that result not with the returns from

DISCOUNT RATE SIGNALS

(1)	(2)	(3)	(4)	(5)	(6)	(7)	(8)
	Buy Signal		Sell Signal		Change During	Accumulated Change	Compound Annual
Investment	Date	Price	Date	Price	Period	to 6-16-78	Average
Stocks	8-30-68	906.95	12-18-68	966.99	+ 6.6%	+ 675.7%	+ 23.2%
Gold	12-18-68	$ 41.70	11-13-70	$ 37.625	− 9.8%	+ 627.7%	+ 23.2%
Stocks	11-13-70	760.47	7-16-71	892.30	+ 17.3%	+ 706.5%	+ 31.7%
Gold	7-16-71	$ 40.90	11-19-71	$ 43.26	+ 5.8%	+ 587.5%	+ 32.1%
Stocks	11-19-71	790.67	1-15-73	1029.12	+ 30.2%	+ 550.0%	+ 32.9%
Gold	1-15-73	$ 64.65	12-9-74	$ 174.75	+ 170.3%	+ 399.2%	+ 34.5%
Stocks	12-9-74	595.35	8-31-77	872.31	+ 46.5%	+ 84.7%	+ 19.2%
Gold	8-31-77	$146.40	6-16-78	$ 184.60	+ 26.1%	+ 26.1%	+ 34.1%

Dates shown are the days the discount rate changed direction.

Prices shown are the closing prices two business days after the signal. *Accumulated Change to 6-16-78* is the gain achieved by acting on all the buy and sell signals from the buy date for that line through June 16, 1978.

Compound Annual Average is the average annual rate of change (compounded basis) from each buy date to June 16, 1978. *Stocks* are the Dow Jones Industrial Average.

PRIME RATE SIGNALS

(1) Investment	(2) Buy Signal Date	(3) Price	(4) Sell Signal Date	(5) Price	(6) Change During Period	(7) Accumulated Change to 6-16-78	(8) Compound Annual Average
Stocks	9-25-68	933.80	12-2-68	977.69	+ 4.7%	+ 197.8%	+ 11.8%
Gold	12-2-68	$ 40.50	3-25-70	$ 35.30	− 12.8%	+ 184.4%	+ 11.6%
Stocks	3-25-70	784.65	5-11-71	936.34	+ 19.3%	+ 226.3%	+ 15.4%
Gold	5-11-71	$ 40.80	10-20-71	$ 42.475	+ 4.1%	+ 173.4%	+ 15.3%
Stocks	10-20-71	852.37	4-5-72	962.60	+ 12.9%	+ 162.6%	+ 15.8%
Gold	4-5-72	$ 48.35	10-24-73	$ 98.25	+ 103.2%	+ 132.5%	+ 14.7%
Stocks	10-24-73	987.06	3-22-74	883.68	− 10.5%	+ 14.4%	+ 2.9%
Gold	3-22-74	$172.25	10-7-74	$155.70	− 9.6%	+ 27.8%	+ 5.9%
Stocks	10-7-74	631.02	7-18-75	846.76	+ 34.2%	+ 41.4%	+ 9.9%
Gold	7-18-75	$165.25	10-27-75	$142.75	− 13.6%	+ 5.4%	+ 1.8%
Stocks	10-27-75	838.63	6-1-76	973.80	+ 16.1%	+ 22.0%	+ 7.8%
Gold	6-1-76	$127.20	8-2-76	$113.40	− 10.8%	+ 5.1%	+ 2.5%
Stocks	8-2-76	992.28	5-13-77	936.48	− 5.6%	+ 17.9%	+ 9.2%
Gold	5-13-77	$147.80	6-16-78	$184.60	+ 24.9%	+ 24.9%	+ 22.9%

See explanation on facing page.

clairvoyance, but with the returns from any other signal that is as easy to use as the discount rate.

Using the Rate

There are twelve Federal Reserve Banks. Each one has its own discount rate, but the rates usually agree. Occasionally, however, one or two banks will change trend while the others don't.

The largest and most important of the twelve banks is the New York Federal Reserve Bank. When the New York bank changes trend, the change is durable. So I use only the New York rate as a guide and ignore the others.

The rate isn't published daily in any newspaper that I know of, not even in *The Wall Street Journal*. However, rate changes are always published as a news item in the *Journal* and also appear in any local newspaper with a good financial section.

Each issue of the Federal Reserve *Bulletin* (described on page 401) includes the rates for the past two years. However, since the *Bulletin* is published monthly, you'll become aware of trend changes several weeks late.

A weekly publication that publishes the rate is described on page 402. Any time you're in doubt concerning the current rate, call the head office of any bank that is a member of the Federal Reserve System.

Keep a record of the discount rate, recording each change as it's published. Whenever a move is in a different direction from the last one, alter your investments accordingly.

SIGNAL

The discount rate is currently the most reliable indicator of the current trend in monetary policy. It wasn't as useful during the 1950s and early 1960s, because monetary inflation was milder and less erratic than it is now. Since the late

1960s, the signal has worked especially well, as the mistakes of the past have forced monetary policy into a stop-and-go pattern.

The discount rate is even more valuable than the monetary inflation rate. It is difficult to know, at any given time, how much monetary inflation is necessary to lift the stock market or the economy. But if the monetary impetus is great enough to push the stock market upward, it will be great enough to push the discount rate downward. If the monetary inflation is too little to help the stock market (as the graph on page 345 indicates was the case in 1977 and 1978), the discount rate will continue to rise. So it is more useful to watch the discount rate than to focus on the monetary inflation itself.

There's no guarantee that the discount rate will produce the same investment results over the next ten years, but there's every reason to believe it will continue to be valuable. In Chapter 30, I'll suggest a safety net you can place under your investments to provide for the day the signal no longer works.[1]

[1] I am grateful to Morgan Maxfield for reminding me of the discount rate in his book *1929 Revisited* (National Youth Foundation, Kansas City).

29

TECHNICAL
INDICATORS

TECHNICAL ANALYSIS BY ITSELF CAN'T PREDICT PRICES. BUT if you expect an investment to appreciate, technical analysis can alert you that the rise has begun in earnest, and it can warn you of the price levels at which the uptrend is likely to stall.

Many investors have a low opinion of technical analysis, and understandably so. Too often, its practitioners give the impression that they practice a mystical art—with all the jargon and ritual of a cult. Not surprisingly, technical analysis is frequently rejected out of hand.

In reality, technical analysis is a branch of fundamental analysis. Both attempt to discover how supply and demand will affect investment prices. However, technical analysis confines itself to examining supply and demand within the investment market itself. How much of the investment is likely to be available for sale at a given price? How much demand will develop for the investment at a specific price?

It isn't possible to poll investors to determine what they're going to do tomorrow, but the technician believes there are clues. He attempts to infer investor sentiment from the patterns he finds on a price graph.

In doing so he applies an understanding of the way investors tend to act. Whenever a price trend seems to overwhelm these tendencies or habits, he knows that investor sentiment is very strong in one direction.

The habits of investors provide the key to technical analysis. A few basic habits explain a great many of the recurring patterns that can be seen on price charts. From a survey of these habits, we can establish some simple rules for spotting trend changes.

BREAKING EVEN

One common habit is the preoccupation with breaking even.

In Chapter 9, I discussed the investor who hangs on to a losing position, telling himself that a "paper" loss isn't yet a real loss. After holding a bad investment for many weeks, months, or years, he'll seize any opportunity to get out without a loss. This phenomenon is so common that its effect is stamped on every chart of investment prices.

Suppose a high volume of trades takes place when a stock is at $50. Afterward, the stock drops to $35, and then begins working its way back up. As the price rises, many of the investors who bought at $50 and have held on will hope for a chance to break even.

When the price reaches $50 again, they will sell gladly—relieved that they have managed to get their money back after all. For the price to continue upward, the market will have to absorb what the break-even investors are so eager to sell.

Because of the large supply available at $50, this price is termed a *resistance* level—meaning a point at which the upward trend will run into a great deal of resistance. The price will usually back off from this level because there are too many sellers. In fact, it may approach and back off several times.

A resistance level can be self-perpetuating. Every time the price reaches the resistance level and break-even investors sell their holdings, new investors inherit an emotional interest in that price level. Should the price retreat, these new investors will welcome the chance to sell when the price returns to the resistance or break-even level.

If an investment's value calls for the price to go up, the price eventually will make it through the resistance level. There are two reasons:

1. The fundamental value of the investment will eventually create buying power of such urgency that it will simply overwhelm the resistance. The price will go through the resistance level once and for all.

2. As the investment's value becomes more apparent, it will attract buyers who will not be willing to part with the investment except at a high price. They intend to hold the investment for its potential. Typically, the investors who were so afraid of taking a loss didn't have a good reason to buy the investment; they merely hoped it would go up. But if there is a reason for the investment to appreciate, sooner or later the holdings will pass into what are called "strong hands"—investors who understand the investment's future and are not likely to sell until the future arrives.

Whenever a price approaches a resistance level, you should expect it to stall. If it doesn't, its progress indicates that there's a great deal of buying power behind the trend— enough to overcome the resistance and thus to take the price much further.

SECOND CHANCE

There are also *support* levels—prices at which a falling investment is likely to attract sufficient demand to stall the decline. Often, a support level comes into being because it was once a resistance level.

Suppose, for example, that many investors break even by selling at a resistance level, but afterward the price moves higher. Some of those who sold are going to regret having been so fainthearted. They'll wish for a second chance—an opportunity to get back on the bandwagon.

If the price drifts back down to the level at which they sold, they get their second chance. They can buy again without having missed any of the advance. Because the price has been the scene of heavy selling by break-even investors, it will now be a support level—a price at which a declining investment will receive support.

Normally a price will bounce upward from a support level many times. But if the selling pressure breaks through the support, this indicates that the downtrend is very powerful, and that the price will continue to fall.

ROUND NUMBERS

Support and resistance usually occur also at any round number—$2.00 as opposed to $2.13; $7.50 as opposed to $7.42; or $150.00 as opposed to $157.35, etc. Round numbers have no mystical significance; it's just that many investors choose them as price objectives.

It's unlikely that an investor who buys at $5 would plan in advance to sell at $8.23. More likely, he'd pick $8.00 or $8.50 as a target. Thus, in an uptrend, you can expect the price to run into resistance when it approaches a round number.

Support usually occurs at round numbers, also. As we've seen, any price that was once a resistance level becomes a support level after the price moves up past it, because sellers will welcome a second chance to buy. In addition, short-sellers pick round numbers as the price at which they'll close out their short position (by buying the investment). And, lastly, round numbers can be obvious prices at which a bargain hunter will plan to buy in the event of a downtrend.

SUPPORT AND RESISTANCE

The result of these investor habits is very simple: *any price at which a great many transactions have taken place is both a support and a resistance level.*

A trend can be expected to stall when it approaches such a price from either direction. If the trend moves through one of these levels, it's a sign that the trend is very strong and likely to continue.

VOLUME

Of course, every price along the way may have one or more investors waiting for it. But it is at prices where investors congregate that support and resistance are found.

To know which prices are significant, you need to know the prices at which there was a heavy volume of transactions. There are two methods of discovering this—the best way and a shortcut.

The best way is to follow daily volume figures. The shortcut is to look on a price graph for price levels that were obvious stalling points during trends. We'll look at each of these methods.

Volume Figures

Volume figures for major investment markets in the U.S. are published in *The Wall Street Journal* and in many other daily newspapers. You can, if you choose, keep a record of these figures or construct a graph from them.

It is much easier, however, to subscribe to a chart service. Such a service provides its subscribers with graphs of investment prices, usually published weekly. Some services cover stocks; others cover commodities and currencies. A few are listed on page 405.

The information is commonly displayed in the form of a "bar chart," such as the one of silver on page 363. The vertical lines forming a path across the middle of the chart indicate prices. For each day of trading, a line is drawn from the highest price to the lowest price. A small tic on each day's line marks the closing price.

The vertical lines at the bottom of the chart show the daily

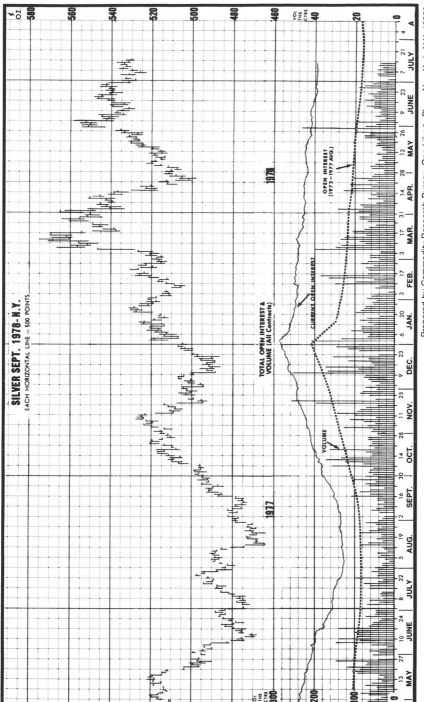

SILVER SEPT. 1978-N.Y.

EACH HORIZONTAL LINE = 500 POINTS

TOTAL OPEN INTEREST &
VOLUME (All Contracts)

1978

1977

OPEN INTEREST
(1972-1977 AVG.)

CURRENT OPEN INTEREST

VOLUME

Prepared by Commodity Research Bureau, One Liberty Plaza, New York, N.Y. 10006.

volume of transactions—the amount bought and sold. The absolute amounts traded aren't important; it's the relationship of the day's volume to the normal volume that matters. The lines that are taller than average identify the days on which high volume occurred; the prices for those days will be significant.[1]

Notice on the chart that high volume frequently occurred at prices near $5.00—on July 22, October 7, November 21 and 22, and on several days between December 9 and 23. Obviously, a lot of investors had an interest in the $5.00 price.

There also were high-volume days when the price was around $5.20 and $5.40. These prices, too, can be considered both support and resistance levels.

We can also see how a resistance level turns into a support level. In July and August, the price was unable to rise through the $5.00 area. It finally made it in October. It rose to $5.28 but then dropped back to the $5.00 area, which was then a support level. A later decline, the following April, also halted at $5.00.

Although U.S. exchanges publish daily volume figures, almost no foreign investment markets do so. In fact, you usually can't obtain even a daily *range* of prices, from which to create a bar chart. All that's published are opening and closing prices.

However, for foreign investments that are also traded in the U.S. (such as gold, silver, and some currencies), it isn't necessary to have foreign price and volume figures. What happens in European markets is usually repeated in the U.S., and vice versa. Consequently, the same price levels will be critical in all markets. You can use the price and volume information from the American markets—even if your investments are in Europe.

---

[1] The prices on the chart refer to the September 1978 silver futures contract traded on the New York Commodities Exchange. The volume shown is the total for *all* delivery months. The total volume is what you want, because the prices for all delivery months will move together. Silver for delivery in the future will be priced higher than silver for immediate delivery. As a result, the prices on this chart are higher than the cash prices for any given day. As September 1978 approaches, the futures price moves closer to the cash price.

Shortcut Method

If you're watching an investment for which no volume figures are available, or if you don't have access to a chart with volume trends, you can learn a lot from a chart that shows only prices. On such a chart, look for two things:

1. Any narrow range where the price remained for several days. You'll probably see that trends in either direction have stalled there. Even if daily volume was low, the total volume over several days would be fairly large.

2. Prices where a trend was turned back, even if only temporarily. These are obvious support-resistance levels. In the case of an investment that has no particular reason to move very far in any direction, a chart will not show any patterns. But if the price is in a definite trend, you'll see a number of obvious support-resistance levels along the way.

This is illustrated by the gold chart on page 367. The chart includes no record of volume, but the support and resistance levels can be discovered fairly easily.

Notice first the periods I've marked with "A." In each of them, gold was trading around $140. In mid-1974, a price decline halted at $127, but most of the trading appears to have been in the $140 range.

In late 1975, the bear market in gold halted for three months in the $140 range. After dropping through $140 in early 1976, a rally began, but it too halted near $140.

When the new bull market got underway in 1976, it encountered major resistance just under $140. And when the price finally cleared $140, its next decline halted at $140.

The $160 area (marked with "B"s on the chart) is also significant. Note the resistance encountered on the way up in 1974, the six months of support on the way down in 1975, and the support again in late 1977.

The periods marked with "C" show trading around the $180 range. There was resistance in early 1974, support in late 1974 and early 1975, and resistance again in 1978.

Support and resistance levels don't get "used up" over time.

A buyer who acquires an investment at one of these levels also acquires the seller's emotional interest in the price. And the investors who habitually wait to break even can wait for years.

The chart also shows that a resistance level turns into a support level and vice versa. The bull market of 1976–1978 sent the price upward in waves. A wave is created because the price encounters a resistance level and backs off. One or more attempts later, a strong uptrend will overcome the resistance. But when the price hits the next resistance level, it backs off once again.

Notice that each of the declines in the bull market halted approximately where a previous advance ended. Resistance levels have become support levels.

SUMMARY

Any price at which a large volume of trading has occurred will become both a support level and a resistance level. A support level is a price at which a decline can be expected to stall. A resistance level is a price at which an uptrend can be expected to stall.

A support-resistance price can be effective for many years. It wears out very slowly.

During an uptrend, expect temporary declines to halt near a price where a previous advance ended. During a downtrend, expect temporary rallies to halt near a price where a previous decline ended. In both cases, the trend can be expected to resume. If it doesn't, there is a good chance that the trend is over.

There's a great deal to technical analysis that I haven't covered in this chapter. But a good part of it is derived from support-resistance theory. Such things as "head-and-shoulders" patterns, "ascending triangles," etc., are merely other ways of expressing the concepts of support and resistance.

With an understanding of support and resistance, you can have a very good idea of the current state of any trend.

In the next chapter I'll suggest trading rules that put these concepts to work.

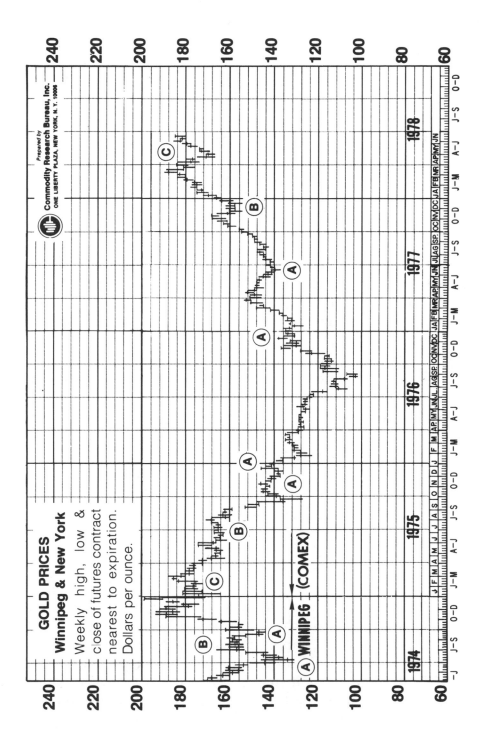

GOLD PRICES
Winnipeg & New York

Weekly high, low & close of futures contract nearest to expiration. Dollars per ounce.

Prepared by
Commodity Research Bureau, Inc.
ONE LIBERTY PLAZA, NEW YORK, N. Y. 10006

30

MAKING DECISIONS

INVESTING WOULD BE SIMPLE IF WE DIDN'T HAVE TO MAKE decisions. We could sit in the shade while the money rolls in—as, in fact, many people did during the two previous investment eras.

Unfortunately, more work and effort are required now, and so are more decisions. The first rule of decision-making is that you *do* have to make decisions; having to make them is the nature of life. The second rule is to limit your decisions to those you can handle.

If you've found the ideas in this book sensible, you'll still have to decide which of them you'll use. One of the standards to be applied to each idea is whether using it will require further decisions that you're not sure you can handle.

STRATEGY

The first choice is about general strategy. If you believe you can't handle the changes involved in managing a variable portfolio, you'll apply the buy-and-hold approach and keep 100% of your capital in the permanent portfolio.

On the other hand, if you believe you can profit by making changes in your investments periodically, you may want to use the twin-portfolio strategy introduced in Chapter 23. In that case, your next decision will be how much of your capital to place in each of the two portfolios.

That choice should be based largely on how confident you feel about managing the variable portfolio profitably. The greater your confidence, the larger your variable portfolio will be.

Permanent Portfolio Decisions

Whatever the division between the two portfolios, you'll need to decide on a distribution of investments within the permanent portfolio.

If all your investments are liquid, so that there will be no difficulty in creating exactly the portfolio you want, I suggest that the primary emphasis be on gold. Compared with what you put into gold, Swiss francs should receive about half as much; warrants should receive about one-quarter as much; and dollar investments should receive about one-tenth as much as gold.

If you have difficulty doing this, it is probably because illiquid investments you own—such as real estate, collectibles, or a business—are getting in the way. In that case, you have three alternatives, none of which may be very satisfactory:

1. Increase the percentage of your total wealth devoted to the permanent portfolio. This will, of course, make the variable portfolio smaller.

2. Plan around the illiquid investments. If you have numismatic gold coins in the permanent portfolio, count their bullion value as part of your gold budget. If you have an interest in a business whose profitability is tied to the economy's general level of prosperity, count the business as part of your warrant holdings. This approach can help as far as it goes, but there may be no correspondence between the investments you would like to have in your permanent portfolio and the illiquid investments you actually own.

3. Sell the illiquid investments. In some cases, selling would be a drastic move. But if illiquid investments are

throwing your portfolio out of balance, that alone is a good reason to consider selling at least part of them.

Variable Portfolio Decisions

The next decision involves the types of investments to include in the variable portfolio.

If you agree with my analysis of the monetary cycles, you'll want to include funds for "gold vs. stocks." Trading gold against stocks requires little supervision or judgment. By following the discount rate (as discussed in Chapter 28), you will keep well enough informed to make the necessary trades back and forth.

If you are more adventurous, you'll branch out into non-cyclical investments—such as silver and currencies—and you'll need to make decisions more frequently.

As to how you should allocate money among the different areas of the variable portfolio, the rule is the same as for choosing the size of the variable portfolio: Let your confidence be your guide. The less confident you are about making trading decisions, the more your variable portfolio should rely on gold and stocks.

Getting Started

The last strategic decision is how to get the variable portfolio started. When you begin, you almost certainly will catch the monetary cycle and the markets in midphase, not at starting points. It may have been a year or more since the last signal from the discount rate.

The first step is to determine what the last signal was. If the discount rate is still in an uptrend, the bull market in gold presumably is still alive; if the rate is in a downtrend, a bull market in stocks is probably underway.

If you read this in late 1978, it is quite likely that gold will be in the final stages of a long bull trend and that the stock market will be in the final, despondent stage of a bear trend. If you confirm this by determining that the discount rate hasn't yet turned down, you have three alternatives:

1. Do nothing with the variable portfolio until the discount rate does turn down, signaling that it is time to enter the stock market.

2. Buy gold bullion and hold it until the discount signal comes.

3. Buy gold options and hold them while you wait for the discount signal.

I much prefer the third alternative. You have no way of knowing whether the current trend will last another week or another year. If it ends soon, the most you can lose with options is 7% of your gold budget; if the trend has further to go, you'll go along with it and profit.

You will face the same decision if you read this book in later years, since you will be entering the market sometime after the latest discount signal. Again, my first choice would be to buy the low-risk, leveraged investment that is appropriate for the current phase of the monetary cycle—gold options if the discount rate has been rising or warrants if the discount rate has been falling.

No matter what the current state of the markets, the permanent portfolio should be initiated immediately, without waiting for signals of any kind.

Choices

The decisions I've summarized here are really decisions about yourself. There are plenty of opportunities in the investment markets, but that doesn't mean everyone will exercise the attention, the patience, and the skill needed to exploit them. You should give a great deal of thought to the basic approach you're going to use. How much work are you willing to do and how much worry are you willing to accept?

This isn't intended to discourage you from getting deeply involved. Obviously, I find the subject very exciting; and

I've emphasized strongly that today the most successful investment programs will need to be more active than in the past. But I think it's equally important not to encourage you to do more than you can do well.

TACTICAL DECISIONS

If you employ only a permanent portfolio, you'll need to tend to it just once each year. Even then, there will be no judgments to make, other than the decision to stick to your plan. You'll need only to restore the investments to the same percentage distribution they had when you initiated the program. This is an administrative chore that can be handled with a $10 calculator and a few instructions to your bank or broker.

Cyclical Investments

If you have a variable portfolio, you'll undoubtedly have all or part of it in cyclical investments—gold and stocks. For these, there will be three tasks: (1) watching the discount rate; (2) choosing specific stocks or warrants; and (3) placing a safety net under the investments.

The discount rate was covered in Chapter 28, and we'll cover stock and warrant purchases in the chapter after this. Here I'll discuss the safety net.

SAFETY NET

The discount rate has worked very well as a market indicator over the past ten years. But as the chaos increases, dangerous surprises become more likely. I believe it's important to have a safety net under your investment program whenever you're in the stock market.

The safety net is a stop-loss order that will get you out

of the stock market if it takes a drop that is too big to be just a temporary setback in a bull market.

An entire bull market in stocks will last in the neighborhood of two years and will include temporary declines as well as the general advance. The safety net isn't a device for taking advantage of these minor back-waves. Instead, its purpose is to make sure you get out in time if a small decline turns into the deflationary crash that might end the present investment era.

Filter Rule

The stop-loss level is determined according to a simple method called a *filter rule*. A filter rule is so named because it "filters out" any movement smaller than the size you believe would be critical. It says that if an investment drops by a stated percentage from its high, it should be sold.

If you are relying on trend changes in the discount rate to tell you when to sell stocks, I believe the most sensible filter to use is 20%. It should be applied to the Dow Jones Industrial Average. Here's how it would work.

Suppose that the stock market has begun a new bull trend from a DJIA low of 600. When the DJIA reaches 647, the discount rate gives a buy signal. You purchase stocks or warrants and watch as the uptrend continues.

Along with your order to buy, you issue a general stop-loss order to your bank or broker to sell all your stocks, warrants, and bonds in the event the DJIA drops to 520 (20% below 650). Thereafter, every time the DJIA rises another 50 points (to 700, 750, etc.), you raise the stop-loss by 40 points— which will keep it 20% below the recent high.

You should never lower the stop-loss. It should always be approximately 20% below the highest level of the current bull market.

Normally, after the DJIA has achieved its final bull-market high, the discount rate signal will come before the market has dropped by 20%, and it will alert you to sell. But one day in the future, the discount signal will fail, and then the filter will be very important.

Filter Rule's Value

Let's say, for example, that the DJIA has passed 950 and you have raised the stop-loss to 760 (20% below 950). Shortly afterward, the market goes into a decline, which it probably has done several times since the start of the bull market. However, this decline goes further—and without a rise in the discount rate to explain why. The DJIA works down slowly to 800, but the discount rate still doesn't give a sell signal.

Suddenly the market seems to fall apart. In one day, the DJIA drops by 25 points, and by 20 points more the next day. The DJIA reaches 755, your stop-loss is activated, and all your stock market holdings are sold. The market continues to drop, and the decline turns into the worst crash since 1929.

Surviving such a crash is the purpose of the safety net. The filter won't help you get out quickly at the top of a bull market. It is a device to protect you when the discount rate signal lets you down—as it is likely to do eventually.

Filter rules have been used for buying and selling investments for a long time. As a normal trading tool, the results have been poor. But we are not in a normal situation. The job the filter rule can do now is to detect the approach of the deflationary crash to which today's market is especially vulnerable.

In previous investment eras, which developed without the cyclical interference we get from today's monetary authorities, the stock market moved in an apparently random fashion. A filter rule was as likely to get you out of the market before a recovery as it was to get you out before a decline.

But we're not investing in the markets of the previous investment eras. The accumulated damage of the monetary cycles has weighted the odds in favor of an eventual crash.

Thus a filter rule in today's market is more likely to sell you out before a disaster than before a rally.

Complications

Submitting an across-the-board stop-loss order based on a market average isn't a common practice, and your broker may not know how to handle it. If your broker won't accept such an order, there are two other possibilities to discuss with him.

First, he could agree to call you promptly if the DJIA drops to a stated level. At that time you would issue individual sell orders for each stock, bond, or warrant in your variable portfolio. Second, you could give the broker a limited power of attorney to sell your holdings in the event the DJIA falls to the stated level. In both these cases, you'll have to revise your instruction every time the stop-loss should be raised.

If you can't make an arrangement that gives you the confidence that the safety net is firmly in place, you'll have to use a "mental stop-loss." Watch the DJIA at least every week or so, and be determined to issue sell orders the moment the filter rule calls for it.

The filter rule will be important even if you regularly place an individual stop-loss order under every stock. Although your stop-loss orders may get you out before a 20% drop occurs, the 20% drop without a discount signal would alert you not to get back into the market, and it would alert you to sell any stocks or warrants that hadn't already been stopped out. The drop would also tell you to sell any other investment, such as bonds, that would suffer during a deflation and that doesn't have a stop-loss of its own.

Economic Consequences

If the filter rule causes your stocks to be sold (without a discount rate signal), you should consider the matter to be serious. It may be an important warning that the economy has finally run out of gas, that monetary inflation has lost its power to stimulate, and that a deflation is in the works.

Once the filter rule provides such a signal, it would make sense to transfer as much of your capital as possible out of the U.S., and to activate any personal emergency plans you've made for a general breakdown of the economy.

Other Investments

A filter rule could be used as a signal to sell gold in the event one of gold's cyclical bull markets turns sour—if you thought that a sudden return to good times was a serious possibility. But that isn't likely. Even if the cheeriest optimist turns out to be right and the era of economic chaos ends without a depression, the recovery will have to be very gradual.

Variable Only

In using the filter rule make sure that any stop-loss order applies only to the holdings in your variable portfolio. The warrants in the permanent portfolio should not be disturbed, despite the conditions suggested by the activation of the filter.

NONCYCLICAL INVESTMENTS

The discount rate signal doesn't apply to noncyclical investments—silver, currencies, and others. Nor does the filter rule apply. To limit your risk and to maximize your profits, it will be necessary to exercise careful judgment in timing your purchases and in selecting stop-loss prices.

The rest of this chapter will cover trading rules for noncyclical investments. If you intend to limit the variable portfolio to gold and the stock market, feel free to skip ahead to the next chapter on page 381.

Basic Rules

There are four basic rules:

1. Buy an investment only when you believe there are fundamental reasons for it to appreciate; buy only if the investment's price is less than its value.

2. Don't buy until the price action has demonstrated that the uptrend has begun.

3. Sell out quickly if the rally proves to be a false signal.

4. Once the rally is confirmed, give the price plenty of room in which to fluctuate; don't sell too quickly.

Procedure

To carry out these rules there is a series of steps you can take for any investment you believe will appreciate:

1. Obtain a price chart for the investment. Using the principles outlined in the last chapter, look for support and resistance levels. Draw horizontal lines all the way across the graph at these price levels.

2. Identify the range in which the investment is currently trading. Specifically, where is the resistance level that has so far prevented the price from taking off?

3. Enter what is called a *stop order to buy*, which instructs your broker to *buy* if the price *rises* to a stated level.

The stop order to buy should be placed slightly above the top of the resistance area that is currently restraining the price. How far above depends on the investment's volatility, but 3% is a useful rule of thumb. Along with this order, you can also issue a *conditional* stop-loss—a stop-loss that becomes effective only after the stop-buy has been activated. For example:

If the price of coconuts reaches $7.21 or higher, buy five tons. If this order is executed, immediately enter a stop-loss order to sell at $6.79.

4. The initial stop-loss order should be placed at a price slightly *below* the resistance level that dictated the stop-buy price. Again, a useful guideline is 3% below the old resistance level—which will become a support level once the price moves above it. The rally will be invalidated if the price moves through that level and back into its old trading range.

5. After the price has broken out of its trading range, don't be surprised if it returns to the top of that range. As I indicated in Chapter 9, many investors who have taken losses are so happy to see a profit that they'll sell almost immediately when the price finally moves up. This can cause a partial retreat.

The price will often move back to the top of the trading range and then resume its rally. As long as it doesn't drop back into the trading range, the rally is still alive.

You might think it would be more profitable to buy after the price makes this retreat, but the retreat doesn't always happen. Sometimes the price moves out of the trading range and runs a long way before encountering resistance.

6. Once the rally is underway, draw new horizontal lines across the graph at each price level where the rally stalls. These are new support-resistance areas.

7. As the price moves up to higher levels, raise the stop-loss order to a price 3% below the *second* support-resistance level beneath the highest price reached in the rally. For example, if the current price is $8.80 and you have identified support levels at $8.50 and $8.00, you would place the stop-loss at $7.76—3% below $8.00.

This means that the price can drop quite a bit from its high without activating the stop-loss order. Once the rally is underway, you want to give it every benefit of the doubt. Don't sell too quickly; don't be afraid that you won't get the last dollar of profit. You *won't* get it, but neither will the person who sells too soon.

8. Never, under any circumstances, *lower* the stop-loss order. The stop-loss is there to sell the investment when the price is dropping; otherwise, there's no reason to have it.

Cyclical Investments

Stop-losses of some kind are necessities for noncyclical investments such as silver or currencies. But they aren't necessary for gold or stock market investments—as long as you watch the discount rate and keep a safety net under stock market investments.

If you're going to trade in and out of the market during a bull trend, stop-losses will be important. But for most people such trading won't be practical and I don't encourage it. And the spreads between buying and selling prices for warrants make them a poor choice for in-and-out trading.

STOP-LOSS PROBLEMS

From what I've said in this chapter, you could easily believe that stop-loss orders will solve every possible investment problem. While they do solve many problems, they aren't magic.

One difficulty is obvious. The price could drop far enough to trigger the stop-loss, then rise to a new high. If you place your stop-losses carefully, this won't happen very often.

The second difficulty is that the stop-loss order may not be executed at the anticipated price. The order instructs the broker to offer your investment for sale in the marketplace after the price has dropped to a stated level. Normally, in a liquid market, there will be a buyer available at a price very close to the stop-loss price.

But occasionally a piece of bad news so undercuts an investment that the price takes a vertical plunge, with no trades along the way. This happens rarely, but it happens.

Particularly troublesome is what is called a *gap*—which is

a pronounced difference between one day's closing price and the next day's opening price. For example, suppose your stop-loss is for $6.75. On Tuesday, the market closes at a price of $6.78. On Wednesday, the market opens at a price of $6.65. In that case, your stop-loss sale will be executed near $6.65— not $6.75.

TRADING

Generally, however, stop-loss orders will serve you well. They are protection against your own emotions and against surprises in the marketplace. I strongly suggest that you use them.

Even with stop-losses, you might find that you don't do as well as you had hoped. Identifying correct stop-loss levels is a skill that must be developed. I hope that the rules I've given will help to speed up that development, if you aren't experienced already. But neither of us can be sure they will.

As I suggested for commodity investments in Chapter 18, it is best to start out slowly, keep your risks small, develop a feel for what you're doing, see some good results, and only then take bigger risks.

Don't expect to conquer the world tomorrow morning; it may take all day.

31

———

SELECTION OF
STOCK MARKET
INVESTMENTS

UNLIKE THE OTHER MARKETS I'VE DISCUSSED, WHEN YOU INVEST in the stock market you have to select specific issues. I've used the Dow Jones Industrial Average as an indication of price trends, but most people won't buy the DJIA. Individual stocks or warrants can achieve results quite different from the averages. So, however you invest in the market, you will want issues that move, as a group, with the averages.

I've suggested buying stock warrants as a way to profit from stock market uptrends while avoiding much of the risk and exposure of owning stocks. However, I'm aware that many investors will decide against purchasing warrants—probably because warrants are unfamiliar.

So this chapter will offer suggestions for selecting stocks, warrants, and mutual funds. In addition, I'll provide some leveraged alternatives to warrants, in case you find that most warrants are overpriced when you're ready to buy. And since bonds move up and down with the stock market, they too will be covered.

TIMING AND SELECTION

If stock market movements weren't cyclical, picking individual winners would be the only way to profit. However, the stock market does move cyclically, and so timing can be enough. When you think the averages will rise, the most important consideration is that your stocks add up to a portfolio that will rise with the tide.

So my suggestions are geared mostly to duplicating the averages.

STOCKS

When the Dow Jones Industrial Average is around 600, for about $86,000 you can buy 100 shares of each of the stocks in the Average. If you have that much in your stock budget, this is the simplest and easiest approach.

Most investors don't have $86,000 to spend on stocks. But it's possible to reduce the capital requirement by buying a handful of the DJIA stocks—at least one or two from each of the six categories explained in the table on page 383. By buying one of each group, your results will be very close to those of the DJIA. At a DJIA of 600, it will require about $17,000 to purchase 100 shares of six stocks.

Beta

Another approach is to select stocks that have historically moved in tune with the overall market. This relationship is called *beta*.

An average stock has a beta of 1.0; a higher beta means the stock moves more dramatically than the market—but tends in the same direction as the market. A beta much less than 1.0 means the stock's movements are more conservative or

30 DOW JONES INDUSTRIAL STOCKS

Grouped by Industry

Consumables
American Brands
American Can
Eastman Kodak
Esmark
General Foods
International Paper
Owens-Illinois
Proctor & Gamble

Oil
Exxon
Standard Oil of Calif.
Texaco

Retailers
Sears Roebuck
Woolworth

Regulated
American Tel. & Tel.

Materials & Chemicals
Allied Chemical
Aluminum Co. of America
Bethlehem Steel
Du Pont
Inco (International Nickel)
Johns-Manville
Minnesota Mining
Union Carbide
U.S. Steel

Durable Goods
Chrysler
General Electric
General Motors
Goodyear
International Harvester
United Technologies
Westinghouse Electric

generally independent of the overall market. The *Value Line Investment Survey* provides a beta for every major U.S. stock.[1]

If you want to approximate the market's volatility, look for stocks with a beta of 1.0; if you want to move with the market but want more volatility, look for stocks with betas higher than 1.0.

Because the betas are only historical tendencies, you can't count on a specific stock to perform in accordance with its beta. You need to construct a portfolio of around 15 stocks to assure that the portfolio will move in line with its average beta. To buy 100 shares of each stock will usually require a budget of around $20,000, but you may find lower-priced stocks that match your beta standard.

If you're not interested in doing the research yourself, your broker may be willing to select stocks with the beta range you specify. However, a Swiss bank isn't likely to do this for you.

Growth Stocks

Growth stocks generally outperform the market averages during a bull market. But this will show up in the betas given in *Value Line*, so you don't need to look specifically for growth stocks.

Market-Makers

Another approach is to look for companies whose fortunes are linked with the success of the stock market itself.

Three major stockbrokers are publicly owned; their shares are traded like any others. The companies prosper during a bull market because their commission income increases as trading volume goes up. And since they are market-makers, carrying inventories of stocks and bonds for sale to customers, the market's rise adds to the value of their assets.

[1] Details for the publication are given on page 407.

The three stocks (and where they're traded) are:

> Merrill Lynch (New York Stock Exchange)
> Bache (New York Stock Exchange)
> First Boston (over the counter)

MUTUAL FUNDS

The prestige of mutual funds has declined drastically since the heyday of the gunslingers in the 1960s. The main reason, I believe, is that the stock market is cyclical and fund managers never seem to know when to get out of a falling market. Consequently, mutual fund values go up and down—just as the market does.

For our purpose this is an advantage. During a super-bear trend, you lose money in the long run by holding a mutual fund through uptrends and downtrends. But if you use the discount rate signal to move with the cycles, a mutual fund can be an appropriate vehicle.

The fund may do better or worse than the averages—as a result of its selection of stocks and the percentage of its assets that it invests in stocks when the market is rising. The main standard for selecting a fund should be its record in matching the averages. Don't try to pick the most astute management; the winners change like players in a game of musical chairs.

Types of Funds

One consideration is the *type* of fund. A mutual fund is just one of two main types of *investment companies*. An investment company is a firm that raises capital by selling shares and investing the proceeds in the stocks of other companies.

A mutual fund is an investment company that continually sells new shares and buys back its old shares, when requested, at the per-share value of its current net assets.

The other type of investment company is the *closed-end investment company*. It issues shares once and then no more. Thereafter, the shares are traded between investors in the open market, just as with normal stock shares. Many of them are listed on the New York Stock Exchange.

A closed-end company's shares usually sell for less than the per-share value of the fund's assets. That discount tends to shrink during a bull market, however, which gives the shares an extra boost, in addition to the effect of rising portfolio values.

The table on page 387 lists nine closed-end investment companies that have generally risen along with the market during previous trends. These companies are called "diversified funds."

Barron's and the Monday *Wall Street Journal* both carry a table ("Publicly Traded Funds") that lists closed-end fund share prices and asset values. A sub-heading of this table identifies the diversified funds.

If you have no desire to buy warrants and no zeal for researching stocks, your best bet may be a fund. A small stock market budget is another reason for choosing a fund. You need diversification to insure that your stocks move up with the averages, and transaction costs can eat up a small portfolio that tries to diversify on its own.

WARRANTS

The leverage in warrants makes them especially appropriate for an investor who is cautious about the stock market. If a stock rises 10%, its warrant may rise 30% or 40%. Thus, you can have an interest in a stock while risking less than the cost of the stock.[2]

However, a warrant isn't a bargain at every price—no more than any other investment is. Nor do all warrants have the same leverage. So you'll need to select warrants that provide

---

[2] Warrants are explained on page 139 of Chapter 12.

DIVERSIFIED COMMON STOCK FUNDS
(Nine Funds Likely to Move with the Market Averages)

Name of Fund	Discount
Adams Express Company	17.3%
Baker Fentress & Co.	29.2%
General American Investors	24.4%
Lehman Corporation	25.1%
Madison Fund	25.6%
Niagara Share Corp.	21.0%
Overseas Securities Co.	9.7%
Tri-Continental Corp.	14.8%
U.S. & Foreign Securities	26.5%

Discount shown is the percentage by which the company's stock was trading under its net asset value on June 30, 1978. *Source:* The Wall Street Journal.

the appropriate leverage and which aren't overpriced when you're ready to buy.

I have a method for picking warrants that's quite simple, but the reasons for the method are complicated. I'm going to explain the reasons so that you can judge the logic of the method. But even if the explanation seems too complicated, you'll find the selection method outlined on page 390 easy to execute.

Leverage

A warrant's leverage is the degree to which the price of the warrant moves, compared with the movement in the price of the underlying stock. Leverage of 4 to 1 means that the warrant's price changes 40% when the stock's price changes 10%.

Two principal factors affect the amount of a warrant's leverage. One is the relationship of the warrant's exercise price to the current price of the stock. The other is the length of time remaining before the warrant expires.

If the current price of the underlying stock is below the warrant's exercise price, the warrant is called *out-of-the-money*. The warrant currently has no exercise value, since it is cheaper to buy the stock directly than to turn in a warrant and pay the exercise price. In general, the further out of the money a warrant is, the higher its leverage.

If a warrant has a long life remaining, there is a better chance that the price of the stock will rise up past the exercise price and thereby give the warrant some exercise value. As a result, a long-life warrant is worth more than a short-life warrant; it usually sells for more and has less leverage.

For example, suppose a warrant has only three months remaining until expiration. Suppose further that its exercise price is $30, while the underlying stock is selling for only $15. The chance of the warrant's acquiring any exercise value within the next three months is very slim; the stock must double in price in three months or less. So the warrant might sell for only 25 cents.

Now let's suppose that the stock moves up from $15 to $17 during the next week. Ah, maybe there's a chance for the warrant. So the price of the warrant might rise from 25 to 50 cents. None of these figures seems important until you realize that a 13% increase in the stock price has caused a 100% increase in the price of the warrant. That's leverage of 8 to 1.

It may seem attractive, but too much leverage isn't a good thing. For one reason, only a dramatic rise in the market would produce a profit on the warrant. If the warrant expires in three months with the stock still under $30, the warrant price will drop to zero. For another reason, you'd have to pay constant attention to warrants that expire soon, frequently replacing expiring issues.

To get enough leverage, but not too much, we can combine the two factors that affect the warrant's leverage. The result is the rate at which the underlying stock must appreciate during each year of the warrant's remaining life in order to rise to the warrant's exercise price. This is the Required Growth Rate, and the table on page 391 will enable you to calculate it.

It would take many additional calculations to compute the actual amount of leverage in the warrant. The Required Growth Rate makes it possible to compare warrants without knowing the actual amount of leverage. A good rule of thumb is that the average warrant in your portfolio should have a Required Growth Rate between 20% and 40%. This will give you leverage in the neighborhood of 4 to 1.

Price

The leverage calculation doesn't consider the warrant's present price. Even if the leverage appears high, you might pay too much for a warrant and fail to get the price appreciation a rising market should bring.

There are formulas for estimating the value of a warrant. These formulas don't consider the fundamental value of the underlying stock. Instead, they evaluate the warrant on the assumption that the stock price is as likely to rise as it is to fall.[3]

None of the formulas is simple but, fortunately, you don't have to work with them. Each week, *Value Line Options & Convertibles* rates warrants and other option-type securities. It is available by subscription and can be found also in some libraries and in most brokerage offices.[4]

Value Line uses a formula to rate the current price of each warrant. A rating of zero means the warrant is priced about where it should be in relation to its underlying stock. A +50% rating means the warrant is overpriced by 50%. For your warrant purchases, select only issues with negative ratings, such as −20%, −30%, etc. These warrants are underpriced and represent bargains.

Selection Method

Value Line's warrant rating doesn't consider the fundamental value of the underlying stock—only whether the warrant is overpriced in comparison to its stock. But if you hold ten to fifteen warrants, each of which is underpriced and has sufficient leverage, you'll do all right when the market goes up.

If you're not willing to replace warrants as they expire, select only warrants that have expiration dates far enough away for your purpose.

To use warrants profitably, you need both value and leverage. To get them, follow these steps:

1. From *Value Line*'s table of warrants, make a list of the warrants that are underpriced as indicated by a minus sign

---

[3] One such formula was developed by John P. Shelton, Associate Professor of Finance at UCLA. The formula is explained in his article, "The Relation of the Price of a Warrant to the Price of Its Associated Stock," reprinted in *Modern Developments in Investment Management*, edited by Lorie and Brealey (New York: Praeger Publishers).

[4] Details of the publication are given on page 406.

REQUIRED GROWTH RATE FOR WARRANTS
(Amount by which Stock Price must appreciate yearly to reach Warrant Exercise Price)

Stock/ Warrant Relation- ship	1	2	3	4	5	6	7	10	15
				Years to Warrant Expiration Date					
1.00	0.0%	0.0%	0.0%	0.0%	0.0%	0.0%	0.0%	0.0%	0.0%
0.95	5.2%	2.5%	1.7%	1.2%	1.0%	0.8%	0.7%	0.5%	0.3%
0.90	11.1%	5.4%	3.5%	2.6%	2.1%	1.7%	1.5%	1.0%	0.7%
0.85	17.6%	8.4%	5.5%	4.1%	3.3%	2.7%	2.3%	1.6%	1.0%
0.80	25.0%	11.8%	7.7%	5.7%	4.5%	3.7%	3.2%	2.2%	1.4%
0.75	33.3%	15.4%	10.0%	7.4%	5.9%	4.9%	4.1%	2.9%	1.9%
0.70	42.8%	19.5%	12.6%	9.3%	7.3%	6.1%	5.2%	3.6%	2.4%
0.65	53.8%	24.0%	15.4%	11.3%	8.9%	7.4%	6.3%	4.4%	2.9%
0.60	66.6%	29.0%	18.5%	13.6%	10.7%	8.8%	7.5%	5.2%	3.4%
0.55	81.8%	34.8%	22.0%	16.1%	12.7%	10.4%	8.9%	6.1%	4.0%
0.50	100.0%	41.4%	25.9%	18.9%	14.8%	12.2%	10.4%	7.1%	4.7%
0.45	122.2%	49.0%	30.4%	22.0%	17.3%	14.2%	12.0%	8.3%	5.4%
0.40	150.0%	58.1%	35.7%	25.7%	20.1%	16.4%	13.9%	9.5%	6.2%
0.35	185.7%	69.0%	41.8%	30.0%	23.3%	19.1%	16.1%	11.0%	7.2%
0.30	233.3%	82.5%	49.3%	35.1%	27.2%	22.2%	18.7%	12.7%	8.3%
0.25	300.0%	99.9%	58.7%	41.4%	31.9%	25.9%	21.9%	14.8%	9.6%
0.20	400.0%	123.6%	70.9%	49.5%	37.9%	30.7%	25.8%	17.4%	11.3%
0.15	566.6%	158.1%	88.2%	60.6%	46.1%	37.1%	31.1%	20.8%	13.4%
0.10	900.0%	216.2%	115.4%	77.8%	58.4%	46.7%	38.9%	25.8%	16.5%
0.05	1900.0%	347.2%	171.4%	111.4%	82.0%	64.7%	53.4%	34.9%	22.1%

INSTRUCTIONS

1. Divide the current stock price by the warrant's exercise price.

2. Find the figure in the left hand column that is nearest to the answer.

3. On that line, find the column headed by the number of years that is nearest to the time remaining before the warrant expires.

The figure in that column will be the approximate average yearly appreciation required for the stock to reach the warrant's exercise price by the expiration date of the warrant.

in the column "Over (+) Under (−) Valued (%)" (column 26 on *Value Line*'s table). Skip any warrant whose "Expiration Date" (column 13) is too soon for your purposes.

2. For each warrant you list, note the recent price of the stock (column 3), the "Effective Per Share Exercise Price" (column 9), the "Symbol" (column 1), the "Exchange" on which the warrant is traded (column 19), and the "Expiration Date" (column 13).

3. Use the table on page 391 of this book to determine the Required Growth Rate for each warrant on your list.

4. Create a portfolio of warrants that has an average Required Growth Rate between 20% and 40%. Not every warrant has to fall in that range, but the average of all the warrants should.

5. When you've created the portfolio, give the list to your broker or Swiss bank. For each warrant you've selected, you should provide the name, the expiration date, the stock symbol, and the exchange where the warrant is traded.

If your account is important to your broker, he may be willing to do this research for you. However, a Swiss bank can't be expected to select warrants.

WARRANT ALTERNATIVES

You may decide not to buy warrants—either because they seem to require too much work or because you discover that they're all overpriced (which isn't likely at the beginning of a bull market).

But you may still want the low-risk leverage that warrants can provide. If this is the case, there are some alternatives.

OPTIONS

There are call options for 150 stocks available on the U.S. stock exchanges. All these options are for major companies. There are two drawbacks to using options, however.

Short Life

One drawback is the short life span. The maximum term available at any time is nine months. This means you'll have to sell the options just before they expire and purchase new ones.

Cost

The other drawback is cost. At the beginning of a bull market, an "on-the-money" nine-month option will probably cost about 8% to 10% of the price of the stock it represents. As the bull trend proceeds, the option's premium will increase with the market's growing optimism. In the later stages, the premium cost of a nine-month option should be in the range of 15% to 20% of the price of the stock.

None of that cost is returned to you when the option expires. When you sell the option just prior to expiration, you will get back the amount by which the price of the stock exceeds the option's striking price. The premium you paid at the outset was for the time remaining before expiration, and that has evaporated.

With a warrant you get back part of the premium when you sell, because the warrant still has some life left. In fact, the premium shrinks at a very slow rate until the warrant's final year. If you buy a warrant nine months before its expiration date, the premium will shrink rapidly, and that's what happens with a nine-month option.

The purpose of an option or a warrant is to provide leverage during a stock market rise. To come out ahead with an option, let alone to obtain sufficient leverage, the underlying stock must rise very fast—whereas with a warrant, the rise needn't be so dramatic.

Use of Options

The best time to buy options is at the beginning of a bull market when most people are afraid to take the plunge. The premium is lowest then.

If a discount rate signal forecasts a new uptrend and the stock market hasn't responded yet, it may be the best time of all to buy options. You'll buy the option with a low, bear-market premium just before what you hope will be the beginning of a new bull market.

On such an occasion, buy an option that has already been traded for three months or so, and thus has six months before expiration. The striking price will probably be higher than the current price of the underlying stock. This out-of-the-money feature will give the option more leverage—just as with a warrant.

For most investors, an option's short life and high cost make it an unwieldy vehicle for stock market speculation. And the short life makes it totally impractical for a permanent portfolio.

DUAL-PURPOSE INVESTMENT COMPANIES

A dual-purpose investment fund can be a suitable replacement for warrants as a low-risk, leveraged way of investing in the stock market. The task of selection is much easier than for warrants, as a dual-purpose fund provides the diversification that a small portfolio cannot achieve on its own.

A dual-purpose fund is like a mutual fund in that it invests its stockholders' capital in a portfolio of stocks. However, the fund originally issued its shares in pairs. One share (the *income* share) receives all the dividends and interest earned by the fund, while the other share (the *capital* share) receives the benefit of all price appreciation in the stocks held by the fund.

This means initially that a rise in the value of the fund's

portfolio will be doubly valuable to a capital share, because it receives the income share's capital gain as well.

In addition, the funds are closed-end investment companies (as described on page 386); no new shares are issued. The existing capital shares trade on the New York Stock Exchange, and they generally trade at a discount from their net asset values. This provides additional leverage in the event of a bull market in stocks.[5]

A fund's leverage can't be determined precisely. However, the table on page 396 lists six useful dual-purpose investment funds, together with a formula for determining the maximum possible leverage a fund offers at any given time.

This maximum leverage will be diluted or ineffective if the fund holds the wrong stocks, or too little in stocks, during a bull market. But the funds usually hold the bulk of their assets in stocks, and most of the stocks are mainline companies.

With this leverage you can invest only 25% to 50% of your stock market budget and still profit from a bull market. Your risk will be limited to that percentage. For diversification, purchase at least three different funds.

A dual-purpose fund is a useful alternative to warrants in that it requires much less effort to make the selection. However, you have more control over the situation when you buy warrants, because a fund might not be fully invested when the stock market goes up.

A dual-purpose fund can be used for either the permanent or variable portfolio.[6]

BONDS

A bond doesn't have inherent leverage, as does a warrant or a dual-purpose investment fund. However, the selection of

[5] The net asset value of a mutual fund share is the total value of the fund's holdings (less any liabilities) divided by the number of shares outstanding. The net asset value changes daily as the value of the fund's holdings changes.

[6] A good explanation of warrants and dual-purpose funds is *Using Warrants* by Terry Coxon, listed in the *Suggested Reading* on page 448. The booklet covers a number of useful details for which only a specialized work can allow space.

LEVERAGE IN DUAL-PURPOSE INVESTMENT FUNDS

Fund	(1) Income Shares Redemption Date	(2) Income Shares Redemption Value	(3) Net Asset Value	(4) Example from June 30, 1978 Net Assets per Capital Share	(5) Example from June 30, 1978 Price	(6) Maximum Leverage
America DualVest Fund	6-29-79	$15.00	$ 9.82	$24.82	$ 8.875	2.8
Gemini Fund	12-31-84	11.00	27.87	38.87	21.125	1.8
Hemisphere Fund	6-30-85	11.44	.33	11.77	1.625	7.2
Income & Capital Shares	3-31-82	10.00	8.25	18.25	6.25	2.9
Leverage Fund of Boston	1-4-82	13.73	18.72	32.45	14.375	2.3
Sudder Duo-Vest	4-1-82	9.15	9.95	19.10	8.00	2.4

Column #1 shows the date on which the holders of the income shares must receive the redemption amount shown in column #2. After that date, the fund's capital shares will contain no leverage. To determine the maximum leverage in a capital share:

1. Find the table "Dual-Purpose Funds" on the Mutual Funds page of the Monday Wall Street Journal or Barron's.

2. From that table, add the "N.A. Val. Cap. Shs." (net asset value per capital share) to the figure shown in column #2 above.

3. Divide that total by the item "Cap. Shs. Price" (price per capital share) shown in the same table in the Journal or Barron's.

The result is the leverage in a capital share — the number of dollars that can be invested in the stock market for each dollar you spend for a capital share. The table above shows an example of this calculation for June 30, 1978. The Redemption Value (column #2) is added to the Net Asset Value (column #3), and totaled in column #4. This is divided by the current Price (column #5). The result is the maximum leverage (column #6).

Sources: Columns #1 and #2 are from Mutual Funds Almanac, 1978 Edition by Yale Hirsch (The Hirsch Organization, Old Tappan, N.J.). Columns #3 and #5 are from The Wall Street Journal, July 3, 1978.

bonds is a simple matter, compared to the selection of stocks or warrants.

As I discussed in Chapter 14, the safest and most advantageous bonds to purchase early in a bull market are U.S. government issues with long periods to maturity and low coupon rates. These will be trading at deep discounts from face value, and their prices will be more volatile than the prices of other bonds.

Bonds are identified by their coupon rates and maturity dates. Six U.S. Treasury bonds are potential purchases for the next bull market:

Coupon Rate	Maturity
3%	February, 1995
3½%	November, 1998
3½%	February, 1990
6¾%	February, 1995
7⅝%	February, 2002–2007
7⅞%	February, 2002–2007

The first three bonds have lower yields, due to certain advantages with respect to estate taxes. However, they have low coupon rates, which makes them more volatile than other bonds.

The last two bonds I've listed are "call bonds." The government can redeem them as early as the first year shown, or as late as the last year shown. In this case the call feature is of no great consequence, since the call date is twenty-three years away.

Although I favor the first three bonds for their volatility, any one of the six will suffice.

Bonds usually don't fluctuate as much during a cycle as stocks do, and there is no inherent leverage in a bond. However, you can add leverage to a bond investment by buying on margin. A U.S. or Swiss bank or a securities broker will lend money on bonds—requiring as little as 10% equity. If you purchase with 40% equity, you'll get more volatility than the stock market averages.

If you buy following a discount-rate signal, the potential

loss is relatively small—even if you buy on margin. The discount rate usually moves after other interest rates have moved; it is a signal that the general trend in rates won't be reversed.

Even if the discount-rate signal turns out to be premature and is later reversed, your potential loss is only about 6% if you don't buy on margin. If you do buy on margin, the 6% is multiplied by however much leverage you use. The leverage is determined by dividing the equity percentage into 100. Thus, 20% equity means leverage of 5 to 1, and a potential loss of about 30%.

Without leverage, the potential profit is about 33% (plus interest collected on the bonds) over the period of the bull trend. With 4 to 1 leverage, the potential profit is around 130%, in exchange for a risk of about 24%. You have to pay interest on the margin loan, but this is largely offset by the interest collected from the bonds.

WHICH INVESTMENT?

For a great many investors, warrants are the most sensible stock market investment. The limited risk makes it easier for someone who's uneasy about the future to expose himself to the stock market.

However, there are investors who won't find warrants attractive—because too much effort seems to be involved or because warrants are unfamiliar. For them, dual-purpose investment funds might be the best choice.

Others just won't feel comfortable without the familiar stock shares. Depending upon the capital available and the objectives, the safest route is to purchase the whole Dow Jones Industrial Average (or buy a part of it) or select stocks by their betas.

For those with a small budget or no desire to select stocks, the purchase of two or three closed-end investment companies is best.

Whichever group you are in, consider putting some funds from the variable portfolio into bonds during a bull market.

The diversification would be valuable, and the potential profits are attractive.

If you keep the safety net in mind, you can invest in any of the alternatives I've given without the fear that a sudden crash could wipe you out.

For the permanent portfolio, only warrants and dual-purpose investment funds are appropriate. The object is to have a hedge, and only an investment with inherent leverage serves that purpose.

32

WHERE TO
GET HELP

I'VE REFERRED FREQUENTLY TO INFORMATION THAT CAN HELP in making investment decisions. How much of this information you'll need will depend upon the kind of program you set up.

This chapter provides a brief survey of the companies and publications that may help you carry out your strategy. I suggest that you first read quickly through the chapter, marking those services that might be of interest to you, and then come back to them later—when you're ready to take action.

All subscription prices shown are for U.S. delivery. In some cases, I've indicated that a publisher will provide a low-cost trial subscription.

GENERAL DATA

Several publications provide general economic and investment data. We'll start with the most obvious sources.

The Wall Street Journal

The *Journal* is the one daily newspaper that will provide almost anything you might want to know about the U.S.

economy and U.S. investments—including weekly money supply figures, price inflation announcements, and changes in the discount rate. It also includes extensive lists of daily prices but very little information about foreign economies or investments.

In many cities, the *Journal* is home-delivered, arriving on the day it's published. Annual mail subscription: $49; 20-week subscription: $20; single-copy newsstand price: 25 cents. *The Wall Street Journal*, 200 Burnett Road, Chicopee, Mass. 01021.

Barron's

Reading *Barron's*, which is the *Journal's* weekly brother, will take up less of your time. *Barron's* provides investment articles and extensive price lists, but little hard news. The articles are generally more skeptical of the prevailing economic and investment orthodoxy than those of the *Journal*. Annual subscription: $32; newsstand price: 75 cents. *Barron's*, 22 Cortlandt St., New York, N.Y. 10007.

Federal Reserve Bulletin

The monthly *Bulletin* includes a statistical summary of all important U.S. economic indicators—money supply, inflation rates, interest rates (including the discount rate), average monthly foreign currency prices, etc. Annual subscription: $20; single copy: $2. Division of Administrative Services, Board of Governors of the Federal Reserve System, Washington, D.C. 20551.

Federal Reserve Monthly Chart Book

The *Chart Book* presents graphs of the figures that appear in the *Bulletin*. Most of the charts go back eight years. A subscription also brings the annual edition of the *Historical Chart Book,* with graphs going back forty or fifty years. Annual subscription: $12; single copy: $1.25. Same address as for the *Federal Reserve Bulletin.*

U.S. Financial Data

Issued by the Federal Reserve Bank of St. Louis, this weekly publication provides graphs and statistics on interest rates (including the discount rate) and on monetary growth rates. It's an easy way to keep in touch with the monetary cycles. There is no charge for a subscription. Federal Reserve Bank of St. Louis, St. Louis, Mo. 63166.

Business Conditions Digest

A monthly publication that includes twenty-year graphs for all major U.S. (and some foreign) economic indicators, as well as the corresponding statistics for the past two or three years. Published by the U.S. Department of Commerce. Annual subscription: $40; single copy: $3.50. Superintendent of Documents, U.S. Government Printing Office, Washington, D.C. 20402.

NEWSLETTERS

It is difficult to suggest newsletters, because the reaction one has to a newsletter is very subjective. It isn't as easy as it might seem to rate a newsletter's record of forecasts, as every newsletter suggests literally hundreds of future events, and has to qualify its expectations to some degree.

I personally subscribe to about a dozen newsletters, but often my purpose is merely to see what the competition is doing. I'll limit my remarks here to two newsletters—my favorite and my own.

Dow Theory Letters

Richard Russell, like most writers, includes many suggestions in each issue of his newsletter (published every two weeks). But unlike most, he has been definite and unequivocal whenever he believed a new major trend in stocks or gold had begun—and he's been right every time for the several years I've been reading him. There's no one I would rely on more to make such judgments.

Each six-page issue contains a chart of the Dow Jones averages and of gold, plus several other graphs of economic or investment significance. Most of each issue is devoted to Russell's view of the current economy and the major markets, and to specific stock recommendations when stocks are in a bull trend.

Annual subscription: $150; 3-issue trial subscription (one time only): $1. *Dow Theory Letters,* P.O. Box 1759, La Jolla, Calif. 92038.

Harry Browne's Special Reports

As I can't give an unbiased opinion, I'll say only that each issue contains monetary inflation graphs (as on page 45 of this book), leading economic indicators, weekly prices of currencies and other investments, the vital statistics of twenty-three currencies (as in the table on page 234), current purchasing power parity status for fifteen currencies (as described in Chapter 16), background articles on investment and economic ideas, and a summary of my current opinions on the various investment markets.

The newsletter isn't published on a calendar schedule. Issues are sent out whenever I feel I have something useful to say, a schedule that works out to about ten issues per year. However, special bulletins are sent to subscribers when there's pressing news that can't wait for a full issue, and every subscriber receives a telegram when the discount rate changes trend.

The subscription price is $175 for the next ten issues.[1] One time only, you may purchase for $5 the latest newsletter excerpt outlining where I believe the major investment markets stand. *Harry Browne's Special Reports*, Box 5586A, Austin, Tex. 78763.

MISCELLANEOUS VIEWPOINTS

Most newsletters are very personal affairs. By reading a typical newsletter, you learn how the author sees the world. Two companies offer something that is, in effect, quite different—a potpourri of many, often conflicting viewpoints.

Because they offer variety, you'll find plenty to disagree with. Their value is in exposing you to many ideas that you might otherwise miss when you stick to those sources you know and respect.

Select Information Exchange

S.I.E. is a clearinghouse for newsletters. The company sells various packages of trial subscriptions—each package providing a short-term look at 15 or 20 different newsletters. A price list that describes the various packages currently available can be obtained by writing to Select Information Exchange, 2095 Broadway, New York, N.Y. 10023.

Inflation Survival Letter

ISL is a biweekly newsletter that publishes viewpoints from a wide range of writers. The newsletter emphasizes hard-

---

[1] $195 as of January 1, 1979.

money investments, but also publishes articles on stocks, bonds, real estate, life insurance, collectibles, U.S. banks, etc. The writer of each article is usually someone dealing in that field, and who thus advocates it as a profitable investment, but the diversity of viewpoints can prod you to remain receptive to new possibilities. Annual subscription: $48. *Inflation Survival Letter*, P.O. Box 2599, Landover Hills, Maryland 20784.

CHART SERVICES

There are dozens of services that mail updated investment graphs weekly, but I haven't tried them all. Here are a few:

Commodity Chart Service

A weekly presentation of about 150 graphs of daily prices on the U.S. commodity and currency futures markets. Gold and silver cash prices are also included. Regular charts cover the most recent year, and periodic supplements provide graphs going back fifteen years or more. Annual subscription: $277; single issue (one time only), $7.50. Commodity Research Bureau, One Liberty Plaza, New York, N.Y. 10006.

International Monetary Market

The International Monetary Market publishes an eight-page weekly summary of price activity in the currency and financial futures markets, including graphs of six currencies, gold, and U.S. Treasury bills. There is no charge for a subscription. International Monetary Market, 444 W. Jackson Blvd., Chicago, Ill. 60606.

Quote Digest

There are two weekly services. One includes charts for all stocks and warrants traded on the New York Stock Exchange; the other covers the entire American Stock Exchange. Each stock's chart is accompanied by financial data—dividends, price/earnings ratio, etc. This is probably the most complete and timely source of stock charts. Annual subscription: $210. *Quote Digest,* P.O. Box 213, Wichita, Kans. 67201.

3-Trend Security Charts

Similar to *Quote Digest,* this service provides a single monthly publication that covers 1,100 stocks (no warrants) from both the New York and American Stock Exchanges. Annual subscription: $79. Security Research Company, 208 Newbury St., Boston, Mass. 02116.

WARRANT AND STOCK DATA

Value Line Options & Convertibles

This weekly publication provides extensive information on all but the most obscure warrants, including an estimate of each warrant's current value. (One use of the publication was explained on page 390 of the preceding chapter.) Each issue also contains information on listed stock options, convertible bonds, and convertible preferred stocks. Annual subscription: $300; 8-week trial subscription (one time only): $29. Arnold Bernhard & Co., Inc., 5 East 44th St., New York, N.Y. 10017.

The Value Line Investment Survey

This service covers 2,000 stocks, updating its analyses of part of the group every week. Each weekly issue also provides summary information on all 2,000 stocks, including their betas.[2] Annual subscription: $295; 10-week trial subscription (one time only): $29. Arnold Bernhard & Co., 5 East 44th St., New York, N.Y. 10017.

Bank & Quotation Record

A monthly publication listing price and volume data for virtually every security publicly traded in the U.S., plus foreign bonds and Toronto Stock Exchange issues. In addition, there are daily prices for the leading stock averages and for forty-one foreign currencies. Annual subscription: $75; single issue: $10. *Bank & Quotation Record*, P.O. Box 450, Whitinsville, Mass. 01588.

The Dow Jones Investor's Handbook

An annual publication listing price ranges for New York and American Stock Exchange stocks, bonds, and warrants; U.S. government bonds; and various stock averages—with summary information for previous years. The price is $4.95. Dow Jones Books, P.O. Box 300, Princeton, N.J. 08540.

Mutual Funds Almanac

An annual publication providing performance results and classifications for over six hundred mutual funds. Perfor-

---

[2] The use of betas is explained on page 382.

mance figures go back ten years. Probably the simplest source of data on mutual funds. The price is $15. The Hirsch Organization, Inc., 6 Deer Trail, Old Tappan, N.J. 07675.

Capital International Perspective

This is the only service I know that surveys the world's stock markets. Each monthly issue charts the averages in eighteen countries, and gives price and financial data for individual stocks. A quarterly supplement provides charts for individual stocks. It is extensive and easy to use.

Annual airmail subscription: $675. Capital International SA, 15 rue de Cendrier, CH-1201 Geneva, Switzerland.

CURRENCY DATA

Some of the publications listed under other headings include currency data. Here I'll provide two publications that concentrate on the subject.

International Financial Statistics

This monthly publication of the International Monetary Fund is the bible of currency statistics. Every 400-page issue includes separate coverage for each of about a hundred countries.

There are statistics for the previous nine months, plus quarterly and annual figures going back seven years. Included are wholesale and consumer price indices, money supply figures, exchange rates, trade figures, government spending, and a great deal more. One issue each year provides annual data going back twenty-five years. And every issue provides a summary table of the twelve-month monetary and price inflation rates for most countries of the world.

The information is usually a month or two old—necessarily so in a monthly publication—but IFS is the most extensive single source of currency data. Annual subscription: $35. The Secretary, International Monetary Fund, Washington, D.C. 20431.

Selected Interest & Exchange Rates

For those who want only a quick overview of current exchange-rate and interest-rate trends, this weekly publication is probably best. It includes small charts of nine foreign currencies, gold, and foreign interest rates. Each chart goes back three years. There is also a table of daily currency prices.

Annual subscription: $15; single issue: 40 cents. Publication Services, Division of Administrative Services, Board of Governors of the Federal Reserve System, Washington, D.C. 20551.

MONEY MARKET FUNDS

Here are four money market funds whose portfolios are concentrated in government securities, making the funds convenient substitutes for Treasury bills. All four allow you to make an instant withdrawal by writing a check on their bank account. The funds' holdings are shown as of March 27, 1978.

Capital Preservation Fund

Capital Preservation is the only fund that invests 100% in Treasury bills and is also the only fund that offers bearer shares (certificates that aren't registered in anyone's name), if desired by the customer. The minimum to open an account is $1,000. Capital Preservation Fund, Inc., 459 Hamilton Ave., Palo Alto, Calif. 94301; (415) 328-1550.

Midwest Income

This fund has 71% of its assets in U.S. government securities and in repurchase agreements that are secured by government securities; the balance is in certificates of deposit. The minimum for opening an account is $500. Midwest Income, Room 508, Terminal Building, Cincinnati, Ohio 45202; (513) 579-0414.

Fund/Govt Investors

Fund/Govt has 20% of its assets in Treasury bills and the balance in short-term bonds issued by U.S. government agencies. The minimum investment is $50,000. Fund/Govt Investors, 1735 K Street N.W., Washington, D.C. 20006; (202) 452-9200.

FedFund

This fund has 92% invested in Treasury bills and the balance in short-term U.S. government and government agency bonds. Individuals can purchase shares only through stockbrokers. The minimum investment is $50,000. FedFund; Loeb, Rhoades, Hornblower & Co., 42 Wall St., 58th Floor, New York, N.Y. 10005; (212) 483-6127.

LIQUID SWISS BANKS

Here are five Swiss banks that are small to medium in size, are equipped to serve Americans, and have high liquidity ratings.[3]

[3] Liquidity ratings are explained on page 300.

All of them handle gold bullion, coins, and options; silver bullion; currency deposits and forward contracts; bonds in major currencies; U.S. government Treasury bills and bonds; money market funds; and stocks and warrants from any country.

Bank assets, liquidity ratings, and account minimums are as of March 31, 1978.

Foreign Commerce Bank

I've dealt with this bank since 1967. It is probably the Swiss bank that has tried hardest to devise procedures that are convenient for Americans. It has created a number of unusual services, including accounts in dollars and other non-Swiss currencies that are a direct obligation of the bank.[4]

Assets: 245 million Swiss francs. *Liquidity*: 127%. *Minimum to open an account*: $5,000. *Contacts*: Bruno Brodbeck, Roger Badet, Frank Bachmann, Andre Rufer. *Street address*: Bellariastrasse 82, CH-8038 Zurich. *Mailing address*: P.O. Box 1006, CH-8022 Zurich, Switzerland. *Telephone*: (01) 45 66 88.

Cambio + Valorenbank

I've known this bank for about five years. Its small size allows it to provide personalized service, and it has officers who specialize in helping North Americans.

Assets: 76 million Swiss francs. *Liquidity*: 130%. *Minimum to open an account*: $5,000. *Contact*: Werner W. Schwarz. *Address*: Utoquai 55, CH-8008 Zurich, Switzerland. *Telephone*: (01) 47 54 00.

---

[4] See page 296 for an explanation of direct obligation vs. "at your risk."

Banque Indiana (Suisse)

This bank also has a good record of service to Americans. The English spoken is especially understandable, which is valuable if you will be dealing by phone.

Assets: 24 million Swiss francs. *Liquidity*: 77%. *Minimum to open an account*: $3,000. *Contacts*: Francine Misrahi, Max Furrer. *Street Address*: 50 Avenue de la Gare, Lausanne. *Mailing address*: P.O. Box 127, CH-1001 Lausanne, Switzerland. *Telephone*: (021) 20 47 41.

Bankinstitut Zurich

I've had fewer dealings with this bank, but I've noticed that it welcomes North American accounts and works hard to satisfy them.

Assets: 31 million Swiss francs. *Liquidity*: 109%. *Minimum to open an account*: $5,000. *Contact*: R. Selna. *Street address*: Grossmunsterplatz 9, Zurich. *Mailing address*: P.O. Box 777, CH-8021 Zurich, Switzerland. *Telephone*: (01) 47 60 63.

Nederlandsche Middenstands Bank [5]

This bank, while providing all the usual deposit and investment services, specializes in forming closely held corporations that aid in large-scale international investing and tax planning.

Assets: 52 million Swiss francs. *Liquidity*: 129%. *Minimum to open an account*: $5,000. *Contacts*: Arthur P. Hediger, Mark Amrein. *Street Address*: Holbeinstrasse 31, Zurich. *Mailing address*: Postfach 151, CH-8024 Zurich, Switzerland. *Telephone*: (01) 34 19 90.

[5] Formerly Transitbank Zurich.

Help in Opening an Account

You can obtain help in opening a Swiss bank account from Economic Research Counselors (listed on page 418).

BIG SWISS BANKS

Although I consider liquidity and service to be the two most important attributes of a bank, I realize that many investors consider size to be just as important. For them, I'll list the five major Swiss banks. I can't name individual contacts for most of them, because the big banks generally won't assign a specific officer to any but the largest accounts.

Bank Leu is one exception. Dr. Joseph V. Buschor handles American accounts for the bank, and several of my clients have reported that the service is very good.

Dr. Joseph V. Buschor
Bank Leu
Bahnhofstrasse 32
CH-8022 Zurich,
   Switzerland

Swiss Bank Corporation
Aeschenvorstadt 1
CH-4002 Basle,
   Switzerland

Swiss Credit Bank
Paradeplatz
CH-8022 Zurich,
   Switzerland

Swiss Volksbank
Bundegasse 26
CH-3000 Berne,
   Switzerland

Union Bank of Switzerland
Bahnhofstrasse 45
CH-8021 Zurich,
   Switzerland

With the exception of Bank Leu, each of these banks has branches all over Switzerland. Although the big banks don't state minimum account sizes (they'll accept any size deposit over the counter), you can assume that a Swiss franc account can be opened by mail for $500.

SWISS BANK SOURCES

You may want to investigate banks on your own. If so, there are international banking directories in most public libraries. You need only copy the names and addresses of a few of the banks and then make your own inquiries.

Swiss Financial Year Book

If you need to have your own directory of Swiss banks, this is the only English-language book that covers every Swiss bank. It categorizes the banks by type, and most listings include total assets, net worth, year established, names of directors, managers, and principal owners, mail and cable addresses, telephone and telex numbers. Similar information is provided on Swiss insurance companies. There is also limited information on the Swiss stock exchanges.

The directory is purely a reference work; no text or commentary about the banks is included. It's nicely put together. The price is $35 ($45 by airmail). Elvetica Edizioni, P.O. Box 694, CH-6830 Chiasso, Switzerland.

Information on Swiss Banks

The *Complete Guide to Swiss Banks* (listed in the *Suggested Reading* on page 449) provides detailed information on the services and types of accounts available and on procedures for using a Swiss bank.

SWISS FRANC LIFE INSURANCE
AND ANNUITIES

Assurex SA, a company in Zurich, specializes in selling Swiss franc life insurance and annuities to Americans. This firm acts as a broker; it represents all the major Swiss companies, from which it earns its commissions.

The firm's written and spoken English is quite good. Every effort has been made to make Swiss insurance intelligible to Americans.

The company publishes a booklet, *Swiss Franc Life Insurance*, which explains the kinds of policies that are available. The price is $10 (refundable if a policy is purchased). Assurex SA, Postfach 129-5, CH-8035 Zurich, Switzerland; telephone: (01) 60 25 10.

COINS AND FOREIGN CURRENCIES

There are coin dealers in most American cities. However, the three companies listed here specialize in low-premium gold coins and bags of U.S. silver coins. All three can deal with you by telephone and mail, if you wish.

Monex International Ltd.

This firm was the first of many to specialize in non-numismatic gold and silver coins and probably is still the largest in its field. Monex sells coins through forward contracts, for immediate delivery, and on margin. I have dealt with the company since it opened in 1967, and I gave a lecture series on its behalf in 1973. Monex International Ltd., 4912 Birch St., Newport Beach, Calif. 92660; (800) 854-3361 or (714) 752-1400.

Deak-Perera Group

Deak-Perera is primarily a dealer in foreign currency and may be the best source if you decide to buy Swiss francs or other currencies in the form of banknotes (cash). The company also sells gold coins. They have offices in many American cities (a list can be obtained from the head office or from the currency exchange counters Deak-Perera operates in many airports). Deak-Perera Group, 29 Broadway, New York, N.Y. 10006; (212) 480-0280.

Investment Rarities

This company specializes in the sale of coins for immediate delivery. Much of its business is done by mail or telephone, and it will ship coins to customers anywhere in the U.S. I filmed a television commercial for them in 1978. Investment Rarities, One Appletree Square, Minneapolis, Minn. 55420; (800) 328-1860.

Coin Futures

Futures contracts for U.S. silver coins (five bags per contract) are traded on the New York Mercantile Exchange. You can take delivery when a contract falls due, thereby acquiring the coins themselves. Any broker that handles commodities can provide information.

INVESTMENT ADVISORS

Choosing an investment advisor isn't simple. In fact, it can be just as hard to pick the right advisor as it is to pick the right investment. One problem is that you may not know how valuable the advisor is until long after you've consulted with him.

A great deal of your success in finding a good advisor will depend upon the kind of help you're looking for. If you're hoping to find someone who can turn ashes into gold, you'll probably be disappointed. And the legendary "prudent man" who conservatively guards his client's capital doesn't really exist anymore; today there are no investments that professionals unanimously consider safe.

The best use to which an advisor can be put is in helping you do the things you have decided are correct but don't know how to proceed with. He can tell you many things you would learn for yourself if you spent all your time working on investments. His knowledge of the many alternatives, together with your knowledge of yourself and what you need, can be a profitable combination.

If you approach an advisor in this light, he can be very useful. He can show you ways by which you can accomplish your objectives. He can help you put together a portfolio that fits your circumstances. He can answer questions, and he can provide an opinion on the soundness of what you're planning to do.

Even so, the investment field, as any other, includes individuals of varying degrees of intelligence, knowledge, and thoughtfulness. You'll have to size up the advisor at your first meeting and try to determine whether he sees the world in the same general way you do. If he doesn't, keep looking.

References from other investors can help a little but not much. Every advisor has some clients who are satisfied and some who are not. The reports clients give will reflect to a large extent what they want from the advisor and how personally compatible they find him. The results he produces for you will depend a lot on who you are.

For me to suggest investment advisors is no easier than for you to select one. Anything I say about an advisor will be far more subjective than my remarks about a chart service or a reference book.

My experience is necessarily limited to the people I've

dealt with. And although I try to deal only with people I respect, my standards may be different from yours. In addition, there are probably hundreds or thousands of competent investment advisors whom I've never had an occasion to meet. The advisor you find on your own may be one of them.

Private Investors

Terry Coxon, the owner of Private Investors, has worked with me for the past four years. He has contributed a great deal to this book, to my book on Swiss banks, and to my newsletter. He is aware of what readers of this book are likely to be looking for, and he's knowledgeable about the alternatives available to achieve those ends. Private Investors, 100 S. Ellsworth Ave., Suite 310, San Mateo, Calif. 94401; (415) 343-7161.

Economic Research Counselors

ERC counsels investors about gold, silver, and currencies, with particular emphasis on Swiss bank accounts. I worked for the company from 1967 to 1970 and have continued to stay in touch with them. Economic Research Counselors, 1760 Marine Dr., Suite 2-12, West Vancouver, British Columbia V7V 1J4, Canada; (604) 926-5476; (800) 426-5270 (toll-free from the U.S.).

Swiss Banks

In addition, most Swiss banks manage portfolios. They can't offer a great deal of assistance as counselors, but they can accept a portion of your capital and manage it for you.

I don't happen to share the opinion that the "Gnomes of Zurich" are necessarily more astute than investment managers elsewhere. The attraction of Swiss banks is that they are free to diversify into precious metals and currencies, while the trust department of a U.S. bank must still operate by a "prudent man" rule that actually prohibits thorough diversification.

Both Foreign Commerce Bank and Cambio + Valorenbank (listed on page 411) offer what are called "Cyclical Trading Accounts"—managed accounts that move back and forth between gold and stocks as dictated by the bank's opinion of trends. I act as an advisor in their handling of these accounts.

Other Swiss banks will also tailor a portfolio to your standards.

GETTING HELP

Naturally, I can offer no guarantee that you'll be satisfied with the service from any company I've mentioned. You'll have to determine for yourself that what they offer is useful. If you begin with small investments or trial subscriptions, committing yourself slowly, you'll determine the value before you've spent too much.

I am a little uncomfortable about referring to myself so often in this chapter, but I'm afraid it's unavoidable. In many cases, I know a firm well enough to mention it only because I have worked with or for the company or have been a customer. Your money is at stake, and any dealings you have with someone I suggest will be a serious matter. I think it's better that you know just what my relationship is.

I hope these listings will save you some time and effort in searching for what you need.

EPILOGUE

33

NEW PROFITS FROM
THE
MONETARY CRISIS

ON PAPER, MAKING PROFITS CAN APPEAR TO BE A SIMPLE TASK.
Schemes, systems, tips, and signals seem to work consistently
when examined in retrospect.

But in the present, the signs are never so obvious. Each
new bit of knowledge raises questions of its own and adds
as much to the uncertainty as it subtracts.

Investing profitably has never been easy. It has always been
hard work for those who are successful. For those who believe
it is easy, it is only expensive.

There are opportunities for profit today, just as always.
I don't agree with those who say that mere survival is the
only realistic investment objective now. Profits continue
under all circumstances, even when the results must be adjusted for inflation. It's just that profit opportunities are rarely
obvious.

Only during the two great postwar investment eras did
investing seem to be easy. But maybe that's why the future
looks so bleak today. Maybe we've been so spoiled by the
spectacular profits, first in stocks and then in precious metals
and currencies, that now it seems unfair that we have to
work so hard.

But possibly the profits weren't quite as easy to get as you remember. If you made money in gold by buying in the early 1970s, you may be forgetting the courage it required to invest in something when no one agreed with you. It will take courage again—this time to buy stocks at the bottom of a bear market, when no one believes the stock market will ever recover.

Investing has never been easy because our ambitions prevent us from settling for the small profits that might come from an easier approach. And because it's difficult, we look longingly at earlier times, when today's problems apparently didn't exist.

We can wish we had the world of the past—when taxes were lower, government interference was less, and the crises were mild. But investment markets then were largely the province of professionals. The primitive state of communications made it very difficult for the nonprofessional to participate profitably. Even leaving money in the bank wasn't an easy way out, as inflation (even then) led to periodic banking crises.

Those problems were as severe and as "unfair" to your ancestors as today's problems are to you. But for the person who was determined to make the most of his life, there was always a way—just as there is today.

The basic problem today is the super-bear trend in the economy and in traditional investments. Such periods have occurred before and they'll come again.

What separates this period from its predecessors is the length of the super-bear trend. It has lasted twelve years already, and it could last another ten. The government has found new ways to push the inevitable, painful future back over the horizon. But the future will arrive, and it will be all the more painful for having been delayed.

And when it arrives, this third investment era will be behind us. The fourth will not be pleasant. It will be the final resolution of the crises created by years of financial deception and wasteful control.

But we should also keep our eyes further ahead—on the

fifth investment era that will arrive just as inevitably. Very
few of us are so old that we won't see it. It will be the
beginning of a new super-bull trend in the economy. And
whether we participate as active investors, we'll enjoy it—
because genuine prosperity ultimately touches everyone.

It's hard to believe that such an era can be born out of
the world that exists today. It's too easy to project the present
into the future and wonder how civilization can survive what
is surely coming. How can runaway inflation be avoided
when every politician is afraid of unemployment? Given the
widespread misunderstanding of the crises, how can a dic-
tator be avoided when the depression hits bottom?

Those things are possible. And it makes sense to be fully
prepared for them—financially, physically, and mentally prepared. But I'm not sure they're going to come. And, contrary
to my reputation, I've never been sure they were coming;
I'd be foolish to be sure.

It's important to recognize what might happen, to try to
foresee the many ways in which the government might make
things worse, to anticipate the events that might trigger a
crisis. But it's dangerous to believe that the future *has* to be
as you expect it. It almost certainly won't be. The wide range
of possibilities you can visualize should make you aware that
there are more possibilities than you can imagine.

In 1945 it was common knowledge that there would be
another crash when the war ended, but it didn't happen. In
retrospect, we can see that the ending of wartime controls
set loose a flood of human energy. It didn't matter that the
economy was less free than it had been ten years before; it
was more free than it had been two years before. People saw
the freedom as an opportunity to work, to build, and to earn
all the things that had been denied them for so long.

Maybe the politicians won't let go this time. But don't be
too sure. Such a thing seemed just as unlikely in 1945 as it
seems today. But somehow enough power was relinquished
then to permit the economy to recover, and to spark the great
bull market of the 1950s and 1960s.

I can't tell you now how that might happen again. But I couldn't have told you in 1945 either. There's too much to this world for anyone to see every possibility. And just as a new bull market always seems to begin when no one wants to buy stocks, so will a new prosperity develop when no one expects it—after the problems of today have finally burned themselves out.

I'm not saying these things to convince you that everything will be all right tomorrow morning. There is a terrible price that must be paid for the damage that has been done to the economy over the past decades. That price will be exacted, and you may have to live through some difficult times—times that, even today, most people refuse to believe are coming.

But that period will probably be brief. Such destruction consumes itself quickly because there's no productive energy to sustain it. And there will be no U.S. government from across the sea to bail us out and allow the distortions to continue. It will come to an end, and come to an end quickly—because destruction is always a faster process than creation.

And when it ends, you'll be glad you were there to see it pass. You'll be glad you worked so hard back in the late 1970s to prepare for it and to see yourself through the difficult times. You'll be glad you took care of yourself financially, and that you were mentally prepared, as others weren't, for what happened.

You'll make it if you're prepared not only for what you can foresee, but for other possibilities as well. You have to accept the future in the way it chooses to come, not in the way you've willed it. And this attitude applies not only to your plans for the future, but to today's investment decisions as well.

Successful investors don't come from a mold, but if they have one trait in common it undoubtedly is *humility*. This is simply the ability to let reality tell you what it is—instead of demanding that reality be what you think it should be.

Most investors lose money because the market acts in ways they know to be impossible. And when the impossible occurs, they deny the reality, they make excuses, they simply refuse to believe their eyes.

The intelligent investor, caught by surprises, stops right where he is and adjusts his actions to the new reality. Then he goes back to his theory—not to justify it, but to examine it, find the flaws, and learn.

The world operates with cause-and-effect relationships that we can discover and use. If we pay attention to the relationships, we can be prepared for the things that others can't imagine. But we can't know exactly how the future will unfold, because the future will flow from more causes than we could possibly be aware of.

We can prepare for that uncertain future by studying what has gone before, realizing that the future will be different in some way, equipping ourselves financially and mentally to deal with it, and being prepared to accept it in whatever way it shows itself.

It isn't easy to have this attitude—at least not at first. It requires effort and attention. It also requires a sense of your own responsibility—a realization that no one is going to take care of you, and that preparation and humility are therefore essential to your survival.

If you survive the crises intact, it will be because of what you do, not because of what "they" do. The good guys and the bad guys will live their lives as they see fit. They're not responsible to your concepts of morality; they're responsible only to themselves. But it's your responsibility to make sure that, whatever they do, you adapt and respond and take care of yourself.

You can abdicate your responsibility if you choose. In fact, there are people who will volunteer to assume the responsibility for your welfare. But it's all talk. In a time of crisis, no one will be there to hold your hand.

And if you suffer, you can blame the evil person who caused it all, or you can blame the good guy who was supposed to have protected you. But that won't make life easier for you. It may be someone else's fault, but it will be your problem.

If you understand that now, you'll see to it that there won't be a problem. You'll accept the responsibility as yours, you'll be careful not to assume too much, and you'll make sure you're prepared.

There are people from whom you can purchase help. Make use of them, but don't expect anyone to give up his own self-interest for yours. The world doesn't work that way.

You must accept my ideas in the same spirit. If things work out pretty much as I've presented them in this book, I'll be back in a few years with more—ready to accept your gratitude and applause. You won't have to call me; I'll certainly call you. But if things don't work out, you may have trouble finding me.

I'm saying that I'm not responsible for your future. I offer ideas and alternatives that may make it easier for you to shoulder the responsibility. But the responsibility never shifts. That's why you must think carefully about my ideas and the ideas of others. Don't believe that, just because you've accepted the thoughts of someone else, you no longer need to think for yourself. The person whose ideas you accept won't experience your consequences—you will.

That doesn't mean I haven't done my best in providing what I believe will help you. I want your business again, and I can get it only if you profit from what I offer. I have to face the consequences of my acts, too. But we each have our own lives to live, and I'm not offering to take care of yours.

When you fully accept the responsibility for your own future, you'll also realize how much control you have over that future. No one has the power to tell you what you must believe, or how you must invest, or how you must prepare. You're free to do what you believe to be best.

The control is in your possession. If that control seems to be frustrated too often, it may be because you're too preoccupied with what you can't control—the lives and futures of others.

You can't control others because they'll do what their self-interest tells them to do. But you don't have to control them. If you don't try to make them be what you think they should be, if you don't make yourself responsible for how they act, you'll discover how easy it is to adapt and respond to whatever they become. You'll realize how much you can control your own future.

And while this discussion may seem far removed from investments, it is really about what investing requires—the humility to accept the world as it is, without preconceived notions about how people should act. There are great opportunities if you let reality show them to you instead of demanding that they be what you think they should be.

And that's the point of this book. Much of the investment philosophy could be summarized:

1. Make your decisions based upon what you are, not what you or someone else thinks you should be.

2. Let the market (and the world) tell you how things are unfolding; be receptive to reality as it is, not just as you had expected it to be.

3. Recognize in advance the losses you can't afford to take, and don't accept a liability you can't handle.

4. Remember that things may not work out as you anticipate. If you make sure that potential losses are covered, you'll be free to relax and enjoy what you have.

5. Don't be afraid to be wrong; admitting a mistake is far cheaper than perpetuating it.

6. When your decisions prove to be right, exploit your success fully. Enjoy it, bask in it, get all you can from what you've achieved. Don't be so afraid that a small profit will get away that you miss the chance for a big profit.

Of course, these ideas aren't limited to the investment world; they're the foundation of a relaxed and joyous life. Investing is part of life, and one brings to the investment world the same nature that he expresses elsewhere.

These ideas aren't new, either. In fact, they're so well known that few people pay attention to them. Maybe that's why it has required so many pages to try to rejuvenate them, to demonstrate their importance.

I hope this book has helped to put some new life into

those old truisms—so that they can be useful, rather than just familiar.

I hope the book has helped you. And I wish you the very best.

HARRY BROWNE

Zurich; July 4, 1978

APPENDICES

A

GLOSSARY OF
ECONOMIC &
INVESTMENT TERMS

HERE ARE DEFINITIONS FOR KEY WORDS THAT HAVE BEEN USED in the book, plus other words that you might come across when studying the economy and the investments I've discussed. A **boldface** word within a definition has its own definition elsewhere in the Glossary.

ADR (American Depository Receipt): A receipt issued by an American bank for shares of stock in a foreign company. The underlying stock certificates are deposited in a bank and the ADRs are traded in their stead.

Agio: Premium.

Annuity: A contract with an insurance company to pay you a fixed amount periodically (monthly, yearly, etc.) over a given period of time or for life.

Arbitrage: The purchase of an asset in one market accompanied by a simultaneous sale of the same (or a similar) asset in a different market, to take advantage of differences in price. The arbitrage principle can be applied to simultaneous buying and selling of related currencies, commodities, or securities, the same commodity with different delivery dates, etc. An arbitrager makes such pairs of trades if he believes that a pair of related prices are temporarily ill-matched and offer an opportunity for profit.

Ask price: The price at which a dealer offers to sell (retail price).

Asset: Anything of value on which a price can be placed.

At the bank's risk: Describing an investment, this means that the bank, not the customer, assumes most of the risk.

At your risk: Describing an investment, this means that the bank's customer will bear any loss from foreign government confiscation, exchange controls, default, or price declines.

Bag: In U.S. silver coin investments, the basic unit of trading—composed of 10,000 dimes or 4,000 quarters ($1,000 face value).

Balance of payments: The sum total of a country's commercial and financial transactions with the rest of the world.

Balance sheet: A financial statement showing a firm's or individual's assets, liabilities, and capital.

Bank holiday: A period during which banks are legally permitted to deny withdrawal requests from depositors.

Banknote: A piece of currency in paper form, as opposed to a bank deposit.

Bankruptcy: The formal recognition of an inability to pay debts or other obligations that have fallen due.

Bear market: A period during which the long-term price trend is downward.

Bearer instrument: Any certificate of ownership that isn't registered or made out to a specific name—and thus is effectively owned by the possessor.

Bearish: Anticipating a decline in price.

Beta: A measurement of a stock's tendency to move in harmony with stock market averages. A beta of 1.0 represents a one-to-one correspondence with the averages. A higher beta means the stock is more volatile than the averages, but moves in the same direction. A lower beta than 1.0 means the stock's movements are more conservative than, or are independent of, the averages.

Bid price: The price at which a dealer offers to buy (wholesale price).

Big Three: The three largest Swiss banks: Swiss Bank Corporation, Swiss Credit Bank, and Union Bank of Switzerland.

Bill of exchange: A short-term debt usually secured by a commodity or product that is in production or in transit.

Book value: An estimate of a firm's net worth derived from its balance sheet; the difference between stated tangible assets and stated liabilities.

Broker: One who acts only as a middleman for buyers and sellers; unlike a dealer, he does not buy and sell for his own inventory.

Bull market: A period during which the long-term price trend is upward.

Bullion: Bars of refined gold, silver, or other precious metal.

Bullion coin: A gold or silver coin that normally sells at a price close to the value of its **content**.

Bullish: Anticipating an increase in price.

Call loan: A loan for which the creditor can demand repayment at any time.

Call option: The right to purchase a given investment at a fixed price any time prior to a specified date.

Capital: (1) The sum of money paid into a company by its shareholders. (2) The net assets of a person or firm.

Capital gain: A profit made from a change in price of an investment asset.

Capital goods: Products that are utilized to produce other products.

Carat: Measures the percentage of gold in an alloy; 24 carats equal 100%, 12 carats equal 50%, etc.

Carrying charges: The interest and storage costs of owning an investment.

Cash: (1) Money in coin, paper, or other spendable form. (2) Paid for without credit.

Cash value life insurance: Life insurance that, in addition to paying benefits in the event of death, accumulates an equity that the owner can borrow against or can receive by liquidating the policy.

Central bank: A bank created by a government and given the privilege of issuing money.

Certificate of deposit: A time deposit, represented by a certificate that is transferable.

CH: The international postal abbreviation for Confederation of Helvetia (Switzerland); it appears in Swiss addresses just before the postal zone number.

Claim account: A bank account by which the customer has a claim to a commodity, rather than actual title to, or ownership of, the commodity itself.

Closed-end investment company: A company that invests its stockholders' money in other investments (usually in securities) but does not continually issue new shares or redeem existing shares. Its shares are traded in the open market. It is also called a "Publicly Traded Investment Fund." (See also **Mutual Fund**.)

Collateral: An asset that is pledged for a loan, to be forfeited if repayment is not made.

Conservative: With regard to investments, involving a minimum of risk.

Consumption: (1) The use or enjoyment of a product or service as an end in itself, rather than as a means to a further end. (2) The using up of something.

Content: The precious metal in a coin, medallion, or token.

Convertible currency: A currency that can be redeemed for a fixed quantity of gold or other precious metal. When two or more currencies are convertible into the same metal, a result is that the exchange rate between them is fixed. In present usage, the expression also means a currency that can be exchanged easily for other currencies.

Convertible security: Any **security** that can be exchanged for another security, on fixed terms, upon the demand of the holder.

Credit: (1) Borrowed money. (2) On a bank statement, an entry that is to your favor (as opposed to a **debit**, which is to the bank's favor).

Currency: (1) The money issued by a government. (2) Banknotes and coins, as opposed to bank deposits.

Current account: (1) A bank account allowing the depositor to withdraw any or all of the funds at any time. (2) A nation's exports of goods and services less its imports of goods and services. (See also **Trade Balance.**)

Custodial account: An account in which the bank stores the customer's property while the customer retains ownership.

Custody account: A **custodial account.**

Cycle: A recurring pattern.

Dealer: One who offers to buy and sell a given investment at stated prices; unlike a **broker,** he **trades** for his own account.

Debit: On a bank statement, an entry that is to the bank's favor (as opposed to a **credit,** which is to the customer's favor).

Deflation: A decrease in the money supply, usually causing a decrease in general price levels. (See also **Disinflation.**)

Demand deposit: A bank deposit that can be withdrawn by the depositor at any time; the funds held in a **current account.**

Deposit account: A bank account on which interest is paid and withdrawal rights are limited.

Depression: A prolonged period of declining standards of living.

Deutschmark: (German mark) the currency of Germany.

Devaluation: The dishonoring by a government, or other issuer, of the promise to redeem its currency at the stated rate of exchange—lowering the currency's value in relationship to gold or other currencies.

Dirty float: See **Floating exchange rate.**

Discount: (1) The amount by which an asset is priced under its **book value,** or under another asset of similar qualities. (2) The amount by which a **forward price** is below the **spot price.** (3) The amount by which a coin is priced under the value of its metallic **content.** (See also **Premium.**)

Discount rate: The interest rate charged by a Federal Reserve Bank for a loan to a commercial bank.

Discretionary account: An account for which the owner empowers a bank, broker, or advisor to make investment decisions.

Disinflation: A period during which the inflation rate declines.

Diversified common stock fund: A **closed-end investment company** that normally holds a diversified portfolio of stocks, and thus tends to change in value in harmony with the stock market averages.

Downside risk: The probability of a decline in price, and its potential extent.

Dual-purpose investment company: An investment fund that issues both (a) income shares, whose owners receive only the interest and dividends earned by the fund; and (b) capital shares, whose owners profit or lose from changes in the prices of the fund's investments, but receive no interest or dividends.

Earned income: For tax purposes, income from wages, salary, or self-employment. (See also **Unearned income.**)

Economics: The study of how people use limited resources to achieve maximum well-being (whether on a personal, commercial, national, or international scale); the art of making decisions.

Efficient market theory: The theory that market prices reflect everything that is known about an investment's value.

Equity: The present market value of an investment less all claims against it (such as loans and accumulated interest, commissions, and any other fees).

Eurocurrency: A bank deposit owned by a non-resident of the country in which the bank is located. The term "Eurocurrency market" usually refers to bank deposits that are owned by foreign banks.

Excess equity: In a **margin account, equity** that is above the amount required by the bank or other lender; it can normally be withdrawn or used to finance an additional investment.

Excess margin: Excess equity.

Exchange control: A government regulation restricting or prohibiting the exporting or importing of currency.

Exchange rate: The price of one currency expressed in units of another currency.

Exercise price: Striking price.

Face value: (1) The **legal tender** value of a coin, banknote, or other token. (2) The amount promised to a bondholder at the expiration date of the bond.

Fiat money: Currency that is not convertible into either gold or silver, and is declared to be **legal tender** by government fiat or edict.

Fiduciary account: Custodial account.

Filter rule: A buy or sell signal caused by a price movement large enough to filter out normal fluctuations.

Fineness: The degree to which bullion is pure gold or silver, expressed as a fraction of the bullion's gross weight. For example, gold bullion of .995 fineness means that 99.5% of the total weight is pure gold. (Sometimes the decimal is omitted, but the figure is meant to indicate thousandth's: that is, 995 means .995.)

Fixed deposit account: A time deposit.

Fixed exchange rate: An exchange rate that is maintained within a prescribed narrow range—usually by government purchases and sales in the open market of the currencies involved.

Floating exchange rate: An exchange rate that is allowed to fluctuate, not influenced by government purchases and sales. A "dirty float" occurs when the government influences the exchange rate through purchases and sales, but does not announce an official, fixed exchange rate.

Fluctuation: A change in price—upward or downward.

Foreign exchange rate: Exchange rate.

Forward contract: A contract for delivery of an asset in the future at a price determined in the present; usually, only a small deposit is required prior to the delivery date.

Forward price: The price for an asset to be delivered and paid for on a given date in the future. (See also **Spot price**.)

Fractional reserve banking: A banking system in which money that is payable upon demand to depositors is lent to others for fixed periods by the bank; thus, a system in which the bank maintains less than 100% reserves against **demand deposits**.

Free market: A market free of government regulation or participation.

Fundamental analysis: A system of investment analysis that considers only factors relating to supply and demand emanating from outside the investment market.

Fungible: Interchangeable.

Futures-contract: A **forward contract** with standardized specifications, traded on an organized exchange.

Gap: A condition created on a price graph when the range of prices for one day's trading does not overlap the previous day's range.

Government: The dominant institution of coercion in a given area.

Grain: In weights and measures, .0648 grams or .002 troy ounces; there are 15.432 grains in a gram, 480 grains in a troy ounce. (The abbreviation *gr.* usually means **gram**.)

Gram: The unit of weight in the metric system. There are 31.1042 grams to a troy ounce; one gram equals .03215 troy ounces. A kilogram is 1,000 grams or 32.15 troy ounces. A metric ton is 1,000 kilograms or 32,151 troy ounces.

Hard-money investments: Gold and silver, as well as currencies that have been subjected to less than average monetary inflation.

Hedge: A relatively small investment purchased to offset possible losses in one's principal investments.

Human action theory: The theory that maintains that every human action is motivated by an individual's desire to increase his own mental well-being or to prevent a decrease in his well-being. The science of human action is also called *praxeology,* and is the foundation for the study of **economics.**

In the money: For an **option** (or a **warrant**), the condition that exists when the price of the **underlying investment** is higher than the **striking price** of the option.

Income (investment): Withdrawals from capital, usually in the amounts of interest and dividends received.

Income account: A portion of a **portfolio** reserved for income payments.

Inconvertibility: The contrary of **convertibility**.

Inflation: See **Monetary inflation** and **Price inflation**.

Inflationary depression: A depression that proceeds simultaneously with **monetary** and/or **price inflation**.

Inter-bank rates: Prices or interest rates that apply only to transactions between banks.

Interest differential: (1) The difference between two interest rates. (2) The net **carrying charges** incurred during a period of time.

Investment company: A company that places its stockholders' money in other investments (usually in **securities**).

Kaffir: A synonym for any South African gold mining company.

Kilogram: See **Gram**.

Legal tender: A form of money that an individual is legally required to accept in payment of debts.

Leverage: Any arrangement (such as a margin purchase or an option contract) that exaggerates the effect of a price change.

Liability: A financial obligation, actual or potential.

Limit order: An offer to purchase at or below a stated price, or to sell at or above a stated price.

Linear scale: See **Ratio scale**.

Liquidation: The sale of an asset.

Liquidity: (1) The ability to turn an asset into cash quickly without a penalty for haste. (2) The relationship of a firm's liquid assets to its current liabilities.

Long position: Buying before selling, usually in expectation of a price increase. (See also **Short sale**.)

Maintenance margin: The **margin** required by a bank or other lender, below which a **margin sale** will occur.

Margin: (1) In a **margin account,** the amount of the investor's **equity,** expressed as a percentage of the investment's current market value. (2) In a **forward contract,** the value of the investor's deposit, expressed as a percentage of the investment's current market value.

Margin account: An investment account in which there is a **call loan** against the assets.

Margin call: A demand by the creditor of a **margin account**

that the borrower reduce the loan—so that the loan amount will remain comfortably below the current market value of the assets.

Margin sale: A sale of assets to satisfy the requirements of a **margin call**.

Market: (1) A group of transactions integrated by geography or items traded. (2) An opportunity to exchange.

Market-maker: A **dealer** who continually offers to buy and sell a given investment.

Marketable: Salable in a liquid market. (See also **Liquidity #1.**)

Maturity: The date on which a contractual obligation (such as repayment of a bond) falls due.

Metric ton: See **Gram**.

Monetary inflation: An increase in the **money supply**.

Money: An asset that is generally accepted in exchange with the intention of trading it for something else; normally, usage is confined to gold, bank notes, bank deposits, coins, or tokens.

Money market fund: A **mutual fund** that invests only in short-term interest-earning securities.

Money market paper: Easily marketable short-term notes and bills carrying little risk of default.

Money supply: Currency held outside of commercial banks plus bank deposits that can be withdrawn on demand.

Moratorium: A period during which a bank, company or individual is legally permitted to delay payment of its obligations.

Mutual fund: A company that invests its stockholders' money in other investments (usually in securities) and is characterized by the obligation to redeem its shares at **net asset value** upon request.

Negotiable instrument: A certificate of ownership that can be sold easily.

Net asset value: The amount, per share, of total assets minus total liabilities.

On the money: For an **option** (or a **warrant**), the condition that exists when the price of the **underlying investment** is equal to the striking price of the option.

Option: See **Call option** and **Put option**.

Out of the money: For an **option** (or a **warrant**), the condition that exists when the price of the **underlying investment** is lower than the striking price of the option.

Paper money: See **Currency** (#1).

Par: (1) See **Par value**. (2) Equal in value.

Par value: The nominal or face value of a security or currency. (A currency is often referred to as being at par value when it is trading at the price announced as official by the government.)

Permanent portfolio: An assortment of investments that remains unchanged from year to year.

Portfolio: An assortment of investments held by an individual or company.

Power of attorney: Signature authority.

Premium: (1) The amount by which a security is priced above its **face value**, **book value**, or inherent value. (2) The amount by which the **forward price** exceeds the **spot price**. (3) The amount by which the price of a coin exceeds the value of the coin's metallic **content**.

Price inflation: An increase in the general price level.

Prime rate: The interest rate charged by commercial banks to their best customers.

Public market: An investment market in which most relevant information is publicly available.

Publicly traded investment fund: A **closed-end investment company**.

Purchasing power: The value of a unit of money or other asset, measured by the quantity of goods and services it will purchase.

Purchasing power parity: The exchange rate at which a country's price level is equivalent to price levels in other countries.

Purchasing power parity theory: The system of currency forecasting that maintains that exchange rates will gravitate toward their **purchasing power parities**.

Put option: The right to sell a given asset at a fixed price any time prior to a specified date.

Ratio scale: On a graph drawn to a ratio scale, a given percentage change in value will cover the same vertical distance, no matter at what level it occurs—so that the significance of the change is graphically illustrated. On a *linear scale*, a given absolute change will cover the same vertical distance, no matter at what level it occurs. (The graph on page 162 is an example of a ratio scale; the graph on page 163 is an example of a linear scale.)

Redemption: (1) The repurchase of a security by its issuer. (2) See **Convertible currency**.

Reserve: An allocation of capital for possible losses or to meet a statutory requirement.

Resistance level: An investment price level at which an unusually large volume of selling is expected.

Restrike: A coin that was minted after the date marked, but is otherwise genuine.

Revaluation: An increase in value or price. (If a currency is revalued, the event is the opposite of a **devaluation**; if the gold reserves backing a currency are revalued to a higher price, the event is the same as a devaluation.)

Round lot: The minimum size of an investment transaction that does not incur special trading costs.

Runaway inflation: A rapid rise in prices aggravated by a widespread desire to decrease holdings of money.

Safekeeping account: A **custodial account**.

Safety net: A stop-loss order placed well below the high-point of a stock market rally.

Secured loan: A loan for which **collateral** is pledged.

Security: (1) A token, such as a stock or bond certificate, representing capital entrusted to another. (2) An asset pledged to secure a loan. (3) Safety.

Share capital: Capital provided by shareholders.

Short sale: (1) The sale of a borrowed security. (2) The sale of an asset for future delivery—whether or not the seller currently possesses the asset. (See also **Long position**.)

Signature authority: The authority given by the owner of an account to another person to transact business for the account.

Specialist market: An investment market in which most relevant information is available only through dealers.

Speculation: Any investment made with the hope of profiting from a change in price.

Speculative: In normal usage, involving more than a minimum of risk.

Spot price: The price for the immediate delivery of an asset. (See also **Forward price.**)

Spread: (1) The difference between the **bid price** and the **ask price**. (2) A form of **hedge** or **arbitrage** in which the purchase of an asset for delivery on one date is balanced by a sale of the asset for delivery on a different date.

Stop-loss order: An instruction given to a bank or broker to sell an investment if the price drops to a stated level.

Stop order to buy: An instruction given to a bank or broker to purchase an investment if the price rises to a stated level.

Striking price: The price at which the holder of a **warrant** or **call option** may buy an asset; also, the price at which the holder of a **put option** may enforce a sale. Also called the *exercise price*.

Strong hands: Investors who are likely to hold a given investment for its maximum long-term profit potential. (See also **Weak hands.**)

Super-trend: A very long **trend** that encompasses normal **bull** and **bear markets**, but which maintains a recognizable upward or downward bias.

Support level: An investment price level at which an unusually large volume of buying is expected.

Swap: (1) An arrangement by which a government borrows foreign currency from the government that issues it, to finance intervention in foreign exchange markets. (2) A **spread** (#2).

Tax: Property, usually money, coercively taken from its owner by a government.

Tax haven: A country whose government offers tax advantages to foreigners.

Technical analysis: A system of investment analysis that considers factors relating to supply and demand only within the investment market.

Technology: Knowledge, skills, and tools that increase the productivity of human effort.

Time deposit: A bank deposit that is not withdrawable until a fixed date.

Tola: An Indian unit of weight, sometimes used for precious metals, equal to .375 troy ounces or 11.664 grams.

Ton, metric: See **Gram.**

Trade balance: A nation's product exports less its product imports. (See also **Balance of payments** and **Current account #2.**)

Trading: Buying and/or selling.

Trend: A persistent movement in one direction.

Troy ounce: The unit of weight used to measure gold and silver. One troy ounce equals 1.097 avoirdupois ounces.

Trust account: A **discretionary account.**

Underlying investment: For an **option** (or a **warrant** or other **convertible security**), the investment for which the option provides the right of purchase or sale.

Unearned income: Interest, dividends, rents, and royalties, when measuring taxable income.

Upside potential: The probability of an increase in price, and its potential extent.

Upvaluation: (Colloquial) The opposite of a **devaluation**; a **revaluation.**

Value date: The date on which payment is considered to have been made, and from which interest charges will be computed.

Variable portfolio: An assortment of investments that is altered as investment prospects change.

Warrant: An option to purchase a share of stock at a fixed price until a specified date. (A warrant differs from a **call option** in that a warrant is issued by the company whose stock is involved.)

Weak hands: Investors holding a given investment who are prone to be easily influenced in their trading by short-term trends or events. (See also **Strong hands**.)

Wealth: Resources that can be used or sold.

B

———

SUGGESTED READING

HERE ARE TWENTY BOOKS THAT MAY ADD TO YOUR UNDER-standing of the investment markets. All were still in print when I wrote this and could be purchased or ordered through any bookstore (except where noted) or from the publisher. Any book that has since become out of print can be ordered from a used-book dealer.

INVESTMENTS

Using Warrants by Terry Coxon. A comprehensive introduction to the subject of warrants and dual-purpose investment funds. (Cardcover: Available only from Investor's Perspective Publishing, Box 1187, Burlingame, Calif. 94010; $10.00.)

Silver Profits in the Seventies by Jerome F. Smith. A useful study that provides the complete background of the U.S. government in the silver market, leading to today's production/consumption deficit. (Cardcover: ERC Publishing Company, Box 91491, West Vancouver, British Columbia, Canada; $12.50.)

A Textbook on Foreign Exchange by Paul Einzig. As the title indicates, this is a textbook explaining the foreign exchange market—not a guide to trading for profit. The best explanation of the workings of the foreign exchange market that I've found. Einzig has also written over a dozen other good books on the subject. (St. Martin's Press, Inc., 175 Fifth Ave., New York, N.Y. 10010; $10.95.)

Handbook of Investment Products and Services by Victor L. Harper. A basic introduction to many investment markets —stocks, bonds, real estate trusts, options, mutual funds, life insurance, commodities, annuities, tax shelters, etc. (Prentice-Hall, Inc., Englewood Cliffs, New Jersey 07632; $17.95.)

Financial Tactics and Terms for the Sophisticated International Investor by Harry D. Schultz. An extensive glossary of many investment terms, with interesting comments and background on the investment markets. (Harper & Row, Inc., 10 E. 53rd St., New York, N.Y. 10022; $10.00.)

TECHNICAL ANALYSIS

Technical Analysis of Stock Trends by Robert D. Edwards and John Magee is the only book I've found that explains *why* certain patterns frequently show up on a price graph. There are many books on the subject I haven't read, but this is by far the best one I've found. (Available only from John Magee, 53 State St., Boston, Mass. 02109; $35.00.)

SWISS BANKS

The Complete Guide to Swiss Banks by Harry Browne. Explanations of the types of accounts available, commission rates, fees, numbered accounts, sample instructions to give to the bank, tax considerations, privacy suggestions, etc.—a guidebook for using a Swiss bank account. (Available only from Harry Browne Special Reports, Box 5586, Austin, Texas 78763; $12.95.)

The Swiss Banks by T. R. Fehrenbach. Although published

in 1966, this is probably still the best book available explaining why Switzerland is and will continue to be the money haven of the world. (McGraw-Hill Book Co., 1221 Avenue the Americas, New York, N.Y. 10020; $9.95.)

U.S. BANKING SYSTEM

The Coming Credit Collapse by Alexander P. Paris. A discussion of the illiquid state of U.S. banks. The reading is a little difficult in places, but the point is well made. (Arlington House, 81 Centre Ave., New Rochelle, N.Y. 10801; $8.95.)

ECONOMIC HISTORY

America's Great Depression by Murray N. Rothbard. A thorough monetary history of the U.S. from 1921 to 1933. The book isn't easy reading, but it's extremely interesting. And it provides a great deal of useful information for anyone who wants to understand the causes of the 1929 depression. (Sheed Andrews & McMeel, Inc., 6700 Squibb Road, Mission, Kansas 66202; $12.00; paperback $4.95.)

The Panic of 1819 by Murray N. Rothbard. This book is easier to read than *America's Great Depression* and its explanation of the inflation-depression cycle is simpler. (Columbia University Press, 562 W. 113th St., New York, N.Y. 10025; $6.00.)

ECONOMICS & MONEY

The soundest and most precise explanations of economics aren't going to be the easiest to read; there is simply too much ground to cover. For the person who wants a deep understanding of the economic events of today, I've listed the books I have found to be the most useful. The readability varies, and I've provided my opinion of the ease or difficulty you might encounter.

With the possible exception of Alchian and Allen, the authors were all influenced by the late Ludwig von Mises. I've included two books by von Mises himself.

Human Action by Ludwig von Mises. The *magnum opus* of economics. This book explains in detail the theory of human action—which, in turn, explains the whole of economics. It isn't easy reading, but it is engrossing. And with a copy handy of *Mises Made Easier* (listed below), you won't have trouble with the terminology. (Contemporary Books, Inc., 180 N. Michigan Ave., Chicago, Ill. 60601; $20.00.)

On the Manipulation of Money and Credit by Ludwig von Mises. This collection of essays was published in English for the first time in 1978. It is much easier reading than *Human Action*, but deals only with the monetary cycles. Although some of the essays were written in the early part of the century, the material is quite relevant to today's problems. (Free Market Books, Box 298, Dobbs Ferry, N.Y. 10522; $14.00.)

Mises Made Easier by Percy L. Greaves, Jr. A glossary of the scientific and possibly unfamiliar terms in the books of Ludwig von Mises. It is virtually a necessity for studying von Mises' work, but it is also interesting reading on its own. (Free Market Books, Box 298, Dobbs Ferry, N.Y. 10522; $6.00.)

Understanding the Dollar Crisis by Percy L. Greaves, Jr. This book is a simplified and easy-to-follow explanation of von Mises' theory of the monetary cycle. It also provides a good introduction to the theory of human action. Highly recommended. (Western Islands, 395 Concord Ave., Belmont, Mass. 02178; $7.00.)

Economics in One Lesson by Henry Hazlitt. A valuable book that demolishes many economic fallacies, written in an entertaining style. (Paperback: Manor Books, Inc., 432 Park Ave. So., New York, N.Y. 10016; $0.95.)

What You Should Know About Inflation by Henry Hazlitt. A sound, easy-to-read primer on money and inflation. (Hardcover: D. Van Nostrand Co., 450 W. 33rd St., New York,

N.Y. 10001; $4.95. Paperback: Funk & Wagnalls, Inc., 53 E. 77th St., New York, N.Y. 10021; $2.25.)

Man, Economy and State by Murray N. Rothbard. While easier reading than *Human Action*, this is still a scholarly work and will require effort in places. It is a complete course in economics, taking the reader from the foundations of human action to specific examples of government and free-market activity. (Green Hill Pubs., 236 Forest Park Place, Ottawa, Ill. 61350; paperback $10.00.)

University Economics by Armen A. Alchian and William R. Allen. This may be the most entertaining economics textbook ever written. While meticulously complete, the authors maintain an interesting and often humorous style for most of the book. The first thirty-one chapters provide an extremely valuable course in economics. For some reason, the chapters attempting to explain macro-economics break down; they are not nearly so readable or sound, and they don't seem to follow from the previous chapters; it's as if a different author took over. The rest of the book is well worth the time and effort, however. (Wadsworth Publishing Co., Inc., 10 Davis Drive, Belmont, Calif. 94002; $14.95.)

How I Found Freedom in an Unfree World by Harry Browne. The first half of the book explains the theory of human action, which is the foundation of economics. It also provides the philosophy that underlies the investment ideas expressed in this book. (Macmillan Publishing Co., Inc., 866 Third Ave., New York, N.Y. 10022; $7.95.)

C

ACKNOWLEDGMENTS

MY ASSOCIATE, TERRY COXON, HAS CONTRIBUTED MORE TO this book than I could describe. For two months, he stayed at my home in Zurich—editing, discussing, and clarifying. A great many of the book's ideas and suggestions originated with him. Unfortunately, it would have been too repetitious to footnote every idea he contributed.

More indirectly, a lot of what I understand about economics has come from the late Ludwig von Mises. I sometimes think he's the only man who ever lived who was capable of understanding the whole world. His books, while not easy to read, provide the ultimate explanation of human action.

I began reading the books of von Mises only in the last few years. Prior to that, I had been exposed to his ideas through the works of his intellectual descendents—particularly Murray N. Rothbard, Henry Hazlitt, and Alvin Lowi—to whom I'll always be grateful.

More down to earth, my wife Ute kept me alive throughout the ordeal of writing the book, and she amazed me by staying up night after night typing the manuscript.

D

U.S. CONSUMER
PRICE INDEX,
1945–1978

FROM THE U.S. CONSUMER PRICE INDEX, IT IS POSSIBLE TO calculate the approximate change in an investment's real purchasing power over a period of time.

The tables on pages 456–459 provide the index numbers from which you can compute the change. I have used the "Consumer Price Index for All Urban Consumers" that was introduced by the U.S. Department of Labor in 1978. You can update the table from items appearing in the press.

There are three possible calculations you might want to make: (1) the amount of price inflation; (2) the depreciation in the purchasing power of the dollar; or (3) the purchasing power change occurring for an investment. The formulas that follow will enable you to make those calculations.

AMOUNT OF PRICE INFLATION

To determine the amount of price inflation that occurred between any two dates:

1. From the table, find the index numbers for the beginning and ending dates of the period involved.

2. Divide the ending index number by the beginning index number.

3. Subtract 1.

4. Multiply by 100.

The answer is the percentage by which prices increased from the beginning date to the ending date.

DEPRECIATION OF THE DOLLAR

To determine how much the dollar depreciated between any two dates:

1. From the table, find the index numbers for the beginning and ending dates of the period involved.

2. Divide the beginning index number by the ending index number.

3. Subtract the answer from the number 1.

4. Multiply by 100.

The answer is the percentage by which the dollar has depreciated in purchasing power value from the beginning date to the ending date.

CHANGE IN INVESTMENT VALUE

To determine how an investment's purchasing power value changed between any two dates:

1. From the table, find the index numbers for the beginning and ending dates of the period involved.

2. Divide the beginning index number by the ending index number.

3. Divide the price of the investment on the ending date by the price of the investment on the beginning date.

4. Multiply the answer to #2 by the answer to #3.

5. Subtract 1.

6. Multiply by 100.

The answer is the percentage by which the investment's value changed—in terms of the products and services that could be purchased by each dollar invested.

U.S. CONSUMER PRICE INDEX, 1945-1978

(All Urban Consumers Index)

Year	Jan	Feb	March	April	May	June	July	Aug	Sep	Oct	Nov	Dec	Year Average	Inflation Rate
1945	53.3	53.2	53.2	53.3	53.7	54.2	54.3	54.3	54.1	54.1	54.3	54.5	53.9	2.3%
1946	54.5	54.3	54.7	55.0	55.3	55.9	59.2	60.5	61.2	62.4	63.9	64.4	58.5	18.2%
1947	64.4	64.3	65.7	65.7	65.5	66.0	66.6	67.3	68.9	68.9	69.3	70.2	66.9	9.0%
1948	71.0	70.4	70.2	71.2	71.7	72.2	73.1	73.4	73.4	73.1	72.6	72.1	72.1	2.7%
1949	72.0	71.2	71.4	71.5	71.4	71.5	71.0	71.2	71.5	71.1	71.2	70.8	71.4	– 1.8%
1950	70.5	70.3	70.6	70.7	71.0	71.4	72.1	72.7	73.2	73.6	73.9	74.9	72.1	5.8%

Source: Bureau of Labor Statistics, U.S. Department of Labor. 1967 = 100.

U.S. CONSUMER PRICE INDEX (Cont'd.)

Year	Jan	Feb	March	April	May	June	July	Aug	Sep	Oct	Nov	Dec	Year Average	Inflation Rate
1951	76.1	77.0	77.3	77.4	77.7	77.6	77.7	77.7	78.2	78.6	79.0	79.3	77.8	5.9%
1952	79.3	78.8	78.8	79.1	79.2	79.4	80.0	80.1	80.0	80.1	80.1	80.0	79.5	0.9%
1953	79.8	79.4	79.6	79.7	79.9	80.2	80.4	80.6	80.7	80.9	80.6	80.5	80.1	0.6%
1954	80.7	80.6	80.5	80.3	80.6	80.7	80.7	80.6	80.4	80.2	80.3	80.1	80.5	− 0.5%
1955	80.1	80.1	80.1	80.1	80.1	80.1	80.4	80.2	80.5	80.5	80.6	80.4	80.2	0.4%
1956	80.3	80.3	80.4	80.5	80.9	81.4	82.0	81.9	82.0	82.5	82.5	82.7	81.4	2.9%
1957	82.8	83.1	83.3	83.6	83.8	84.3	84.7	84.8	84.9	84.9	85.2	85.2	84.3	3.0%
1958	85.7	85.8	86.4	86.6	86.6	86.7	86.8	86.7	86.7	86.7	86.8	86.7	86.6	1.8%
1959	86.8	86.7	86.7	86.8	86.9	87.3	87.5	87.4	87.7	88.0	88.0	88.0	87.3	1.5%
1960	87.9	88.0	88.0	88.5	88.5	88.7	88.7	88.7	88.8	89.2	89.3	89.3	88.7	1.5%

U.S. CONSUMER PRICE INDEX (Cont'd.)

Year	Jan	Feb	March	April	May	June	July	Aug	Sep	Oct	Nov	Dec	Year Average	Inflation Rate
1961	89.3	89.3	89.3	89.3	89.3	89.4	89.8	89.7	89.9	89.9	89.9	89.9	89.6	0.7%
1962	89.9	90.1	90.3	90.5	90.5	90.5	90.7	90.7	91.2	91.1	91.1	91.0	90.6	1.2%
1963	91.1	91.2	91.3	91.3	91.3	91.7	92.1	92.1	92.1	92.2	92.3	92.5	91.7	1.6%
1964	92.6	92.5	92.6	92.7	92.7	92.9	93.1	93.0	93.2	93.3	93.5	93.6	92.9	1.2%
1965	93.6	93.6	93.7	94.0	94.2	94.7	94.8	94.6	94.8	94.9	95.1	95.4	94.5	1.9%
1966	95.4	96.0	96.3	96.7	96.8	97.1	97.4	97.9	98.1	98.5	98.5	98.6	97.2	3.4%
1967	98.6	98.7	98.9	99.1	99.4	99.7	100.2	100.5	100.7	101.0	101.3	101.6	100.0	3.0%
1968	102.0	102.3	102.8	103.1	103.4	104.0	104.5	104.8	105.1	105.7	106.1	106.4	104.2	4.7%
1969	106.7	107.1	108.0	108.7	109.0	109.7	110.2	110.7	111.2	111.6	112.2	112.9	109.8	6.1%
1970	113.3	113.9	114.5	115.2	115.7	116.3	116.7	116.9	117.5	118.1	118.5	119.1	116.3	5.5%

U.S. CONSUMER PRICE INDEX (Cont'd)

Year	Jan	Feb	March	April	May	June	July	Aug	Sep	Oct	Nov	Dec	Year Average	Inflation Rate
1971	119.2	119.4	119.8	120.2	120.8	121.5	121.8	122.1	122.2	122.4	122.6	123.1	121.3	3.4%
1972	123.2	123.8	124.0	124.3	124.7	125.0	125.5	125.7	126.2	126.6	126.9	127.3	125.3	3.4%
1973	127.7	128.6	129.8	130.7	131.5	132.4	132.7	135.1	135.5	136.6	137.6	138.5	133.1	8.8%
1974	139.7	141.5	143.1	143.9	145.5	146.9	148.0	149.9	151.7	153.0	154.3	155.4	147.7	12.2%
1975	156.1	157.2	157.8	158.6	159.3	160.6	162.3	162.8	163.6	164.6	165.6	166.3	161.2	7.0%
1976	166.7	167.1	167.5	168.2	169.2	170.0	171.1	171.9	172.6	173.3	173.8	174.3	170.5	4.8%
1977	175.3	177.1	178.2	179.6	180.6	181.8	182.6	183.3	184.0	184.5	185.4	186.1	181.5	6.8%
1978	187.2	188.4	189.8	191.5	193.3	195.3								

THE AUTHOR

HARRY BROWNE WAS BORN IN NEW YORK CITY IN 1933 BUT grew up in Los Angeles. After graduating from high school, his intention to get a college education resulted in a total of two weeks spent at a junior college.

During the next twelve years he had a variety of jobs, mostly in sales and advertising. In the advertising business, he discovered economics indirectly by attempting to explain to clients why their marketing plans were unrealistic.

In 1962, with two partners, he founded a newspaper feature service, which he managed for five years. He continued to develop his ideas about economics and devoted most of his own newspaper columns to explanations of seemingly difficult economic subjects. In 1964 he began giving courses in economics.

In 1967 he acquired the Los Angeles agency for Economic Research Counselors, an investment service that helps customers establish Swiss bank accounts. He also began giving seminars to show how investors could profit from the eventual devaluation of the dollar.

He published his first book, *How You Can Profit from the Coming Devaluation,* in 1970 and was surprised to find that there was a wide audience for his economic and investment ideas. Thereafter he devoted all his time to writing and investment counseling.

How I Found Freedom in an Unfree World was published in 1973, followed in 1974 by *You Can Profit from a Monetary Crisis,* which remained on the best-seller lists for eight months. In 1974 he also began publication of an investment newsletter, *Harry Browne's Special Reports.* In 1976 he published the *Complete Guide to Swiss Banks.*

He moved to Vancouver, Canada, in 1971 and to Zurich, Switzerland, in 1977, where he now lives with his wife, Ute. Outside of economics and investments, his main interests are classical music, opera, sports, and fiction.

At the present time he is working on two new books. One, *Inflation-Proofing Your Investments,* is co-authored with Terry Coxon and will be published by William Morrow in 1979. The other, *Why People Hate Opera,* will be published by Macmillan in 1980.

INDEX